THE CORPORATION AS FAMILY

THE
LUTHER
HARTWELL
HODGES
SERIES

ON
BUSINESS,
SOCIETY,
AND THE
STATE

William H. Becker, editor

THE

THE GENDERING OF CORPORATE WELFARE

The University of North Carolina Press | Chapel Hill and London

CORPORATION

as Family

1890–1930 | NIKKI MANDELL

Designed by April Leidig-Higgins
Set in Ehrhardt by Copperline Book Services, Inc.
Manufactured in the United States of America

The paper in this book meets the guidelines for
permanence and durability of the Committee on
Production Guidelines for Book Longevity of the
Council on Library Resources.

Library of Congress Cataloging-in-Publication Data
Mandell, Nikki. The corporation as family: the gendering of corporate welfare, 1890–1930 / by Nikki
Mandell.
p. cm.—(Luther Hartwell Hodges series on business, society, and the state)   Includes bibliographi-
cal references and index.
ISBN 0-8078-2685-5 (cloth: alk. paper)
ISBN 0-8078-5351-8 (pbk.: alk. paper)
1. Industrial welfare—History. I. Title. II. Series.
HD7261 .M23 2002 331.25'5'—dc21 2001043101

cloth 06 05 04 03 02   5 4 3 2 1
paper 06 05 04 03 02   5 4 3 2 1

To my parents
and in memory of
my grandparents

CONTENTS

PREFACE

THIS BOOK GREW out of my inability to stay focused on the task at hand. As I planned a study of class and urbanization, my thoughts kept drifting to two bits of historical trivia. One incident involved the 1940–41 organizing campaign at Ford Motor Company. Charles Sorensen, a close advisor to Henry Ford, attributed Ford's final decision to sign the United Automobile Workers contract to Mrs. Ford's influence. Sorensen recalled that when Ford wavered at the last minute, it was Mrs. Ford who persuaded him to put pen to paper and sign. In a similar vein, Nettie Fowler McCormick played an instrumental role in convincing her son, Cyrus McCormick Jr., to settle a 1913 strike at International Harvester. Faced with possible antitrust action, Mrs. McCormick argued that the company could ill afford the critical scrutiny of an antagonistic public and a suspicious government. Women knowledgeable about the finances and politics of modern business management? Women involved in crucial business decisions? Weren't women excluded from the masculine boardroom, particularly from the politically charged and violent battles between labor and management? Were these isolated incidents, or had women played a role in business management during the heyday of industrial expansion?

I kept returning to these questions. Perhaps the most intriguing aspect of this line of questioning was the opportunity it afforded to consider gender in an arena that had so far remained impervious to the new women's history. Joan Scott's challenge to use gender as a "useful category of historical analysis" was exciting (and, at that time, freshly issued). Scott had asked "How have social institutions incorporated gender into their assumptions and organizations?" Alice Kessler-Harris cast the same issue in the form of a research agenda. "A gendered exploration of the past," she wrote, "explores how the social relations of men and women create and inhibit expectations and aspirations and ultimately help to structure institutions as well."[1] Here, in these bits of historical trivia, was an invitation to pursue that exploration. I jumped in. I soon discovered that women's involvement in labor relations was more pervasive than these few family interventions suggested. That involvement, as the following pages reveal, was no accident. Rather, it was intimately tied to turn-of-the-century constructions of gender.

As with all research, I have followed unexpected paths, confronted frustrating roadblocks, and benefitted enormously from the advice and generosity of others. I am indebted to the many librarians and archivists whose familiarity with their collections made it possible to study the mid-level people and policies that are at the center of this book. Their expertise proved indispensable in identifying documents buried in the language of traditional finding aids. I also want to thank the many archive staffers who uncomplainingly (at least to me) hauled box after box of letters and reports from the depths of storage to reading room tables.

I owe an enormous debt of gratitude to the advisors who worked with me as this project grew from a vague set of questions, to a dissertation, to final publication. David Brody taught me to uncover the complexities of my subject. Although I tested his editorial patience, I benefitted enormously from his editorial expertise. I will be forever grateful for his advice that analytical complexity is best expressed through clear and simple prose. Roland Marchand's early interest and insightful questioning guided me around many a pitfall. His careful reading of multiple drafts and his generosity in sharing his own research with me has enriched this work. I am saddened that those conversations are no longer possible. One of the unexpected pleasures of working on this project was the opportunity to become reacquainted with Joe Trotter. I thank him for his generous support, which came at a particularly difficult juncture.

Friends and family offered a different, although equally essential, kind of support. I particularly want to thank Lil Taiz. As both friend and scholar, she generously shared the woes, joys, and lessons of historical research. My children have grown up with this project as a third sibling. Although for different reasons than mine, they too are happy to see this book go to press. I thank them for their patience with my unpredictable schedule and for the great fun we have had along the way.

THE CORPORATION AS FAMILY

Introduction

In 1884, John Patterson, an ambitious coal dealer, sold his business and purchased a controlling share in the failing National Manufacturing Company of Dayton, Ohio. During the first year under Patterson's leadership, the company's thirteen employees produced 500 cash registers. Patterson quickly gave his firm a more descriptive name, the National Cash Register Company (NCR). He directed his staff to improve the reliability of the company's registers and embarked on an aggressive marketing campaign to boost demand for this new type of machine. Orders began pouring in. Over the next five years, Patterson hired hundreds of new workers and rebuilt the factory, expanding it from 800 to 15,000 square feet. Less than twenty years after Patterson bought the company, 1,000 NCR employees working in three large factory buildings were producing over 15,000 cash registers annually. By the early 1920s the NCR workforce had grown to 6,000.[1]

This phenomenal growth is only one measure of the changes that took place at NCR. As the company prospered, Patterson found it increasingly difficult to maintain the personal oversight that he believed was essential to quality production and sales. "When the business was smaller," he told his biographer, "I used to travel about through the shops a great deal, knowing everyone, and taking pains to ask them if they had anything to suggest."[2] By the 1890s, this was no longer possible. The executive offices were far removed from the production floors of the new multistoried factory buildings. The growing distance between Patterson and his employees became painfully clear in 1894, when a $50,000 shipment of registers was returned from England for faulty workmanship. This costly disaster led Patterson to seriously reconsider his labor practices, practices that had fostered a disgruntled workforce with little interest in turning out quality machines.

In typical fashion, Patterson turned his prodigious energy to solving his labor problems. In a show of solidarity with his workers, he temporarily moved his office back to the factory floor. He wanted to "discover what the troubles were by living with them." Patterson later recounted the workmen's complaints: the factory was dark, dirty, and cold; workers had no clean water for washing up; only a privileged few had lockers; and so on. He came away from these encounters determined that he "simply had to make that place decent to work in or go out of business."[3]

Patterson arranged for the factory floor to be kept clean, installed lockers, and supplied his employees with clean water. As it constructed new buildings, NCR pioneered factory designs with more window space to permit better lighting. In 1897, Patterson hired a local home missionary, Lena Harvey, to direct a multitude of new activities for NCR employees and their families: boys' and girls' clubs, a women's club, music clubs, garden contests, home visiting, factory beautification, a company library, and restrooms. Although other company officials questioned the cost of these innovations, Patterson was confident that such welfare work was the key to creating an ideal class of workers—"enthusiastic, loyal and intelligent."[4] In the ensuing years, the NCR welfare program became even more elaborate, including the building of Welfare Hall, which housed dining and meeting facilities for company employees, and the NCR Schoolhouse, at which employees could enjoy movies, listen to company-sponsored lectures, and attend regular company meetings. By Patterson's account, his workers responded cautiously at first, but soon became enthusiastic about the new company policies.

Despite Patterson's optimism, NCR's labor problems were not entirely resolved. He faced a growing union movement after 1897. Although Patterson easily repressed unionism at first, a four-day strike late in 1899 led him to sign contracts with more than twenty unions. He apparently persuaded himself that unions would make workers feel involved in company affairs and thereby boost loyalty and productivity. While minor problems arose, Patterson honored the contracts and enjoyed relatively peaceful labor relations in return. However, one foreman in particular refused to abide by the contracts. This contributed to a series of escalating grievances and finally to a strike and complete factory closure in 1901. Although Patterson publicly stood behind his foreman's decision, he granted the man a "long vacation" to find other work.[5]

The offending foreman and strike leaders were not the only ones to lose their jobs. When the factory reopened, Lena Harvey, NCR's welfare manager, was not invited back. Her firing seems to have been a response to employee and management anger at the welfare program. Yet welfare work did not stop at NCR. In fact, over the succeeding years, Patterson employed a series of welfare managers and greatly expanded the company's welfare program. Welfare Hall and the NCR Schoolhouse, for example, were both constructed after the 1901 strike.

The greatest change seems to have been the context within which welfare work proceeded. Shortly after the end of the strike and Harvey's firing, Patterson created the nation's first personnel department. He chose a former plant superintendent, Charles Carpenter, to direct the new Labor Department. Under Carpenter's guidance, the Labor Department instituted systematic policies for hiring, promotions, and firing. Welfare work was folded into the responsibilities of Carpenter's Labor Department.

THE LABOR PROBLEMS that accompanied NCR's rapid growth were shared by most businessmen at the turn of the century. Employers were concerned on a daily basis with improving efficiency and productivity, as well as with the threat of periodic strikes. Patterson's responses to those problems may, at first, seem unusual. Relatively few employers acquiesced so easily to their workers' demands for union recognition. More typically, they responded as Patterson did in the Spring of 1901, by locking out workers and refusing to employ union leaders. By most accounts, his experimentation with welfare work was equally unusual. Most historians accord welfare work only passing mention, portraying it as a minor and failed experiment undertaken by a few progressive businessmen.[6] Yet a growing body of evidence suggests that welfare work was a more widespread and significant development than has been previously recognized.

While welfare programs varied widely from company to company, most advocates agreed that any program worthy of the name should first promote health and safety at the workplace. This encompassed improvements such as ventilation systems, clean drinking water, and belt guards on machinery. It also entailed provisions such as on-site medical care, locker rooms and washrooms, clean toilets, lunchrooms, well-appointed restrooms, and manicured factory gardens. Patterson introduced all of these features at NCR.

A second group of welfare activities focused on health and safety in workers' homes. As at NCR, welfare workers undertook home visits, counseled workers in their personal affairs, created mothers' clubs, home garden contests, and sewing and cooking classes for employees and their families.

Companies also offered a wide variety of educational, recreational, and social activities to employees. These ranged from English classes for immigrants to noontime dancing and fully equipped clubrooms. NCR employees, for example, were encouraged to join the company's chorale and instrumental clubs.

Finally, financial benefit plans comprised a fourth category of welfare activities. Employers developed many plans of this type, from savings and loan plans to sickness benefit associations, pension plans, stock or profit-sharing plans, and, after World War I, life and health insurance programs.[7]

It is difficult to determine exactly how many American companies engaged in welfare work. Contemporary reports provide some rough indications, but these suffer from severe limitations. Proponents of welfare work, who wrote most of these accounts, were primarily interested in generating enthusiasm and conveying enough details to persuade more employers to adopt this strategy. Thus, they were more likely to list a few hundred nationally and regionally well-known firms than to compile comprehensive records of such companies.[8] Historians of the welfare movement have done the same.[9]

Nevertheless, scattered reports provide strong evidence that millions worked for firms offering some type of welfare program. A 1904 meeting of welfare workers in New York City, sponsored by the National Civic Federation (NCF), drew representatives from companies employing an estimated 500,000 workers.[10] A limited survey completed by the Bureau of Labor Statistics in 1916 provided detailed information on 431 firms employing 1,662,000 people. Yet only two years earlier the National Civic Federation knew of 2,500 companies conducting some form of welfare work.[11] One study in the mid-1920s estimated that 80 percent of the nation's largest companies conducted at least some type of welfare work.[12]

These firms were scattered nationwide, with heavy concentrations in the more industrialized and urbanized Northeast and Midwest. A 1915 study identified 223 businesses distributed across 107 cities: with 58 percent located in the Northeast, 34 percent in the Midwest, 4 percent west of the Rockies, and 3 percent in the southern states.[13] Some industries demonstrated a marked tendency to favor welfare work, particularly department stores, telephone and insurance companies, textile and machinery manufacturers, and the iron and steel industry. However, welfare work was certainly not limited to these sectors. The 431 companies included in the Bureau of Labor Statistics' 1916 survey represented more than twenty-two industries. Almost 15 percent of the firms were scattered so widely that they were grouped together under "other."[14]

Historical interest in welfare work has been episodic and, with only a few exceptions, has arisen in the course of studying other topics. Beginning with Irving Bernstein's *The Lean Years*, in 1960, early analyses of welfare work focused on its adoption as an anti-union device. Bernstein argued that employers added welfare work to their anti-union arsenal in a failed attempt to co-opt workers' loyalty. David Brody, most notably, took issue with Bernstein's conclusions, arguing that workers were willing to forgo unionism in exchange for good welfare programs. However, when employers curtailed welfare work during the Great Depression, workers no longer felt constrained from taking action.[15]

In the late 1970s and early 1980s, Daniel Nelson and Sanford Jacoby refocused the spotlight. Sidestepping anti-unionism, Nelson and Jacoby examined welfare work in the context of business efforts to rationalize the factory system. Welfare work emerges from this historical scrutiny as little more than an ill-formed, and quickly abandoned, first step toward systematizing labor policies.[16]

The continuation of corporate welfare work through the Great Depression and into the post–World War II era is a clear indication of the limits of this scholarship. Welfare work, as recent studies reveal, did not end.[17] If businessmen did not abandon welfare work, what did happen to the vibrant turn-of-the-century welfare movement? If employers continued to offer welfare benefits to their employees, how did such activities fit into the new system of personnel management that defined corporate labor policies by the mid-1920s?

The difficulty of fixing a chronology for the "rise and fall" of welfare capitalism highlights a larger dilemma. While there is widespread agreement that employers designed welfare work to solve their labor problems, we know very little about why they chose that particular strategy at that particular time. Recent case studies begin to address this question, suggesting that employers wanted to do more than deflect workers from unionism; they wanted to reform their workers' character. Broadening the older anti-union framework, and frequently benefitting from the insights of gendered analysis, this new scholarship suggests that employers designed welfare work to promote middle-class standards of morality. However, this picture is not well developed. Most of the new work appears in case studies focused on issues of workers' control. This literature addresses welfare work as a tangential issue rather than as the central issue.[18]

Against this backdrop of renewed interest, Andrea Tone's *The Business of Benevolence* stands out as the first study of turn-of-the-century welfare work in a quarter century.[19] Similar to the existing scholarship, Tone is interested in employer motivations. In contrast to earlier accounts, however, Tone is more concerned with welfare work as part of an emerging business-state relationship than with welfare work as it affected the labor-management relationship. *The Business of Benevolence* places welfare work within the larger context of Progressive Era reform, arguing that employers promoted welfare work as an antistatist strategy intended to persuade various constituencies that business was benevolent and, thus, government regulation was unnecessary. This analysis begins to answer the question of why employers turned to welfare work at the particular time they did; businessmen wanted to foster an antistatist public culture to counteract growing support for state intervention.

The welfare strategy appealed to a broad constituency of reformers, consumers, and laborers, Tone argues, largely because employers gendered discrete welfare features to promote Victorian notions of manhood and womanhood. On this level, *The Business of Benevolence* moves beyond recent case studies, explaining why welfare work emerged at a particular historical time and, in the process, embedding gendered analysis into the history of labor relations. Yet, in doing so, it leaves a number of fundamental questions unanswered.[20]

Ironically, Tone's focus on business-state relations precludes a thorough analysis of labor-management relations. Did welfare work simply deflect calls for welfare statism, or did it fundamentally alter the relationship between employers and employees? *The Business of Benevolence* examines the effects of welfare work on demands for state intervention; it does not investigate the internal impact of welfare work on the firms themselves. If gender shapes institutions and relationships, as well as discrete actions, what impact did the Victorian construction of manhood and womanhood have on the development of modern labor relations?[21] What happened when gender constructions changed? Tone does not, for example, carry gendered analysis beyond the Victorian era into her discussion of personnel management in the 1920s. Nor does her analysis explain how turn-of-the-century business benevolence differed from the benevolent paternalism of the early nineteenth century. Neither *The Business of Benevolence* nor earlier case studies fully address these issues.[22]

Sanford Jacoby's new study, *Modern Manors*, begins to address this for the post–New Deal era. Jacoby argues that corporate welfare practice changed from a pre–World War I feudal system of corporate paternalism to a post–New Deal system in which "genteel paternalism," grounded in ideas of "brotherhood," "bridge[d] fissures of ethnicity and race."[23] This intriguing argument reveals both the potential and the current limitations of this type of analysis. On the one hand, Jacoby asserts that businessmen purposefully gendered labor practice to gain the cooperation of white male employees and to attack unions. On the other hand, it is not clear how corporate brotherhood related to broader social constructions of brotherhood and masculinity in the post–New Deal era, or how employers constructed labor policies for their female employees. If gender served as a powerful shaper of corporate labor policy, we must be able to locate those policies within the larger gender system.

The lack of clarity in this regard may account for the significantly different characterization *Modern Manors* gives to early welfare capitalism than do Tone and others. This latter scholarship highlights the Victorian underpinnings of early welfare features. In contrast, Jacoby characterizes the same activities as feudal, referring to welfare companies as "industrial manors." Certainly feudal and Victorian were not the same. The gendering of labor relations suggested by these most recent works needs considerably more fleshing out.

At the same time, a number of questions about welfare practice, rather than employer motivations, remain unanswered. If, as this newer scholarship argues, welfare work sought to reform working people according to the standards of middle-class morality, why did welfare work vary so much from company to company? Why, for example, did some firms develop elaborate educational programs, while others concentrated on stock-purchase plans? And, given this wide variation, which labor policies should be categorized as welfare work and which should not? Historians have shown considerably less interest than did welfare advocates in delineating the boundaries of this movement. Certainly, educational programs and stock-purchase plans were welfare work. What about other practices included by some historians but not by others—factory redesign, employee representation, YMCA (Young Men's Christian Association) clubhouses, company towns, Saturday half-holidays? Without a clear sense of the content of welfare work, it is difficult to assess its role in labor-management relations. This vagueness may also account for the difficulty of determining if and when the welfare movement ended. Personnel management seemed to dominate employer-based labor policy in the 1920s. Yet, as we know, corporate welfare work continued through the 1920s and into the post–World War II era. What was it that continued, and how did it differ from welfare practices at the inception of this movement?

Searching for answers to these questions requires broadening the investigation beyond the traditional focus on employer motivations. I was curious about the specific content of welfare work and how welfare programs actually functioned. Further, I wondered about the nature of labor-management peace that might have descended on corporate America if welfare advocates had succeeded in solving the labor problem. This line of inquiry revealed the importance of assessing welfare work as part of a *system* for managing labor relations rather than as a reflection of employer goals.

As I argue in this book, progressive businessmen, welfare managers, and wage-earning employees jointly created the corporate welfare system. Businessmen and welfare managers clearly held the upper hand, defining the goals and initiating the practices that came to characterize the welfare system. They promised that welfare work would solve the labor problem by transforming contentious labor-management conflict into a harmonious labor-management partnership. By the early 1900s, these welfare advocates had settled on the nineteenth-century Victorian family as the model for this harmonious partnership. Like other Progressive Era reformers, welfare advocates drew lessons about personal behavior from the Victorian ideal. They assumed that social conflicts could be overcome by teaching their poor working-class clients to live according to the gendered ideals of the Victorian family. Thus, it is not surprising that many welfare activities paralleled those introduced by philanthropic reformers in the public sector. My research confirms that welfare work did seek to control labor relations by reforming workers' character. As I document in the pages that follow, welfare activities were carefully tailored to meet the assumed inadequacies of different segments of the laboring population. However, the ultimate object was not simply to make working people over in their employers' image, but to prepare them for their role in the new business partnership.

In this respect, welfare advocates applied the family model in a second, less understood, way. They called for transferring the relational structure of the Victorian family to the private corporation. Within the private family, individuals had inescapable obligations toward one another determined by their position in the family hierarchy. Welfare advocates asserted that a comparable set of reciprocal obligations (and rewards) should animate the corporate family. In this manner, advocates of the familial model sought to create an organic interdependence between what had been conflicting parties. More than a collection of discrete reforms, welfare work became the vehicle through which American business asserted an entirely new relationship between labor and management.

A distinctly gendered conception of labor and management animated this new relationship. Within the corporate family, employers assumed the authoritative role of fathers and assigned the subordinate role of children to their employees. Yet this was not simply another version of the traditional two-party struggle for power. The Victorian model, as well as the growing complexity of corporate management, demanded a third party to make the partnership work. Businessmen hired welfare managers to act as corporate mothers. Like mothers in the Victorian family, welfare managers assumed responsibility for creating a harmonious household. In this capacity, welfare managers played a defining role in the corporate welfare system. Businessmen asserted that they had neither the time nor the expertise to foster the desired partnership. They hired welfare managers to build the bridges that would bring them and their employees together in a cooperative partnership. This unique gendering of the labor-management relationship temporarily opened the managerial doors to an eclectic group of women (and men), whose very femininity seemed to qualify them for positions in an otherwise masculine world of business management. In most cases, employers left it to female welfare managers to design and implement the myriad activities that characterized corporate welfare programs.

Until now, historians have neglected this aspect of the corporate welfare system. Assuming that welfare work was simply a new battleground with the same combatants, historians approached welfare work as a two-party contest between labor and management.[24] Historical accounts of welfare managers are skimpy at best, serving primarily to demonstrate workers' opposition to the welfare system—an opposition that often expressed itself in animosity directed at the welfare workers.[25]

However, welfare workers were more than surrogates for busy employers. Although sympathetic to their employers' needs, welfare managers were not simply automatons carrying out orders from above. They had a distinct agenda of their own, which often placed them at odds with their employers. They brought a commitment to the familial ideal that differed in significant ways from their employers', particularly regarding the nature of the obligations corporate fathers owed to their corporate children. In addition, welfare managers sought to establish labor management as a permanent function of modern business operations and to carve out positions of authority for themselves in the new managerial bureaucracy. In order to achieve this, they found it necessary to define their tasks, their expertise, and ultimately their contributions in more androgynous terms. Rather than claiming authority as corporate mothers, they recast themselves as models of a new professional business manager.

Employers generally accepted welfare managers' efforts to bring employees into the partnership with programs designed to reform employees into loyal, productive workers. Employers balked, however, when welfare managers recommended that they fulfill their own obligations within the partnership. Furthermore, businessmen refused to grant welfare managers the authority they demanded within the new corporate bureaucracies. Although they praised welfare managers' special expertise, businessmen were unprepared to equate what they believed were feminine instincts with business expertise.

In the end, employers refused to implement such a radical reconfiguration of the labor-management relationship. Against the advice of their welfare managers, they applied the family model in a limited form, supporting programs designed to reform individual workers, but not the corporation itself. For their part, employees rejected the role of children, and, recognizing their employers' lack of commitment to real reciprocity, they supported only those welfare activities that they could turn to their own advantage.

By the mid-1920s, most large employers turned to a different model of the labor-management relationship: personnel management. Advocates of personnel management challenged the welfare system's familial model, arguing instead that the labor-management relationship actually resembled the modern consumer marketplace; employers needed to be discriminating purchasers of productive labor and recognize that working people were similarly discriminating in their search for good employers. From this perspective, the manager of corporate labor programs needed to combine the skills of an expert purchasing agent with those of a good salesman. Personnel managers asserted that these were essentially masculine qualities. Rather than the nurturing and domestic skills of welfare management, personnel management called for expertise in the "manly art of handling men." Welfare work lived on, not as a system to promote corporate partnership, but as a collection of benefits designed to "sell" the corporation to potentially discriminating employees.

This regendering of corporate labor relations ended the nascent welfare movement, and with it, the assumption that the modern corporation bore an inherent responsibility for the general welfare of its employees. In her role as corporate mother, the welfare worker had symbolized the familial labor-management partnership. When the welfare ideal gave way to personnel management, welfare workers lost their special positions in the managerial bureaucracy. Those who remained found themselves subordinated within new, more powerful, and male-directed labor departments.

Chapter One

Redefining the Labor Problem

rior to the advent of welfare work, employers had pursued one of two general strategies in their dealings with employees. Confronted with rebellious workers, an employer might look to the example set at Homestead in 1892. There, company management spent months preparing for an armed showdown with employees, stockpiling inventory and turning the factory into a defensible fortress. One Georgia textile manufacturer summed up this repressive approach to the labor problem when he told an interviewer that "in an acute situation where I had only men to deal with I'd just as soon get a gun and mow 'em down as not."[1] In addition to violent confrontations, the repressive model included the use of company-paid spies to ferret out union organizers and sympathizers, the immediate discharge of those employees, blacklisting, and the yellow-dog contract. This antagonistic method incorporated more subtle strategies to solve problems of inefficient labor. Whether or not they engaged in outright repression of strikes and union sympathizers, most employers manipulated wage rates, work rules, and production processes in a concerted effort to force greater output from their workers.

By the turn of the century, public officials, the courts, and industry trade groups lent a degree of legitimacy to this strategy. In a practice reminiscent of 1877, for example, government troops broke the Pullman strike and boycott in 1894. At the same time, the courts became increasingly sympathetic to employer appeals for protection of property, issuing numerous antistrike injunctions after the mid-1890s.[2] In 1903, the National Association of Manufacturers adopted an aggressive open-shop platform. Association membership accorded a degree of respectability to employers advocating the "big stick" solution to the labor problem.

Despite these sanctions, some employers turned to a tradition of benevolent paternalism to solve the labor problem.[3] As far back as the founding of the Slater Mills in 1790, some employers proffered the carrot, rather than the stick, to ensure themselves an industrious, loyal workforce. Samuel Slater promised an education in the company's Sunday School to attract young farm boys to the new mill.[4] Other textile manufacturers, facing similar labor shortages, developed more elaborate programs to entice hard-working, tractable workers to remote mill towns. Textile mills built in Lowell, Massachusetts in the 1820s and 1830s drew most of their workers from among the daughters of area farmers. Cheaper and less troublesome than men, women were an ideal labor force for the nation's first large-scale mechanized factories. However, manufacturers had to convince apprehensive parents that mill life would not strip their daughters of familial protection. Nathan Appleton, a founder of the Lowell Mills, recalled that in order to protect the virtue of their women workers the "most efficient guards were adopted in establishing boarding houses, at the cost of the Company, under the charge of respectable women with every provision for religious worship."[5] Mill owners soon added a full complement of protective institutions—schools, hospitals and churches—to the boarding-house system.

Dependence on water and coal power forced many nineteenth-century manufacturers, like the textile mill owners, to locate their plants far from towns. Isolated from established institutions, employers in company towns pioneered in providing for the physical and moral well-being of their workers. However, paternalism was not limited to company towns. Prior to industrialization, most apprentices and journeymen lived and worked as junior members of the master craftsman's family. As production with waged labor replaced the apprentice system in the nineteenth century, employers continued to claim some responsibility for their workers' welfare, especially when the employers' own welfare was at stake. Employers frequently tried to help both their employees and themselves by loaning money, counseling temperance, retaining aged workers on the payroll, or supporting benefit associations.

Henry J. Heinz, struggling out of bankruptcy in the late 1870s, regularly admonished intemperate employees for the harm they were doing to themselves. In 1878, he sent an intoxicated jellyman home, demanding that the man return only "when his head would be clear," and presumably when he would be able to make the jelly clear as well.[6] Heinz's temperance campaign included a talk given in his home to all wagon salesmen. At the end he extracted a pledge from each not to drink.[7]

Like Heinz, many nineteenth-century employers provided for their employees' welfare as a personal responsibility. Gerald Zahavi describes similar practices at the Endicott Johnson Company.[8] For example, George Johnson often attended to injured workers and, when needed, fetched the doctor himself. Employers' wives played an important part in this system of benevolent paternalism. In the 1890s, Mrs. George Johnson taught sewing and domestic arts to local girls in her home.[9] Mrs. Joseph Bancroft performed similar duties for the children of Bancroft and Sons Company employees, baking turnover pies for each of the fifty children in the company's town at Rockford, Delaware.[10]

By the early 1890s, a number of employers began to question whether either method, repression or benevolent paternalism, would ever solve the labor problem. As continuing strikes and organizing drives demonstrated, workers showed no sign of being beaten into permanent submission. Large employers in particular began to find repressive strategies increasingly problematic. Aggressive anti-unionism opened the door to a public scrutiny that was damaging to both personal and corporate reputations. Nor were employers satisfied that they were extracting the most work possible from their employees. While mechanization gave employers a means of controlling the pace and quality of production, it raised the potential for costly slowdowns and sabotage by disgruntled employees.[11]

THOSE EMPLOYERS who began to search for new strategies for solving the labor problem did so in an environment very different from the earlier ones that had fostered either the repressive or paternalistic approaches. Mechanized production and an expanding national marketplace were transforming the work experience dramatically. NCR's growth was admittedly spectacular. Still, the average workforce per plant more than doubled in size in most major industries between 1870 and 1900. While workforces numbering in the thousands were common only in the steel and textile industries in the 1880s, after 1900 numerous other industries, from meat packing to electrical equipment, employed thousands of workers per plant, and steel and textile workforces grew to the tens of thousands.[12] New industries, especially the giant department stores and telephone companies, employed similarly large numbers of workers.

These larger workforces were called on to perform different kinds of jobs than were their predecessors. In some industries the demand for unskilled, and particularly for semiskilled, labor exploded. By the turn of the century, semiskilled operatives performed virtually all production jobs in the textile industry and were the fastest growing group in many other industries. Newer sectors of the economy, such as the department stores and the telephone and insurance companies, created new types of jobs. Combined with an expansion of bureaucracies within American business, retail and clerical jobs offered new options for women, who entered the workplace in ever greater numbers throughout the early twentieth century. Workers vying for jobs in this changing labor market, often seeking to protect skills or autonomy in the face of changing production processes, did not submit quietly to the new industrial landscape.

At the same time, the great merger movement of 1895–1904 resulted in the consolidation of one-quarter to one-third of the nation's manufacturing stock. Thousands of firms disappeared through mergers, leaving a small number of powerful corporations in many key industries.[13] In a number of cases these mergers prompted increased labor activism, especially as unions struggled to protect hard-won recognition in the face of corporate efforts to consolidate power over both their markets and their labor forces. This was the underlying motivation for the 1892 lockout and strike at Homestead. A decade later, when the McCormick and Deering families, along with three other firms, formed the International Harvester Corporation, union organizers found sympathetic ears among workers at both the McCormick and Deering plants. In the wake of a 1903 strike at the Deering works, one investigator reported that "if William Deering had kept the business, the trouble would not have come, but the people say 'the Company has gone into a Trust; why should we not combine?'"[14]

As at NCR, important changes in the relationship between employers and employees accompanied expansion of this magnitude. These changes affected the way many employers understood the labor problem. Small shop production in the mid-to-late nineteenth century generally entailed the employer's direct involvement in daily operations. While few may have been as persistent as Patterson, both his proximity to the factory floor and his supervision of production were typical of the era. However, as workforces and factory spaces grew, and as mechanized, mass production replaced made-to-order or small-batch production, foremen increasingly replaced owners as front-line supervisors. By the late nineteenth and early twentieth centuries, employers in mass-production and mass-marketing industries had entrusted most aspects of daily operations to foremen. In addition to overseeing production itself, foremen generally hired, trained, and disciplined workers; they set the pace of work and frequently set wages as well.[15] To the extent that foremen replaced employers as supervisors on the shop floor, workers remained subject to a highly personal and often autocratic control of their work lives.

Employers, however, experienced these changes differently. Over time, all but the smallest firms added layers of management between workers and employers.[16] In some respects the expansion of the managerial hierarchy rivaled the growth of the wage labor force.[17] While the numbers of wage-earners in manufacturing, mining, and transportation grew by almost 30 percent between 1910 and 1920, the growth among supervisorial employees exceeded 65 percent. By the early twentieth century, as many as four layers of managers might separate employers and employees in the largest American firms. Sitting at the top of the hierarchy, employers lost direct contact with their employees.

This separation was exacerbated further by the increasingly different tasks each performed. The executive of the modern firm devoted less and less time to daily operations, where contact with workers might occur. Instead, he concentrated on long-range planning and finance, often in home offices distant from the firm's many plants or in executive suites isolated from the shop floor.[18]

Employers in rapidly expanding industries felt this loss of intimate contact with their employees in a number of ways. As lines of communication spread across layers of management, workers, like those on strike at Deering in 1903, were less inclined to balance their interests and needs with those of an infrequently seen employer. Equally troublesome, employers were not entirely confident that foremen transmitted either their orders or their employees' concerns very faithfully. Reporting on conditions at the Colorado Fuel and Iron Company in the aftermath of reforms in 1914, Ivy Lee noted that "the mine superintendents and petty bosses have all the faults of their kind and the Company has no assurance that its policies are being carried out."[19]

The experience at NCR was typical. Despite a belief that his office door was always open, John Patterson had to admit that by the late 1890s a worker would have needed the "agility of a Rocky Mountain goat" to have reached him over the walls thrown up between subforemen, foremen, department heads, and the president. This loss of contact, he claimed, deprived the company of good ideas and left ambitious workers with little hope of recognition or advancement.[20] While an expanded management hierarchy promised greater productivity by rationalizing business operations, the consequent loss of personal contact between employer and employee might also entail costs.

Employers searching for a new solution to the labor problem frequently cited the lack of personal contact with their employees as a new and serious problem to be remedied. Under present conditions of industrial production, noted a speaker at a 1902 conference on the labor problem, "there remains no longer the personal touch, and sympathy is lost in estrangement."[21] In fact, nostalgia for a mythic golden past of close, caring relations between employer and employee tinged many turn-of-the-century accounts of the labor problem. As late as 1919, the president of an urban railway company attributed an unmeasurable loss of efficiency to the "failure to protect and continue in effect that close intimate relationship which obtained during the days of small organizations when the proprietor or general manager knew each man by his first name, was familiar with his family affairs, and had more or less first hand knowledge of the hopes and ambitions of each member of the organization."[22]

A growing number of executives concluded that a reformed, humanized business system must overcome this lack of intimacy. Trying to recapture this familiarity through the benevolent paternalism of an earlier era was unrealistic. How could an employer provide a timely home loan to a hard-working employee if he did not even know he existed? How could he offer sage advice to a troubled worker he had never met? They needed, as one employer phrased it, a "personal contact mechanism" between themselves and their expanding workforces.[23]

Beyond the changed environment inside the modern corporation, employers also confronted a new environment outside the factory walls. When the nation moved through the first industrial revolution and into the post–Civil War era, entrepreneurs had pointed to the invisible hand of market forces to explain the dynamics of American capitalism. Arguing that the American economy was open and competitive, businessmen claimed that concentrations of market power were the uncontrollable consequence of natural competition and that such concentrations of economic power need not be feared. The pursuit of one's personal interests, classical liberalism theorized, redounded to the benefit of all. Thus, the entrepreneur could be neither too greedy nor too successful in the competitive marketplace.

Throughout the last quarter of the nineteenth century, however, the American economy conformed less and less to the model of the classically competitive marketplace. With the rise of cartels, pools, trusts, and, eventually, integrated corporations, market control in many industries became concentrated in monopolies or in a handful of giant oligopolies. Concentrations of economic power no longer seemed to be the result of some invisible hand, but rather the consequence of active manipulation by corporate owners and financiers.[24]

With increasing frequency, corporations found themselves subject to attack from journalists, academics, and politicians. Exposés of unethical business practices, shoddy or harmful products, and abhorrent working and living conditions shocked readers of popular magazines. A new generation of economists challenged the classical theory that unfettered pursuit of one's self-interest promoted the common good.[25] Politicians, riding a groundswell of public outrage, frequently weighed in against the large corporation, as well. Corporate efforts to solve the labor problem took place in an environment that increasingly questioned the legitimacy of corporate power.[26]

One progressive reformer summed up the situation: "The alert and intelligent member of the capitalist group is aware of the fact that he and his class are under surveillance today; that they are distrusted by many of the people, and that the situation demands, not an arrogant defiance of this irrational attitude, but an earnest effort to justify their place in the social organism."[27] Business executives could hardly ignore these challenges.

The thousands of employers who adopted welfare work believed they were embarking on a new path toward harmonious labor relations. It was a path that promised to boost productivity, recapture the intimacy of a bygone era, and legitimize their place in modern society. The key to achieving these ends lay in rethinking the relationship between employers and employees. A group of prominent employers, labor leaders, government officials, and scholars gathering in Minneapolis in 1902 to discuss the "puzzling and sometimes distressing labor problem," gave voice to this new sensibility. All concurred that the nation's labor problem would remain intractable as long as capital and labor waged war on each other. Their aim was to find "some plan by which the industrial forces of the country may be thoroughly harmonized, the work of the country may be carried forward in the spirit of peace, and our whole people may advance."[28] The debate, conference participants argued, needed to be reframed and the language of conflict rejected. Modern industrial capitalism required cooperation between capital and labor and, significantly, promised mutual benefits to both. The business community, they contended, possessed the ability and bore the responsibility to initiate this transformation. It could do so by embracing the general movement toward welfarism.

Like participants at the Minneapolis Conference, welfare advocates argued that business success depended on a sustainable partnership between employers and employees. They rejected claims that an inherent conflict existed between these two groups. Employers and other welfare advocates often blamed labor problems on employees' failure to understand this. They believed that workers frequently misunderstood company goals, either because they lacked intelligence and sophistication, or because unreasonable and antagonistic union leaders led them astray.[29] The loss of personal contact between employers and employees exacerbated the problem. In addition to conflicts arising from misunderstandings, other confrontations were blamed on the inordinate selfishness of one party or the other. The task at hand was to help managers and workers recognize and overcome these problems. A good welfare program would create an environment in which workers and employers could understand their common interests and act in partnership for their mutual benefit.

When welfare advocates adopted the language of partnership, they joined a public discourse in which the idea of partnership appeared as an antidote to late-nineteenth-century social conflict. Some of that discourse, like calls by the Knights of Labor and Populists for worker and farmer cooperatives, was anathema to American businessmen. However, other strands spoke directly to their own experiences and interests. In the political arena, liberal Republicans who were influential among industrialists in the early 1870s urged closer cooperation between labor and capital. In place of labor's campaign for the eight-hour day, which they condemned as divisive class legislation, liberal Republicans promoted profit sharing as a form of "industrial partnership" that would lead to social harmony.[30]

A cultural debate about the meaning of the work ethic in the late nineteenth century also focused on the idea of an employer-employee partnership. The work ethic had promised success in the form of independent entrepreneurship to those who were industrious, thrifty, and honest. However, as opportunities for independent entrepreneurship shrank with industrial expansion, some promoters of the work ethic redefined success in terms of a business partnership. Throughout the 1880s and early 1890s, a vocal minority of businessmen and reformers publicized profit sharing as a modern form of proprietorship. Like the liberal Republicans before them, these late-nineteenth-century advocates of industrial partnership envisioned a society in which class harmony replaced class conflict.[31]

At the same time, the Social Gospel movement elevated cooperation between employers and employees to a religious duty. Washington Gladden, a leading minister of the Social Gospel movement, called on both capital and labor to lay aside their quarrels and apply the Golden Rule in their dealings with each other. While many businessmen may have questioned Gladden's assertion that cooperative relations must ultimately lead to the abolition of the wage system, they found great comfort in his prescriptions to workers. He advised workers to turn inward and find reward for their labor in the dignity of a job well done rather than battle over how the profits of industry ought to be divided. Gladden warned workers away from the "noisy, crazy, crack-brained creatures" who led labor unions.[32] On the other hand, he instructed employers to replace selfishness with a genuine concern for their employees, demonstrated by caring for their health, comfort, and religious and moral welfare. Gladden's moderate wing of the Social Gospel movement showed businessmen a way to integrate their spiritual lives with their worldly lives. It was a path that demanded little real sacrifice, yet promised considerable returns in the form of a more cooperative workforce.

Given the tenor of these public discussions, it is not surprising that the idea of partnership proved attractive to those in search of new strategies for solving the labor problem. However, they did not support the idea of partnership indiscriminately. Nor were they simply insincere in their use of this language. Instead, welfare advocates infused it with a set of meanings that clearly defined the labor-management partnership on management's terms. John Patterson referred to this partnership as a "give-and-take proposition of mutual benefit and mutual responsibility."[33] Management's responsibilities within this partnership generally included the provision of safe, sanitary work spaces and fairness in employment. In return, workers were expected to adopt the work ethic as their guide: to be industrious, disciplined, honest, and sober. A pamphlet distributed to all employees of the Endicott Johnson Company obligated managers to know their jobs, be fair, and act like gentlemen. Reciprocally, workers were to assume responsibility for maintaining machines in good order, demonstrate good morale, and earn their annual bonus.[34] Clearly, workers were not invited to join employers as partners in the executive boardroom. Nor did employers propose to join workers on the line or behind the counter.

Just as mutual responsibilities did not imply identical responsibilities, mutual benefits did not entail identical benefits. Welfare advocates promised lower costs, higher productivity, and greater profits if both partners fulfilled their responsibilities. If successful, there would be a larger pie to divide between capital and labor. As business prospered, workers could look forward to more stable employment and perhaps to higher wages as well. Companies that adopted welfare work boasted wage rates at or above those paid by other firms. By 1914, for example, the Metropolitan Life Insurance Company enforced an internal minimum wage of $9.00 per week for all female employees.[35] Welfare advocates pointed to the long-term benefits of financial security—cleaner and safer homes, time to cultivate healthy recreation, and better educated children who could escape the insecurity of low-wage jobs.

Workers could enjoy the benefits of partnership on the job, as well. In addition to safer and healthier workplaces, welfare advocates held out the possibility of shorter working hours. In 1902, for example, clerks at Filene's Department Store enjoyed a fifth of July holiday, while clerks at other Boston stores worked.[36] At the same time, the Kilbourne and Jacobs Manufacturing Company of Columbus, Ohio, inaugurated a five-day workweek, turning the Saturday half-holiday into a full holiday with no loss of pay.[37]

Welfare work offered tangible rewards to employers as well. Businessmen could expect larger profits and an edge over the competition. Yet, as attractive as these rewards might be, the intangible benefits of the welfare partnership were even more important. First, welfare work promised to solve the labor problem without seriously altering the way in which the economic pie was divided. When President Augustus Loring of the Plymouth Cordage Company considered the best way to distribute the "extra profits" generated by his firm's welfare program, he proposed a new profit-sharing plan rather than a general wage increase. In support of the profit-sharing plan, he asserted that the firm's current rates of "dividend and . . . wages [should be] considered the regular return [to] which the stockholder and employee are entitled, for their respective investments and labor." Loring assumed that the existing distribution of profits between capital and labor was equitable, and that "extra profits" ought to be divided in the same (unequal) proportions with "payment to the employee [at] the same rate of dividend on his yearly salary that is paid to the stockholder as an extra divided."[38] In 1916, the Bureau of Labor Statistics determined that a fairly comprehensive welfare program could be maintained for only 2 percent of a firm's annual payroll.[39]

Equally important, the welfare partnership promised to solve the labor problem without affecting the traditional power of employers vis-à-vis their employees. President Loring's willingness to share profits with employees of the Plymouth Cordage Company did not imply any willingness to share power. At the same time that he proposed the profit-sharing plan, Loring rejected a recommendation that he establish a welfare advisory board comprised of workers. He insisted that corporate officers and the board of directors continue to make all decisions about the company's welfare program.[40] Employers who established a welfare partnership with their employees decided which amenities they would offer and how each would be administered. Virtually all financial welfare plans, for example, asserted the employers' power through clauses that conditioned eligibility on the employees' "good behavior" and granted employers sole discretion to alter or abolish the plans. In the case of pension plans, employers' control over their employees continued into retirement. Most pension plans allowed management to withdraw benefits if retired employees engaged in unacceptable behavior (read: strike support or union activities). Most plans also placed caps on the total income a worker could receive in retirement, lowering company-paid benefits in proportion to income received from other sources.[41]

Thus, the welfare partnership encompassed a hierarchical relationship in which management retained its traditional powers and prerogatives. Welfare advocates saw no contradiction between this and their belief that such a partnership could produce cooperation and industrial harmony. In fact, they entrusted the success of the welfare system itself to management's privileged role. As noted earlier, welfare advocates attributed much of the labor problem to workers' selfishness and lack of intelligence. Working people, they argued, were not mature enough to take on the responsibility of a more equal partnership with management.[42] Therefore, management ought to use its power to institute welfare programs that would educate employees up to their responsibilities. As one employer explained it, the employers' superiority within the labor-management partnership placed them in a position to "help [their] employees to help themselves."[43]

Although welfare work bore some resemblance to traditional strategies of both repression and benevolent paternalism, it developed into a wholly different approach to the labor problem. Whereas repressive strategies were designed to give employers the upper hand in this conflict and benevolent paternalism reflected a type of noblesse oblige exercised by the upper class toward the lower class, the new welfare strategy assumed that the interests and values of employers and employees were essentially the same.

The contrast with repressive strategies is obvious. In place of violence and spying and the animosity such methods produced, welfare work promised to fight labor activism by weakening the attraction of unions and redirecting workers' loyalty to the company. The DuPont Company, for example, awarded annual bonuses to those who contributed "either by invention, unusual ability, industry or loyalty . . . to the general good of the Company."[44] Despite the rhetoric touting bonuses as a reward for past service, executives clearly adopted the bonus plan as a peaceful anti-union device. Alfred I. DuPont wrote that the plan would "eliminate or reduce to [a] minimum demands for increased wages . . . [and] discourage efforts toward unionism. In case of strike this plan would exert influence with [the] men benefitted," since continuous service would be required for eligibility.[45] Welfare work provided other strategies for fighting unions, as well. The chair of International Harvester's Recreation Committee believed that company-sponsored athletic, social, educational, and economic organizations could capture the interests of employees "to the exclusion of outside attractions."[46] Rather than fighting rebellious workers, employers could reform them into a cooperative workforce.

Much less understood is the fact that good welfare programs differed as much from benevolent paternalism as they did from repressive labor strategies. Traditional paternalism fostered dependency among employees. Employees in the Lowell Mills boarding-house system, for example, depended on their employers for shelter, food, and even religious services. Fifty years later, the Greenhut-Siegel-Cooper Department Store subjected its sales clerks to a similar kind of paternalism. They could enjoy annual vacations only if they went to the company's cottage on Long Island. When Isabelle Nye began her work as welfare manager at Greenhut-Siegel-Cooper, she discovered that only a few of the department store's clerks took vacations, and they did so very reluctantly. Female clerks, Nye recalled, felt that such a "vacation" was really charity, and many preferred no vacation at all rather than accept charity.[47]

Welfare advocates recognized that workers took great offense at such treatment. Instead, they argued that employers should respect and encourage their workers' desire for independence. "Wholesale, indiscriminate charity," wrote the president of Dennison Manufacturing Company, "harms both giver and receiver."[48] A Carnegie Foundation study of pension plans went so far as to recommend only those plans that required employee contributions. The report reminded employers that "the responsibility of protecting oneself against dependence in old age belongs to the individual. . . . The duty of society does not lie in relieving the individual of this duty, but rather in providing the machinery under which the individual shall be able to discharge his obligations."[49] Welfare work, unlike traditional paternalism, promised to provide the machinery needed so that workers could care for themselves.[50]

This rejection of charity distinguished the welfare movement from traditional paternalism in a second way. While businessmen in the nineteenth century clearly expected their employees to be more loyal and industrious in return for paternal care, few justified their actions in this way. The Lowell textile manufacturers claimed that the boarding-house system was designed solely to protect their young female charges.[51] In the 1870s, Henry Heinz approached temperance as a moral crusade, not as an imperative of business success.

In contrast, welfare advocates argued that betterment work was simply good business, not philanthropy. Lee K. Frankel, vice-president in charge of employee and policyholder welfare at the Metropolitan Life Insurance Company, reported to the National Civic Federation in 1916: "We have for quite a number of years attempted to care for our people, not with any thought of philanthropy. I think it is safe to say that we do it because it pays . . . the proper care of the employee is a good business proposition." Frankel explained that the company's free lunch program was "not a gratuity; it means instead of giving them approximately a dollar a week more in wages, we are spending that money for them."[52] The company freely admitted that better nourished workers were more productive workers. While the paternalism inherent in Metropolitan Life's free lunch program is undeniable, it is equally important to recognize that welfare advocates firmly believed that pragmatic business considerations, rather than paternalism, guided their policies. Henry Dennison, president of Dennison Manufacturing Company and an enthusiastic advocate of welfare work, praised the National Cash Register Company because its program was "founded on economy, an economy which looks ahead for its returns."[53] John Patterson, president of NCR, posted signs throughout the factory with the simple message "It Pays."[54]

The argument that welfare work was a business proposition, not charity, shifted responsibility from the shoulders of the individual entrepreneur to the more abstract entity of the modern corporation. In contrast to the informal and ad hoc paternalism of the nineteenth century, welfare work emerged as a systematic and bureaucratic strategy for addressing the labor problem. This meant that policies designed to ensure employee welfare were often formally debated and adopted by top management, put in writing, and then offered to all who met eligibility standards.[55] Welfare work took shape as company- or plant-wide policy rather than as special favors granted on a case-by-case basis at the employer's discretion. Whereas nineteenth-century employers had exercised benevolent paternalism as isolated individuals, those who engaged in welfare work participated in a national movement that defined labor relations as an essential management responsibility.

The establishment of local and national organizations to promote welfare work added to the distinctiveness of this new labor relations strategy. H. H. Vreeland, chairman of the NCF Welfare Department, recalled that the organizing meeting for the Welfare Department in 1904 was the "first time that employers who were giving especial consideration to the welfare of their employees had been brought together, and that each one had an idea that this welfare work was an individual effort on his part in his particular locality, and that he was rather like the mole groping in a dark passage."[56] The National Civic Federation, the American Institute of Social Service, local chambers of commerce, numerous trade organizations, and a variety of trade and popular magazines supplied information to interested members. Employers' access to this kind of systematic information contributed to more elaborate and uniform labor practices than would have been imaginable in an earlier era. A company planning to add a lunchroom could obtain detailed budgets and equipment lists, as well as recommendations on menus. The executive charged with developing a pension plan did not have to reinvent the wheel. Through his trade group or the National Civic Federation, he could obtain explanations of the pros and cons of various plans. Upon request, he might also receive copies of specific plans that, with a few alterations, could be adopted in toto by his own company. In addition to gathering and distributing information, these organizations contributed to the bureaucratization of employee welfare by encouraging the formation of welfare departments directed by welfare managers.

Welfare managers are the least understood element of this new approach. Yet they were one of the crucial innovations of the corporate welfare system. In a business world that had grown increasingly complex, employers were not able (or willing) to devote the time needed to build a truly viable partnership with their employees. As they were beginning to do in more and more areas of operation, businessmen created a new level of corporate management to act in their name—the Welfare Manager.

Patterson's decision to hire Lena Harvey in 1897 exemplifies this new trend. Welfare managers, like Harvey, functioned as the "human contact mechanism," whose purpose was to breathe life into the concept of the business partnership. Along with the employers who hired them, welfare managers invented a labor relations system in which they served as the indispensable bridge between employers and employees. The way in which employers and welfare managers defined this new managerial position is central to understanding the kind of labor relations system that took shape.

Chapter Two

Like a Family

In the mid-1890s, the Bancroft and Sons Company housed its 500 textile workers in company towns. Yet owner John Bancroft found himself in a situation similar to Patterson's at the National Cash Register Company. He no longer knew all of his employees. Over the next decade, the Bancroft and Sons workforce almost tripled.[1] The majority now lived in independent communities near the mills, not in company towns. In 1902, Bancroft decided to address the growing separation between himself and his workers by placing the firm's traditionally paternal relations on a more systematic basis. He wanted all his employees to feel the "warmth of his interest" in their welfare.

Bancroft turned to Elizabeth Briscoe to undertake this work. The company initially hired Briscoe as a schoolteacher in 1879. Her personal interest in the welfare of her charges, combined with a religious call to be of service to others, led Briscoe to expand her activities beyond the classroom. By the time John Bancroft appointed her as the company's first welfare manager, Briscoe had, on her own, already established educational and religious clubs for young female employees. She encouraged the women to share their problems with her and offered sympathy and advice in return.[2] Here was a woman who could project Bancroft's personal concern for his employees' welfare. As welfare manager, she could devote the time necessary to broaden this personal relationship to all employees. Briscoe clearly understood her responsibilities as a continuation of the firm's traditional paternalism. She later explained to a class of social workers that she was "simply carrying on the work initiated by the elder Mrs. Bancroft."[3]

Although Bancroft appointed her to manage a new Welfare Department, he defined her responsibilities only vaguely. He announced to employees that she would engage in "special service."[4] Briscoe later recalled that neither she nor Bancroft had any definite plans for her work.[5] Briscoe first sought to gain the trust and friendship of the workers she was hired to serve. She made a practice of visiting sick and injured workers in their homes. When she found cases of financial distress or need, she recommended loans or material assistance.

Over time, employees came to expect Briscoe's involvement in a wide range of personal problems. Acting in the company's name, Briscoe intervened to return a young girl to her mother in England, supported the wife of a drunken employee, and helped a discharged worker regain employment. Yet her assistance was not indiscriminate. The drunken husband, for example, was warned to sober up or he would be responsible for his family's eviction from company housing. She thoroughly investigated employees' work habits before arranging for them to be rehired.[6]

By 1907, the role of the Welfare Department was fairly well developed. The Bancrofts had defined Briscoe's job as "'interpreting the position of the employer toward the employees,' and acting as 'the representative of the employees, bringing before the firm any grievances that affect the employees individually or collectively.'"[7] Briscoe continued to visit workers and their families in their homes, to lend a sympathetic ear to all employee grievances, and to present the company's point of view in differences with employees. She also developed a broad range of welfare activities designed to make the Bancroft workers' lives healthier and happier. She managed the firm's safety program, taught sewing and cooking to the young women, organized team sports for the men, held weekly religious services, carefully selected reading material for the company library, and installed dining rooms, washrooms, and restrooms.

ELIZABETH BRISCOE, like Lena Harvey at NCR, helped to set the pattern for the kind of business partnership that would characterize the corporate welfare system. It was a partnership that responded to employers' desire for intimacy and cooperation with their workers, while ensuring that employers maintained absolute power. No model of such a partnership existed in the business world. Thus, employers and their welfare managers had to look elsewhere. Through trial and error they settled on a model from the private world—the Victorian family. In a nation wracked by social conflict, the late-nineteenth-century Victorian family stood out as a working example of a cooperative partnership.

Forged during the economic transformations of the early nineteenth century, this family ideal was uniquely responsive to the demands of the industrial marketplace.[8] In its ideal form the Victorian family performed a dual mission. First, it was charged with training children to take their proper place in industrial society. The Victorian ideal assumed that children were highly malleable and in need of constant guidance and instruction as they matured. Young boys and girls were to learn discipline, frugality, and deference to authority. Boys would be trained to be self-reliant, Christian gentlemen and educated to take their place as leaders in the commercial world. Girls would be encouraged to develop nurturing and pious characters and instructed in the domestic arts and social graces.

At the same time that the Victorian family prepared its children to join industrial society, it made the home into a refuge from the harshness and insecurity they would find there. This family ideal recognized that greed, unbridled aggression, and tempting vices awaited the young men, and their fathers, who were sent into the business world. (Such a world was deemed unfit for women's finer nature.) In compensation, the home and family were expected to be bastions of civilization, harmony, and morality. The layout and furnishings of the Victorian home contributed to the proper atmosphere. Libraries, sitting rooms, and formal parlors separated their occupants from the general bustle of household chores, as well as from the outside world. Middle- and upper-class families furnished their homes with books, pianos, pictures, hanging plants, and upholstered furniture that bespoke the value placed on high culture and genteel behavior.

Within this setting, men, women and children were assigned distinct, but interdependent, roles. As industrialization shifted production out of the household, these roles reflected new definitions of the character and duties of the sexes. The man who lived up to the Victorian ideal was resolute and unsentimental. Masculine passions—ambition, aggressiveness, and competitiveness—distinguished the true man from timid and self-effacing women. Unlike women, the Victorian man was an individualist; he prized autonomy in his own life and mastery over the lives of others. Such a character might produce the brute and result in social chaos. However, the Victorian gentleman avoided this disruptive possibility by exercising self-control and social responsibility. He channeled his passions and energy toward material success. He eschewed idleness and avoided vices that might dissipate his energy and distract him from productive ends.

Whereas an earlier generation might have proved its manhood in warfare, the Victorian gentleman fought his battles in the economic arena. "A man's business makes him," asserted one self-help author; "it hardens his muscles . . . works up his inventive genius, puts his wits to work, arouses ambition, makes him feel that he is a man, and must show himself by taking a man's part in life."[9] Following such prescriptions, Victorian men measured their manhood according to their success in the world of business. In the early-to-mid nineteenth century, this generally meant establishing oneself as a proprietor or professional; the personal autonomy enjoyed by this class of men was perhaps the most important mark of manly success. By the late nineteenth century, the increasing difficulty of achieving this type of manly autonomy, combined with the financial rewards in big business, contributed to a reweighting of the measures of manhood. Leadership and control over others (evidenced through executive positions in large corporations) became new marks of manly independence, valued as highly as had been personal autonomy for an earlier generation. At the same time, wealth assumed new importance as a measure of manhood. If, as was assumed, masculine character played out in the struggle for business success, then one could measure manhood by running the equation in the opposite direction: wealth must reflect the measure of one's manhood. Thus, work was at the core of Victorian masculinity. Men's familial responsibilities, as role models to their children and as breadwinners for their families, were necessarily derivative of their success in the workplace.[10]

It fell to the Victorian woman to raise her sons to resist corruption and to use only honorable means in their pursuit of such success. In addition, she was charged with creating a harmonious environment at home, one that would afford relief from the harshness of her husband's work-a-day world. As it was defined at the end of the nineteenth century, woman's temperament fitted her perfectly for these tasks. Popular literature, religious sermons, and numerous professionals asserted that women were inherently more moral, nurturing, sympathetic, self-sacrificing, pious, and domestic than men.

Women were to exercise these characteristics within the private household. They qualified women to instill moral values and habits of discipline and deference in their children. Women were expected to apply their domestic instincts to food preparation, cleaning, and shopping, as well as to child-rearing. Combined with domestic skills, women's aesthetic sensibilities helped them furnish the Victorian home in a fashion that reflected its occupants' sophistication and advertised their husbands' status. If they succeeded, Victorian women presided over islands of loving security and harmony.

However, that harmony derived from a clear sense of hierarchy and duty. Men's and women's temperaments and responsibilities were understood to be quite distinct, but complementary. Men acted as breadwinners and role models to their children. Women managed the household and reared the children. Whereas men were unsentimental, women were sympathetic. While men engaged in individualistic, competitive struggle, women sacrificed themselves to nurture others. Together, spouses provided for the welfare of their sons and daughters by supplying their material needs, ensuring a well-ordered household, building character, and maintaining discipline. They tempered the harshness of their authority and discipline with love. In return, children were expected to show respect for their parents. Family members resolved differences either by deferring to a parent or husband or by repressing such differences out of deference to family loyalty and order. Children and wives were expected to stifle their own will for the good of the family. Family unity and morale derived from each member fulfilling his or her obligations.[11]

Interestingly, the attractiveness of the Victorian family as a model of business partnership did not reflect the vibrancy of such families. Rather, efforts to pattern the employer-employee relationship after this family model were rooted in a turn-of-the-century debate over a "crisis" in the family. The failure of a growing number of families and individuals to live up to this ideal sparked the public debate. Participants bemoaned the weakening of the Victorian family. Instead of abandoning the Victorian ideal, however, they reasserted its importance and strongly promoted it as a viable and desirable family model.[12] Interestingly, efforts to strengthen this traditional family form focused not on the middle class where it might seem most appropriate, but on the growing working class. A number of factors combined to shift the focus of the debate in this direction.

Many attributed the breakdown in the family to middle-class women who seemed unwilling to fulfill their prescribed roles. By the early twentieth century, a growing number of women were obtaining college educations, joining the paid labor force, and choosing not to marry.[13] These women often rejected the limitations inherent in the role of the Victorian housewife and mother. They argued that the home could not be an island of harmony and morality in a sea of corruption and vice. Led by reformers like Jane Addams, many educated middle- and upper-class women redefined their housekeeping duties to include the public as well as the private sphere.

As they cast their nets more broadly, they discovered the greatest need among the working class. Here, lifestyles and living conditions departed most dramatically from the Victorian ideal. Working people, many of them immigrants, lived without the order, discipline, and economic security that lay at the center of the Victorian ideal. Initially blamed as a root cause of the crises in the family, middle- and upper-class women turned the tables and claimed the moral authority of Victorian womanhood to legitimize their efforts on behalf of the working class.[14] Through reform movements promoting temperance, charity, the abolition of child labor, antiprostitution, and other causes, Victorians made a concerted effort to bring non-Victorians into the fold, to remake them as Victorians.[15]

At the same time, sociologists began to study the impact of modern industrial society on the "breakdown" of the family. By the 1910s, a growing body of literature had concluded that industrial society made it impossible for families to fulfill many of their traditional tasks. Unstable economic conditions threatened men's authority as breadwinners and heads of household, limited their ability to control the conditions of their employment, and often left little choice as to which family members would work for wages. Families lost control over the conditions of their housing and neighborhoods in the face of largely unregulated urban growth. The expansion of commercial amusements removed young people from the direct supervision of their parents. Again, working-class families seemed most vulnerable to the disruptive effects of urban, industrial society.

Although sociologists began their studies of the crises in the family by chronicling dramatic changes in the education and employment levels, birth rates and divorce rates of middle- and upper-class women, their prescriptions for reform generally focused on the working-class and immigrant families that failed to emulate the Victorian norm in any way. They argued that other institutions must gradually take on responsibilities traditionally located in the family. In 1910, for example, a social worker noted that the school was "fast taking the place of the home, not because it wishes to do so, but because the home does not fulfill its function."[16]

While schools were seen by some as an appropriate institution to perform services not provided by the family, other institutions might suffice as well. Speaking at the Minneapolis Conference in 1902, Elizabeth Wheeler, welfare manager at the Shephard Company, asserted that the modern corporation had a responsibility to step into the breach. Working girls' extravagant expenditures on amusements, clothing, and even chewing gum belied their lack of culture, thrift, and discipline. Since many left school at a young age, it fell to the employer, Wheeler argued, to provide the guidance and discipline they lacked.[17] Officials at the Colorado Fuel and Iron Company similarly claimed that their employees' unsatisfactory home life obligated the company to undertake welfare work. In an effort to explain the advantages of such policies, they provided reporters with detailed vignettes of the violence, dysfunctional families, and unsanitary living conditions that existed in company towns prior to the introduction of welfare work. Such stories "illustrate[d] the environment the workmen made for their children, the dwellings they provided for themselves, the manner in which they handled the liquor problem, and the way they amused themselves, when left to their own devices."[18]

This type of advocacy for welfare work reflected a unique marriage of the concurrent debates over the breakdown of the family and the causes of the labor problem. It accepted social reformers' conclusions that immigrant and working-class families suffered from economic insecurity, poor health, and bad habits and that these contributed to social instability. It parted company, however, with those who railed against the modern corporation as the source of these problems and who looked to expanded government or reform organizations to enforce solutions. Instead, welfare advocates like Wheeler argued that employers' desire to reestablish personal contact with their employees meshed perfectly with employees' needs for guidance and support. They took business success as proof that employers possessed the habits and values they found lacking in working people.

It was at this juncture that welfare advocates counterposed images of the businessman as self-made man to reformers' portrayals of the businessman as Simon Legree. The self-made man was a widely used trope in nineteenth-century success literature, which both validated business success and explained business failure. Grounded in the ideals of Victorian masculinity, the myth of the self-made man assumed a linear relationship between character and business success. Old standards, like Benjamin Franklin's *Autobiography*, were joined in the nineteenth century by life stories of men whose primary claim to fame lay in amassing great fortunes. From P. T. Barnum's popular *The Life of P. T. Barnum, Written by Himself* (1854), to William Makepeace Thackery's widely read collection of biographies of famous businessmen, *The Ethics of Success* (1893), to hotel tycoon Orison Marden's *Pushing to the Front* (1894), which went through 250 editions, the literature of the self-made man shared a number of common themes.[19] Popular novels reinforced in fictional form the essential lessons of these real-life rags-to-riches stories. By the late nineteenth century, captains of industry replaced religious or military figures as literary heroes.

The key to success lay in individual character—ambition and hard work tempered by discipline, thrift, and a steady moral compass. As one "prophet of success" explained, "the things which are really essential for a successful life are not circumstances, but qualities . . . not the things which surround a man, but the things which are in him."[20] And how did one acquire the requisite moral character to become a self-made man? Even the most casual reader of nineteenth-century success literature discovered that lessons learned in childhood served as the foundation for future success. Rural origins and youthful poverty seemed to offer ample opportunities to work hard and struggle against destructive temptations. In this respect, the poverty of the urban working classes might be construed as an asset; the working poor were well positioned to become self-made men (or the women behind the self-made men, as we will see). Neither race nor the "misfortune" of foreign birth need hold a man (or woman) down.

Progressive employers ascribed to themselves the virtues of the self-made man. They rejected critics' aspersions on their character and offered themselves as role models. They proposed to use their own business success, and the character on which it necessarily must rest, to inculcate habits of discipline, thrift, and hard work that both they and their critics found lacking in working people. In the process, employers would achieve a second objective: nurturing new workplace relations that would bring them closer to their employees.

Despite the implications inherent in the term "self-made man," businessmen did not presume that they could accomplish these tasks alone. Character-building, the key to business success, after all, depended on the gentle guidance of Victorian mothers. Eulogizing mothers' crucial role, success-writer Orison Marden informed his readers that "the testimony of great men in acknowledgment of the boundless debt they owe to their mothers would make a record stretching from the dawn of history to today. . . . Few men indeed, become great who do not owe their greatness to a mother's love and inspiration."[21] Businessmen agreed with their critics that dysfunctional families contributed to the social problem. On the other hand, "functional families" lay at the heart of personal success and societal progress.

Thus, the Victorian family ideal, with its particular constructions of manhood and womanhood, served as the model for establishing a new mutually beneficial relationship between employers and employees. The corporation assumed that workers and managers, like members of a family, differed in abilities, responsibilities, and authority. Yet the contributions of each were essential to the success of all. The familial paradigm provided both a justification and a model for a system of close contact between employer and employee that would produce friendly, cooperative relations. Welfare work was introduced with the expectation that it would solve the labor problem by convincing workers that they were members of a compassionate community or family.[22] In this way, welfare work promised to satisfy the needs of both employers and employees and to promote social stability and harmony in the process.

Companies that engaged in welfare work frequently replaced the word "company" with "family" when referring to their businesses. The American Telephone and Telegraph Company, for example, redefined itself as the "Bell Family" and claimed that restrooms, matrons, and pleasant surroundings helped to create a family feeling among its employees. The company held an annual "Parents Night," at which operators' real parents could observe their daughters at work and in the care of their Bell Family.[23] The National Malleable Castings Company established a social club for its black employees to "build up the family spirit." When a strike by the firm's white employees forced it to lay off these black workers, company officials "advised them to get work elsewhere, but to remember that we still considered them members of our industrial family."[24] The Gilbert and Barker Manufacturing Company welcomed its new employees by informing them that they were "member[s] of a large family." Although the Gilbert and Barker family was too large for everyone to know each other personally, it was not too large for all to work together harmoniously.[25]

As at Gilbert and Barker, few firms allowed the size of their workforce to interfere with efforts to cast the company as a happy family. Employee magazines, published as part of many welfare programs, sometimes projected the family idea directly into their titles. "The Family Wash," "Curtis Folks," "Monitor Family Circle," "The United Clan," and "Sperry Family" addressed readers as members of a corporate family, not as faceless employees earning a pay envelope.[26] The Endicott Johnson Company paper informed its readers that "a business concern ought to be like a family as much as possible."[27]

The hired welfare manager played a central role in the new corporate family—she was the mother. Businessmen often selected women to fill these new managerial positions. This is somewhat astonishing at first glance, considering the crucial role that welfare work was designed to play (improving productivity, cementing worker loyalties, and fighting unions). However, progressive employers seeking to recreate the intimate and friendly relations they ascribed to a bygone era understood that masculine competitiveness and lack of emotion were ill suited to this task. Instead, they believed that the very qualities that traditionally excluded women from the world of business, their assumed selflessness, compassion, and domesticity, were just the skills needed to build a happy corporate family.

Thus, welfare work, conceived in both familial and gendered terms, created unprecedented opportunities for women in business management, where men monopolized virtually all positions of authority. Out of the twenty-seven social secretaries referred to in a 1906 article explaining this new occupation, about half were reported to be women.[28] Placement lists maintained by the Welfare Department of the NCF include the names of 144 women and 188 men involved in corporate welfare work. Over 25 percent of those listed as "special workers," and more than half of those identified as welfare managers, were women.[29]

Despite the large proportion of women engaged in welfare work, this was never an exclusively female occupation. Men always comprised a significant proportion of the nation's welfare managers. In many cases, men held the more authoritative and highest-paid positions within the field. Whereas women with little experience might earn between $700 and $900 per year, men with similarly limited backgrounds could expect to begin at $1,200 per year. Commensurate with their smaller salaries, women often entered welfare work on a more limited basis, perhaps beginning with the introduction and management of a lunchroom. In contrast, the evidence suggests that men in similar positions were expected to embark on more ambitious agendas, with emphasis on improvements in factory conditions that often required significant changes in plant facilities. Once they had gained experience, however, men and women were expected to undertake the same types of programs. Nevertheless, salaries and titles continued to favor male welfare managers. While top salaries for female welfare managers ranged from $1,800 to $2,500 per year, reports of men's salaries ranged up to $3,000 to $5,000 per year, with a few reports of salaries as high as $7,000.[30]

While women's "femininity" seemed to naturally fit them for the multifaceted role of corporate mother, welfare advocates never assumed that sex was the most important asset one brought to welfare work. Rather, welfare work attracted people who shared a sympathy for the difficulties of working-class life and a belief that community, not conflict, should characterize employer-employee relations. They chose to imbue their work with a feminine character because this seemed the most promising method for transforming the impersonal and conflict-ridden corporation into a harmonious family. As a consequence, welfare work drew from a rather heterogeneous group, including not only women and men, but also middle-class reformers and lifelong workers, the college educated and those with little formal education.

Gertrude Beeks, one of the earliest and most widely known welfare managers, represents the kind of person historians most typically associate with welfare management.[31] Beeks had been active in Chicago reform and businesswomen's organizations before her employment as International Harvester's first welfare secretary in 1901. Those activities brought her into contact with both Jane Addams at Hull House and the McCormick women, who were very active in the Chicago reform community.[32] While it is not entirely clear which of these connections persuaded Cyrus Mc-Cormick Jr. to hire Beeks, Jane Addams actively supported Beeks's plan to expand welfare benefits to the company's male employees.[33] In addition to Beeks, Addams helped to place at least one other Hull House resident, Mary Thaon, at International Harvester.[34] Other International Harvester welfare workers also had direct ties to the settlement movement, not only in Chicago, but also in Boston.[35] Beeks and those who followed her at International Harvester were not unique among welfare workers. Her voluminous correspondence with both employers and welfare workers reveals that quite a few had spent time either as settlement residents or with charity aid societies.[36]

While some employers relied on their connections with local civic reformers, others turned to the Social Gospel movement to find someone to conduct their new welfare programs. In 1897, NCR's John Patterson decided that Lena Harvey's work as deaconess of a local home mission qualified her to develop welfare work among his factory workers. Elizabeth Briscoe's religious meetings with factory women probably account for at least part of her attraction to John Bancroft. Other employers were drawn to the apparent expertise of the YMCA, and chose to recruit their welfare managers from among social workers in the YMCA's Industrial Relations Department. In 1911, Clarence Hicks, who later became a Rockefeller protégé and exponent of employee representation, talked his way into a position as welfare manager at International Harvester from a YMCA position at the company's McCormick Works.

Welfare workers drawn from these public sector reform movements brought with them a scientific knowledge of, and a sympathy for, the instability and insecurity of working-class life. They eagerly adapted their reform skills, and the social housekeepers' spirit of service, to the more limited arena of a single corporation.

However, experience in social housekeeping was not the only, or even the most important, training ground for corporate mothers. A significant proportion of welfare managers came from working-class families. Henry Heinz, for example, selected a former pickler, Aggie Dunn, to serve as welfare manager for his female employees. Beginning work at the age of thirteen in a Civil War munitions factory, Dunn spent ten years as a seamstress before becoming a pickler at the Heinz factory in the early 1870s. She left Heinz in the mid-1870s to marry, only to return by the end of the decade; when she returned, Dunn was a widow and the sole supporter of both her infant son and her father. After being elevated to the position of forewoman and then matron in the 1880s, Dunn slowly expanded her duties until, by 1924, she had responsibility for interviewing, hiring, counseling, and directing welfare activities for 1,200 women. Dunn remained loyal to her working-class roots throughout her career at Heinz, including dressing in factory apron and cap long after she had left the factory floor.

While the social housekeeper's training alerted her to the numerous inequities of modern life, welfare workers like Dunn brought an intimate understanding of the difficulties of daily life to this work. She knew "what it was to work, and worry, and skimp to make ends meet." In place of the social housekeepers' commitment to serve the lower classes, Dunn's commitment to her girls grew out of empathy. "These girls Mr. Heinz wanted me to look after were just so many Aggie Dunns over again!" she recalled. "They were traveling that same old bumpy road over which I had just come! . . . I understood these folks, plain like myself, and they understood me."[37]

Many welfare workers brought both the expertise of the social housekeeper and the empathy of a fellow worker to their new duties as corporate mothers. The vast majority, it seems, were self-supporting, attracted to the work as much by their own economic needs as by an altruistic spirit of reform. Catherine Brannick, for example, had been a factory worker before she entered Smith College. Brannick was trained as an agent by the Associated Charities of Boston in 1902 and spent time working with the South End House settlement in Boston before moving into welfare work, first at Curtis Publishing and then at International Harvester.[38] Although Brannick believed in the reforming mission of welfare work, her first priority remained her own financial well-being. Frustrated during her first months at International Harvester, Brannick informed Beeks that she would willingly leave welfare work and return to "business pure and simple" if she did not gain the confidence of employees and support from management soon.[39]

Regardless of whether an employer hired a woman or a man, a middle-class reformer or a lifetime worker, the welfare manager's responsibilities and powers clearly mimicked those of the Victorian mother. It was the welfare manager who directly supervised and implemented a firm's welfare program, just as the Victorian mother took direct responsibility for raising the children. The welfare manager's success depended in large part on her (or his) ability to project a feminine character into the work. The welfare manager was expected to exercise sympathy, persuasion, and a strong code of morality as she counseled employees on personal matters of health, love, drink, and how they spent their wages. Managers at Bancroft and Sons Company consciously exploited these feminine qualities in Elizabeth Briscoe. Noting that the firm's unskilled workers were particularly prone to drinking too much, Briscoe related that "if a man is away and his foreman suspects the reason [to be drink], I am sent after him. This is very humiliating and mortifying for him; he usually comes right to work that afternoon and is just as mad as he can be with the foreman for sending a woman after him."[40]

Like the Victorian mother, the welfare manager was also self-sacrificing in her efforts. Marion Brockway, House Mother at the Metropolitan Life Insurance Company, noted that "Mothering a family is at all times an exacting piece of work . . . but think of mothering a family of some nine thousand or more children."[41]

Beyond her feminine temperament, the welfare manager also needed domestic and aesthetic skills to properly care for her corporate family. Welfare managers supervised meal planning and food preparation in company lunchrooms, selected reading material for company libraries, and arranged classes and entertainment for employees. One supporter of welfare work praised the domestic skills of welfare managers by asserting that it was "doubtful whether even a medical inspector would be more useful in a tannery or any dirty business than a woman who knows how to clean house."[42] Here were the roots of many factory safety programs.

In addition, the welfare manager was charged with creating a pleasant, homelike atmosphere for employees. Welfare advocates believed that factory conditions could influence workers, just as the physical appearance of the Victorian home shaped the behavior and values of family members. Welfare managers carefully selected furnishings for lunchrooms, reading rooms, and men's smoking rooms to promote their ideas of genteel behavior and culture.

Female welfare managers assumed their parental role more openly than did their male counterparts. At H. J. Heinz, employees addressed the welfare manager as "Mother Dunn." When asked why she was called Mother Dunn, a company officer replied: "It's the one word which fully explains her. . . . She *is* a mother, as much so to the girls in her charge as she is to her own son." He noted that she "handles all those girls under her as if they were her very own daughters." Mother Dunn "worried" with her girls, visited them in their homes, and in a single month attended twenty of their weddings.[43]

When Metropolitan Life hired a new welfare manager in 1919, the president assured home office employees that she was an experienced mother, having raised a family of her own, and assigned her the new title of House Mother. A few months later, the company magazine, *The Home Office*, highlighted Mrs. Brockway's motherly role when it printed a laudatory letter, presumably addressed to President Haley Fiske.

In leaving Mrs. Brockway's office today, I tried to thank her for what she has done for me. I promised to tell the other girls that she really *can* help us. . . . I came to New York City about six months ago, quite alone, and found both the people and the ways of the city strange to me. One day I woke up to the fact that I very much needed advice. I am sure there are other girls with cases similar to mine. . . . Please, Mr. Fiske, accept my sincerest thanks for providing us such a "Mother" as I have found and the other girls will find Mrs. Brockway to be.[44]

Whether real or created, this letter clearly revealed the roles and relationships that animated the corporate family. President Fiske fulfilled his masculine duty by providing a good mother to his employees. By listening patiently to this young woman's problems and offering sympathy and advice, Mrs. Brockway provided the support and moral guidance that children might expect from their mother. Through the new occupation of the welfare manager, the businessman who promoted welfare work was relieved of direct participation in the more feminine aspects of this system. Contrary to most accounts, welfare work represented not corporate paternalism, but corporate maternalism.

Along with fulfilling maternal responsibilities toward their corporate children, welfare managers frequently attempted to reform their employers, the corporate fathers, as well. Despite the fact that employer sponsorship of welfare work would seem to demonstrate a progressive outlook, welfare advocates argued that management did not always understand or fully discharge its duty to ensure the health, safety, and security of its workforce. In this respect, welfare managers assumed responsibility, as did the Victorian wife, for taming her employer's more aggressive and uncouth behaviors. On a general level, welfare managers attributed antagonism to workers, low wages, long hours, and unsafe working conditions to excesses of personal aggression and intense competition. They purposefully lobbied businessmen to refine their behavior toward workers and to treat them as allies rather than as enemies in the marketplace.

In 1902, Elizabeth Wheeler explained to an audience of employers that the "heartless proprietor" needed to be "shamed into something better."[45] A decade later, Gertrude Beeks still included managerial reform as a central responsibility of welfare work. Despite progress, she asserted, "it is not to be contended that all employers are humane."[46] Welfare workers' efforts in this area extended to the entire range of the managerial hierarchy. In addition to the heartless proprietor, the "tyranny of the ignorant foreman" needed to be banished from the workplace.[47] It was the welfare manager's responsibility to observe "defects" in managerial attitudes and policies and make "timely suggestions for their remedy."[48]

Such remedies included calls for less autocratic control by foremen and line supervisors and for specific instruction to teach them how to replace repression and arbitrariness with cooperation and fairness in the management of workers.[49] Beyond efforts to "civilize" lower levels of management, welfare managers tried to persuade their employers that low wages and long hours were not beneficial competitive strategies, but rather a misapplication of cutthroat competition to a group that should be their partners in business. From her earliest days at International Harvester, Beeks lobbied the McCormicks to institute a fair wage scale. "While I have been very hopeful that under the [newly formed International Harvester corporation] the problems of wages and hours would be simplified," she wrote to Stanley McCormick in 1902, "it would not change the need of looking into inequalities in my estimation. I have talked of this matter for a year and I feel that it, together with attention to sanitary conditions and ventilation, are the foundation—rather should be—of all this work. I cannot say enough to emphasize the necessity of a fair wage scale."[50] Gertrude Beeks reminded an audience of welfare workers that cooperation by management was as important as cooperation by employees. "Welfare work will not succeed unless all the underlying principles of fair dealing are observed."[51]

This required the education of employers not only in the necessity of equitable wage rates and wage scales, but also in the need for shorter hours of labor. Based on expertise acquired through her work at Bancroft and Sons, for example, Elizabeth Briscoe lobbied the Delaware legislature to pass a nine-hour bill. To her disappointment, lawmakers passed a ten-hour bill applicable to female workers only. Although the Bancrofts opposed the nine-hour bill, Briscoe continued to press them to shorten the workday at their textile factories. "One of the things I am trying to do in my position," she reported, "is to bring employers to realize the poor grade of future work they are storing up for themselves" by requiring such long hours of labor, especially by children who "will become uneducated adult employees."[52]

Like the Victorian mother and housewife on which she was modeled, the welfare manager was defined in relationship both to those above and those below her in the corporate hierarchy. Above her, of course, was the employer. Within the corporate family he was cast as head of the corporate household. Whether he was an owner-manager or a hired manager, the fatherly role suited the businessman well. While industrialization made it impossible for most men to achieve the economic independence associated with Victorian manhood, employers comprised the minority of Americans for whom those standards might seem relevant. They and their immediate families often came closest to emulating the strict division of labor prescribed for members of the Victorian family. Those who presided over businesses with a history of family ownership or benevolent paternalism might easily see their employees as part of an extended family for which they bore some responsibility.[53] NCR's John Patterson explained his firm's elaborate welfare program as no more than an extension of his own family. "It all comes down to this," he said: "In our farmhouse my mother nursed the hired men and cared for them just as though they had belonged to her; she felt that they did. They came to feel so, too. The factory has now taken the place of the farm."[54]

As managerial hierarchies grew at the turn of the century, corporate executives began occupying private offices that expressed in physical form this interweaving of their domestic role as head of the household with their identity as businessmen. Furnished like Victorian parlors, these offices used essentially private and domestic symbols to express the businessman's power in the public sphere. At the same time, the homelike office created an illusion that the factory or store was simply an extension of his personal domain.[55]

The fatherly role allowed the employer to take an active and personal interest in the well-being of his employees without seriously challenging either his business acumen or his masculinity. In an era when intense competition quickly separated the winners from the losers, businessmen took pride in their ability to minimize costs and maximize profits. Few were willing to let other issues distract them from the pursuit of ever-higher profits and larger market share. Arguments that welfare work was simply good business, not charity, reflected this focus.

At the same time, these claims provided some protection against charges that employers were meddling in the feminine sphere of philanthropy. In the latter part of the nineteenth and early twentieth centuries women spearheaded the bureaucratization and rationalization of charity in America. Similarly, women led many of the public sector reform initiatives to improve housing and working conditions. Agitation and support for public sector reforms emphasized their inherent femininity. Reformers highlighted women's ascribed roles as mother, housekeeper, and protector of morality to legitimize both their public roles and the reform agenda. Private sector welfare work shared many of the assumptions, if not always the methods, of public sector social reform during this era. The hard-headed businessman could not afford to be portrayed as a social housekeeper. This was his wife's or daughter's role. Although feminine values of self-sacrifice, nurture, morality, and piety characterized private sector welfare work, the progressive businessman could claim to be no more effeminate than a loving father.

In fact, many executives consciously assumed the fatherly role in their effort to increase worker productivity and loyalty, or to burnish the corporate image. Julius Rosenwald's "fatherly interest" in his employees, for example, included an attempt to increase efficiency on the job by forbidding Sears employees from entering saloons within eight blocks of the plant as well as a strategy to check the power of foremen by threatening dismissal for unwanted advances made to female employees.[56] George Johnson of the Endicott Johnson Company purposely cultivated his fatherly image for similar reasons.[57] The company magazine highlighted Johnson's fatherly bearing in picture and print; a company marching song included the line "George F.s the daddy of this family"; and Johnson made a point of personally visiting the neighborhoods where his employees lived. Referring to these sojourns, he explicitly acknowledged his part in the corporate family. "As I go among my foreign neighbors, I am their 'Father'— even [to] some . . . older than myself. . . . This is a great reputation."[58]

Managerial discipline could be softened by playing father to unruly employees. Like a father who remained head of the household regardless of whether he was gentle or harsh, the executive who took this role to heart could experiment with less repressive methods of discipline without necessarily admitting that this weakened his authority. B. J. Greenhut of Greenhut-Siegel-Cooper, for example, tried to incorporate friendly advice for success on the job when reprimanding employees.[59] When Rowland Macy introduced welfare work at his department store, he continued to impose fines for infractions of store policy. However, in some cases such fines were charged against the employees only for the "moral effect"; employees were not actually obliged to pay.[60] Like various financial, educational, and recreational welfare activities, discipline meted out by a caring father figure might help to build employee character.

Framing the employer-employee relationship in this way allowed the businessman a wide latitude in responding to employee demands for a greater voice in company policy. He might agree to requests for paid vacations, safety guards on machinery or locker rooms, but claim that his superior knowledge and responsibility did not allow for a (more costly) general wage increase. Consistent with the fatherly role, management reserved the right to make all financial decisions for the family-company and its children-employees. Sometimes those decisions benefitted workers. More frequently, as when management refused demands for wage increases or shorter hours, they benefitted the company and its owners at the workers' expense. In this respect, the deference due to the Victorian head of household overlapped perfectly with the needs of American businessmen.

Employees, of course, filled out the picture as children in the corporate family. Officials of the Metropolitan Life Insurance Company, which adopted the familial role with both its employees and its policyholders, explicitly addressed their employees as children. "We are a family," President Haley Fiske told a convention of salesmen in 1916. He reminded them that as "children" of Mother Metropolitan they must act as "elder brothers" to policyholders.[61] While the familial metaphor became a part of Metropolitan Life's public and private persona, most firms assumed the familial role only toward their employees. Writing of the illness of two employees and the need to send a third away for convalescence, Bancroft and Sons' Elizabeth Briscoe noted that "in other respects our family are all well."[62] Laura Ray, welfare secretary at Greenhut-Siegel-Cooper Company similarly referred to the department store's employees as children in her corporate family. She proudly reported that store clerks rarely applied to charity organizations "because we take care of our vast family as far as we can."[63] The dramatic growth in the female and immigrant workforces at the turn of the century, and of black workers after World War I, lent strength to this construction. These were generally the least experienced and most dependent workers in the labor force. Popular images of these groups made it possible to see them as childlike and in need of supervision and guidance.

By the late nineteenth century, writers of popular romance stories and activists in a variety of social reform movements had shaped a stereotype of female workers as "women adrift."[64] This popular image assumed that workingwomen, as women, shared the purity, sympathy, and emotionalism ascribed to their Victorian sisters. Their innocence, often bordering on naiveté, made women adrift vulnerable to the many dangers and evils of urban and industrial life. Thrust into the world without parental protection, working girls became the victims of designing men, false advertisements, and uncontrolled desires to share the high life. While this stereotype bore little resemblance to the real lives of workingwomen, it did shape reformers' efforts to improve their lives.[65] Reformers crusaded to protect young workingwomen with boarding houses, social clubs, lunchrooms, antivice campaigns, protective legislation, and moral suasion.

Welfare advocates shared many of the assumptions that shaped this stereotype. However, unlike some of their contemporaries, welfare workers recognized that female employees worked out of economic necessity.

In response, they offered welfare work as proof that the modern corporation was a protector, rather than a corrupter, of young women. The adoption of welfare work frequently coincided with sudden increases in a firms' female workforce. Thus, it was no coincidence that the American Telephone and Telegraph Company, the nation's largest employer of female workers by the early twentieth century, became an early supporter of welfare work.[66] The McCormick Reaper Company, with a payroll of 5,000, instituted welfare features only after opening a new twine mill that employed 400 women in 1901. Sensitivity to the influence of mill work on the virtue of their female employees, and to the McCormick family's reputation, prompted this decision. Gertrude Beeks, hired to develop the new welfare program at the Twine Mill, expanded her activities to the company's male employees only gradually, and after first demonstrating their value amongst the women.[67] Like the McCormicks, Henry Heinz first introduced welfare work for his growing workforce of female picklers. By 1901, his company provided, among other amenities, a dining room, dressing room, bathrooms, and a matron, "Mother Dunn," to see to the girls' needs.[68]

Companies were often quite explicit in attributing their interest in welfare work to their employment of women. For example, a clear calculation of the feminine character informed Heinz's decision. "There is something about a woman's nature," he wrote, "which leads her to appreciate more highly these little conveniences than a man would do."[69] Marshall, Field and Company proudly explained that its welfare program "endeavored to throw about the girls employed in the establishment an atmosphere of protection."[70]

A dearth of statistics makes it nearly impossible to quantify the relationship between the introduction of welfare work and the hiring of female workers. However, broader labor market trends bear out the coincidence of these two developments. Two million women engaged in paid employment in 1880. More than 1 million women entered the workforce each decade over the course of the next forty years. By 1920, 8 million women, 25 percent of the nonfarm labor force, worked for wages.[71] Both in sheer numbers and in rates of employment, workingwomen became increasingly visible and integral to the American economy. Women's segmentation into a narrow band of occupations reinforced this visibility. Employers in a number of industries with high proportions of female workers enthusiastically took up welfare work—including those in textile and shoe manufacturing, printing and publishing, food processing and packaging, electrical supplies, department stores, and telephone and insurance companies.[72]

Popular images of immigrant workers similarly cast them as incapable of succeeding on their own. Two basic ideas informed attitudes toward the growing immigrant population at the turn of the century.[73] First, immigrants were characterized as Old World peasants leading unstable lives in the industrialized New World. Many explained the immigrants' tenuous existence by pointing to their un-American lifestyles. Immigrant women, according to this argument, lacked the domestic skills and feminine sensibilities of Victorian women. Their husbands drank too much and lacked the industry of American workmen. A less sympathetic characterization portrayed immigrants as particularly prone to radical politics and trade unionism. From this perspective they posed a real threat to American society. Whether immigrants were viewed benignly or as dangerous elements, reformers who addressed the subject shared a belief that immigrants needed assistance to join the mainstream of American life.[74]

Again, welfare advocates argued that employers had a role to play in these efforts. They claimed that daily contact gave businessmen a special understanding of the problems faced by their immigrant workers and a good grasp on the best way to solve those problems. One young welfare worker noted that "foreigners must have some one give them the initiative and that many of them [are] anxious to improve if some one showed them the way."[75] The corporate family could provide this initiative and guidance through welfare work. A consultant hired by the Plymouth Cordage Company in 1911 left little doubt that the ethnicity of the firm's employees must shape its labor policies. "It is also true," reported H. K. Hathaway, "that the lower the grade of labor employed, the greater the necessity for welfare work."[76]

By the early twentieth century, large firms like the Plymouth Cordage Company relied heavily on immigrant labor. Immigrants and their children comprised over 70 percent of the population in the nation's major cities and filled over half of all industrial jobs. In some industries close to 80 percent of all laborers were foreign-born or the children of immigrants.[77] Employers of large immigrant workforces were among the most likely to engage in welfare work.[78]

A small body of evidence suggests that welfare work also targeted black employees, another "dependent" group within the social structure. Even more than women and immigrants, black Americans had long been stereotyped as childlike. The Sambo image, which informed white attitudes well into the twentieth century, portrayed blacks as simple, docile, and manageable. Yet, like a child, Sambo had the potential to be lazy, cruel, and devious. Whether one dwelled on the dangers posed by black

Americans' assumed bestiality or on their potential for loyalty and docility, racist beliefs cast whites as caretakers and overseers of black people.[79]

Welfare work directed at black laborers extended this role to the modern corporation. It often attempted to capitalize on stereotypes of blacks as both highly loyal and manageable. The Tennessee Coal and Iron Company, a subsidiary of U.S. Steel, had this goal in mind when it introduced welfare work for its black employees in 1908. Company officials believed that they could embark on a small-scale program that would teach their black workers to become more reliable employees. In addition, prevailing prejudices led management to experiment on these black laborers as they planned a more comprehensive welfare program for their white employees. After three years of experimentation, the program was extended to the company's white employees in 1911.[80] The Chicago Urban League took advantage of white prejudice when it encouraged welfare work for blacks as part of its efforts to "recreate" southern black migrants by inculcating values of punctuality, industry, and ambition.[81]

Some industrialists lent a sympathetic ear to the advice of the Urban League. Very few, especially outside the South, had had experience with black workers. Yet they quickly saw the potential of welfare work, both as a strategy to promote divisions between white and black employees and as a way to ensure the loyalty of black employees.[82] Frequently hired as strikebreakers by industrialists in the Northeast and Midwest, black laborers quickly became a small, but permanent part of the industrial labor force. As the numbers of black laborers increased, their employers in meatpacking, steel production, and a handful of other industries introduced various forms of welfare work.

The dramatic growth in the size of the female, immigrant, and black labor forces resonated well with a system that cast the labor-management relationship in the mold of the middle-class family. Yet welfare workers did not restrict their efforts to these groups alone.[83] They often approached native-born, skilled men and women as more mature children in the corporate family. Welfare workers assumed that these employees already understood the value of hard work, discipline, and thrift. The corporate family simply needed to provide them with the encouragement and resources that would unloose the industrious worker lurking inside.

Thus, as one welfare worker argued, the program at Sears, Roebuck and Company, which employed largely native-born workers, was not universally applicable to other companies.[84] A welfare worker at the Chicago Telephone Company noted that her firm's welfare program was shaped not only by the unique conditions of the telephone industry, but also by the type of workers employed. "Being largely American," she explained, "they are consequently quite intelligent, preferring to have their own initiative." As a consequence, the Chicago Telephone Company did not promote educational or recreational welfare activities.[85] An employer's sense of the "maturity" of his workers directly affected the type of welfare activities offered.

The family metaphor, which cast the welfare worker as mother, the employer as father, and employees as children in the corporate family, offered many advantages to employers as they searched for a more cooperative relationship with their employees. Most obviously, it allowed them to play the role of compassionate benefactor, rather than ruthless or uncaring exploiter. Employers and welfare workers fully expected their employees to work more loyally and industriously for a company that treated them well.

At the same time, welfare advocates pointed to the familial relationship to demand cooperation from employees. They reminded workers that each member of the corporate family had distinct, but complementary, powers and responsibilities. While workers should *want* to repay their employers' kindness with steady and productive service, this was not simply a matter for their own discretion. Rather, workers were *obligated*, as were children in the middle-class family, to be loyal to the corporate family through bad times as well as good.

James Kilbourne, president of the Kilbourne and Jacobs Manufacturing Company, proudly related an incident of this type of loyalty to an audience at the 1902 Minneapolis Conference. One morning in 1893, a group of workmen bearing serious countenances filed into Kilbourne's office. Fearing the worst (labor problems), Kilbourne waited patiently for them to speak up. Finally a spokesman rose, and expressing their understanding of the present business depression, offered their personal savings for the company's use.[86] Kilbourne's employees had clearly understood and fulfilled their duties within the corporate family.

Yet the influence of the family metaphor, and its salience to the corporate welfare system, went far beyond prescriptions for good behavior. Welfare advocates applied their construction of the "corporation as family" to the knotty problem of endemic class conflict. By doing so, they redefined class conflict out of existence. If the corporation was indeed a family, there could be no systemic or permanent conflict between labor and capital. In fact, the appropriation of the family metaphor reduced workplace conflicts to issues of individual grievances or needs rather than recognizing them as issues of opposing groups or of collective rights and obligations.

The New England chapter of the National Civic Federation announced that its "whole design" rested on the "principle that there is no 'inevitable' conflict between the interests of labor and capital." It attributed labor-capital conflict to a long list of "very largely preventable causes," including "misunderstandings, lack of the spirit of fairness . . . lack of self control in the use of power, arbitrary demands [and] lack of personal acquaintance." Instead, capital and labor needed to recognize that they were engaged in a "common effort to make nature yield a constantly increasing return."[87] The welfare system would provide the structure and guide the employer-employee relationship to this mutually beneficial and harmonious end. As it evolved, the largest task of all was to prepare workers for their role in the corporate family.

Chapter Three

Raising the Children

Despite their obvious interest in strengthening the employers' hand, welfare advocates demonstrated a genuine sympathy for the instability, poverty, frustration, and even anger that characterized the lives of most working people at the turn of the century. This was particularly true of the welfare managers who assumed the role of mothers within the corporate family. They found in the model of the Victorian family a strategy that promised both to harmonize labor-management relations and to improve the welfare of working people as citizens in their own right. That strategy depended on addressing workers as members of their corporate families *and* as members of their private families simultaneously. In fact, it assumed a kind of interdependence between the two, presuming that security and harmony in workers' private lives was a prerequisite for security and harmony at the workplace. As a consequence, welfare workers searched for ways to help working people achieve a semblance of middle-class stability.

That search led in two directions—one economic, the other cultural. By definition the breadwinner in the middle-class home held a secure job at which he earned a steady income. That income was sufficient to provide for the necessities of life and to ensure that his family enjoyed uplifting recreations, his children were well educated, and his wife was never forced into wage work. His job rarely posed any threat to his physical well-being; it offered possibilities for advancement, and it allowed adequate leisure time in which he could enlighten himself. Whether he was a professional, an independent entrepreneur, or one of the growing number of salaried managers, the middle class breadwinner attributed his good fortune to his own industriousness. He understood that both his family's security and his own social status depended on his diligence.

This understanding of the economic roots of middle-class security led welfare workers to argue that the payment of fair wages was an essential ingredient in any sound welfare program. "Not to pass upon the questions of wages in considering schemes of welfare work," advised one prominent advocate, "is to neglect the supreme economic question in which the wage-earner is interested; for his whole life depends on wages."[1] A "just, reasonable and fair" wage, according to another promoter of welfare work, must enable the worker to "live decently."[2] By promoting a "living wage," welfare advocates distinguished themselves from those who claimed that wages simply rewarded productivity or reflected supply and demand. Instead, they argued that productivity and labor market stability followed from workers' physical and mental well-being. These, in turn, depended on the quality of housing, food, recreation, and even family relations afforded by a worker's wages. Wages served as an inextricable link between work and home.[3]

Gertrude Beeks referred to fair wages as the foundation of all welfare work. She began lobbying the McCormicks to institute equitable wage rates as early as 1901. In the aftermath of a 1903 strike at International Harvester's Deering Plant, she advised the general manager that he should systematically distribute information on wages, piece rates, and the fining system. Workers who knew what to expect in their pay envelopes could budget their money better. They would also be less inclined to blame their employer for their poverty if they felt that the general wage policy was fair.

A 1914 Metropolitan Life Insurance Company report listed employee salaries as the first item under the heading "Welfare Work for Employees." The report proudly noted the continuation of a $9.00 per week minimum salary for female employees. Women had earned an average of $11.06 per week during the previous year. The company claimed that at these salaries self-supporting women could afford decent housing and nutritious meals. They might also resist the trade in sexual favors that scandalized their sisters in the retail trades. Regular employment and a differential that accorded men an average weekly salary of $22.51 brought many of Metropolitan Life's male employees into the middle class.[4]

While exponential growth in the insurance industry made it possible for Metropolitan Life to offer fairly steady work, this was more the exception than the rule during this period. More typically, uncertain labor markets forced workers to change jobs frequently in a constant struggle to support their families. Welfare advocates argued that the inability to count on a steady income created both mental worry and discontent. In response, they promoted employment stabilization as another component of the economic agenda. The chair of the National Civic Federation termed employment stabilization "a wonderful piece of welfare work" whose effect on workers' private lives would translate into greater stability and efficiency at the workplace.[5]

A few firms adopted employment stabilization as a conscious part of their welfare programs. This often required changes in the production process itself. The Westinghouse Air Brake Company, for example, altered its inventory and repair procedures in order to establish a "no shutdown policy." Managers reported that they kept the plant running at full capacity even when this was not necessary for filling orders. The no shutdown policy was an integral part of a welfare program designed to "keep labor pleasant."[6] The Eastman Kodak Company counted scientific achievements that extended the shelf life of film as a significant step toward employee welfare since it allowed the company's workers to produce at a steady pace rather than as demand required.[7] The Wagner Electric Manufacturing Company reported that efforts to standardize their product resulted in more stable employment and wages, improving the welfare of their employees.[8]

Welfare managers used their understanding of the relationship between home and work lives to argue for shorter hours as well. The Westinghouse Air Brake Company, for example, also introduced a no-overtime policy. Company officials explained that this was a significant part of their welfare system because it afforded their workmen more rest time, which in turn made them more efficient.[9] The National Cash Register Company tied its hours policy even more directly to concerns for the stability of employees' personal lives. NCR's female employees saw their paid workday reduced from ten to eight hours in order to allow more time for them to fulfill their domestic obligations.

Although higher wages, steady employment, and shorter hours were deemed essential, welfare advocates never believed that these alone could solve the labor problem. Theoretically, the security and harmony enjoyed by the Victorian family rested on more than high salaries. Middle-class Victorians attributed their security to their adherence to a code of ethics that valued discipline, hard work, thrift, and sobriety. Men and women felt compelled to use family resources in carefully prescribed ways: to furnish pleasant homes, purchase nutritious food, educate their children, and save for the future. Money and leisure time alone were no guarantee of security and stability. Rather, one looked forward to a secure future only to the extent that he or she honored the middle-class work ethic.

Based on this understanding of the cultural foundations of middle-class stability, welfare advocates offered workers a broad agenda of programs designed to inculcate the middle-class work ethic and foster a desire for a middle-class standard of living. Of the two strategies, economic and cultural, the latter proved to be the most popular among welfare advocates and came to dominate the actual practice of welfare work. Two factors account for this development. Most obviously, employers resisted both the challenge to their authority and the costs associated with raising wages, stabilizing employment, and shortening hours. Hired welfare workers generally reinforced their employers' preference for cultural strategies over economic ones. On a practical level this minimized the potential for conflict between welfare workers and their employers.[10] It focused the welfare worker's energies in an arena where she, rather than her employer, could claim expertise—teaching and enforcing proper standards of conduct.

At the same time, both employers and their hired welfare workers persuaded themselves that paying higher wages or cutting hours would be the equivalent of putting the cart before the horse. Workers who lacked middle-class values and habits would be no better off than before, even if their wages rose. They would be inclined to waste higher wages on gambling, frilly clothes, or extravagant weddings and would spend extra leisure time at the saloon or dance hall. In addition, an employer had no guarantee that a more generous wage or hours policy would translate into greater cooperation at the workplace. Harmony at the workplace depended on workers exercising the same values and habits that built security and stability for the family.

As a consequence, welfare advocates built a labor relations system that directed most of their reforming energies at workers rather than at employers. They argued that workers who received the proper education and guidance would, like children, mature into responsible members of society and better workers. In fact, having cast workers as children within the corporate family, they generally interpreted disloyalty and inefficiency as signs of immaturity. They assumed that such behavior could be reformed by teaching discipline, thrift, sobriety, and the value of hard work. Once acquired, the middle-class work ethic, along with a desire for a middle-class standard of living, would ensure that workers performed their jobs more efficiently and loyally, without the necessity of repressive measures.

The task at hand was to devise specific programs and policies that would inculcate these values and habits. Not surprisingly, welfare advocates chose to duplicate the methods of the Victorian family as much as possible. Their efforts fell into four general areas. They called on employers to create safe and healthy workplaces, patterned as much as possible after the fashion of the middle-class home. They organized educational, recreational, and social activities in which workers could learn to enjoy middle-class leisures and which would impress on them the constructive and sober use of leisure time. They offered a variety of financial plans to develop the "savings habit" and help workers achieve the economic stability on which middle-class life depended. Finally, employers and welfare workers joined in a concerted effort to provide the kind of moral guidance and protection that middle-class parents offered to their children as they confronted the daily temptations and uncertainties of modern life.

Inherent in these efforts to reform working people into hard-working, thrifty, and sober middle-class citizens was an acute sensitivity to the distinct and interdependent roles of men and women within the Victorian ideal. While both sexes were instructed in the work ethic, welfare programs subjected them to lessons that taught that ethic in gender-specific ways. Welfare activities directed at male employees consciously promoted their responsibilities as family providers and role models and encouraged them to value promotions (rather than mere wage increases) as the path to financial stability.[11]

While male employees were expected to become budding Horatio Algers, welfare work tried to groom female employees for the role of Mrs. Alger. Welfare workers recognized that economic necessity drove women into the workforce. They also knew that most left full-time employment for marriage. As a result, welfare work directed at women had a two-fold purpose. First, as with that designed for male employees, it sought to inculcate middle-class habits that would make women more industrious and loyal workers. Second, the welfare system assumed a fundamental responsibility to teach female workers to be good housewives and mothers. It was through these latter roles that the working-class woman could contribute the most to solving the labor problem. The well-fed, healthy breadwinner married to a wife who appreciated a well-appointed home and uplifting recreation was more likely to be a stable, loyal, and productive worker.

While welfare workers continually reminded others that each business situation was unique and there was no one complete or perfect package of welfare programs, a brief look at typical welfare work in each of the four program areas will demonstrate the extent to which Victorian ideas of family and gender underpinned the corporate welfare system. We turn first to activities designed to improve the workplace. "The beginning of all welfare work," Gertrude Beeks told an audience of welfare workers, "must be directed toward meeting the pressing necessities for the physical well being of the employees in their place of work."[12] In accordance with Beeks's priorities, businessmen commonly initiated welfare work with programs to improve safety, health, and comfort at the workplace.

The program of factory improvement at the National Cash Register Company served as a guidepost for many firms.[13] When John Patterson directed the construction of a new NCR factory in 1888, his primary concern was to ensure more floor space to house the machines and people needed to produce for his growing market. According to Patterson's biographer, the new plant "followed the plans of most factory buildings of the time. . . . The windows were small, the light was poor, and no attention at all had been given to ventilation."[14] By 1894, when growing demand forced Patterson to build an even larger factory, labor concerns as well as production needs shaped the plans.[15] He insisted that the new factory have as much glass and as little masonry as possible. In addition to flooding the factory with light, NCR "painted all the machinery in a light colour, arranged hoods to absorb dust . . . had first-class baths and locker rooms, restrooms for the women, hospitals and first aid stations." Ferns ornamented machine rooms, and walkways bordered by flower beds and shrubs beautified the new factory grounds.[16]

What did Patterson hope to gain by expending so much money and space on windows, baths, and landscaped gardens? Obviously he expected that pleasant surroundings would induce his employees to work more faithfully and industriously. Yet this was not his only motivation. Patterson believed that a safer, more comfortable factory would not, in and of itself, change the attitudes of his employees. He attributed high turnover rates, inefficient labor, and vandalism at the factory to the "thoroughly undesirable" character of the surrounding working-class community of Slidertown. "A man cannot come out of a hovel," he noted, "have a dirty breakfast, go into a dark, noisome factory, and then do a good day's work."[17] In Patterson's words, Slidertown was in need of a "complete cleansing."[18] He undertook factory improvement not only for the effect that a lighter, quieter workplace would have on employee morale, but also as a purposeful example for his employees to emulate at home. "I arranged flower beds and shrubs around the factory building, sodded the ground, and put in neat walks," he recalled, "as an example to the neighborhood."[19]

He claimed that his employees learned the lesson well. Slidertown soon disappeared, to be replaced by "South Park—a clean, neat suburb filled with good-looking, comfortable houses in which anyone might live." Vines and blossoming flowers bedecked older homes, covering their run-down condition.[20] Whether or not NCR's new factory and the model it set for the local community actually contributed to any transformation in Slidertown, Patterson and his welfare workers believed it did. They also believed that NCR benefitted from its employees' healthier, more comfortable home lives. NCR was not alone in undertaking factory improvement as a way to teach working people to change their homes and lifestyles. An officer of the Natural Food Company of Niagara Falls reported that while most welfare work at his company focused on the plant itself, the goal was "to surround the employees with ideal working conditions, thereby creating a desire for better things in the home as well as factory."[21]

As these examples suggest, welfare advocates rarely distinguished between essential improvements at the workplace and similar needs in workers' homes. The Victorian belief that the home shaped character directly informed the welfare system, which approached workplace and home improvements as two sides of the same coin. Having cast the corporation as a surrogate family, welfare advocates envisioned "ideal working conditions" in much the same way that they pictured the ideal home. Safety guards on machinery, pure drinking water, and well-lighted and ventilated workrooms were indispensable, but not sufficient to qualify as ideal working conditions. In addition to a safe and clean "home," welfare workers tried to provide an uplifting environment for their corporate families.

Just as the Victorian home was designed with special rooms for different activities, welfare workers called on employers to provide separate spaces for employees to work, eat, and rest. Almost two-thirds of the firms surveyed for the Bureau of Labor Statistics' 1916 report provided a separate lunchroom for their employees.[22] These were intended to be much more than spaces where workers could eat their meals away from the noise or clutter of their regular work areas. The careful attention given to menu planning, seating arrangements, service, and table coverings belies a multitude of lessons that welfare workers hoped to pass on to their firms' employees.

Not surprisingly, welfare workers furnished men's and women's lunchrooms quite differently. These differences reflected welfare workers' assumptions that male employees needed a dose of the work ethic, while female employees required training as middle-class housewives. Men's cafeterias were typically austere rooms designed to service as many people as possible in a short period of time. NCR furnished its men's dining room with ten long rows of tables, seating over 100 workmen each. The Natural Foods Company provided its male workers with lunch counters arranged in a horseshoe shape.[23] In recognition of men's unsentimental nature and dirty work, furniture and table coverings were chosen to be efficient and easily cleaned. The Bureau of Labor Statistics' investigators found that stationary stools and wood or oilcloth-covered tables were preferred for men's dining rooms.[24]

These lunchrooms offered plenty of wholesome food to satisfy men's hearty appetites and nutritional needs. Employers often hired workers trained in domestic science to plan and prepare meals. Welfare advocates believed that better diets would have both short-run and long-run benefits. First, workmen would have more energy for the rest of the day. This, along with generous provisions of coffee, were expected to keep workmen out of the saloons. Second, welfare workers hoped that the example of tasty, nutritious meals at work would encourage workmen to demand better diets at home. For ten cents, workmen at the Natural Foods Company could purchase a lunch of puree of oyster plant, Triscuits, creamed codfish, escalloped potatoes, vegetarian baked beans, cold meats, sliced tomatoes, wheat bread and butter, vanilla ice cream, apple pie, and tea.[25]

Managers of women's lunchrooms similarly chose menus that would both sustain workers throughout the day and instill habits of good nutrition. However, developing an appreciation for good meals was only part of the lesson for workingwomen. As future housewives, they needed to be able to plan and prepare these meals. Welfare workers assumed that workingwomen either did not or could not learn these lessons from their mothers. Thus, their corporate family took on this responsibility. The Metropolitan Life Insurance Company, whose home office force was overwhelmingly female, carefully divided and labeled different food groups in its cafeteria line—with separate sections for hot and cold dishes, soups, vegetables, desserts, and beverages. The dietician clearly marked the food value of each item on the menu. Not satisfied that even these precautions would ensure that workingwomen would eat well-balanced meals, and taking advantage of women's assumed submissiveness, the company posted inspectors at the end of the cafeteria line "to preclude the possibility of an employee trying to make a meal of ice cream and dessert only."[26]

In addition to teaching habits of good nutrition, women's lunchrooms were designed to develop an appreciation of (and a desire for) a well-set table and proper dining atmosphere. Anna Doughten, welfare manager at the Curtis Publishing Company, noted that lunchrooms should not only be clean, comfortable, and convenient, but also attractive, artistic, and homelike. This was important "for the indirect, quiet influence of such surroundings often is stronger, farther reaching, and more lasting than any attempt at direct influence."[27] With this goal in mind, welfare workers generally furnished women's dining rooms with smaller tables, seating from six to twenty, to encourage companionship and quiet conversation. In contrast to the long tables in NCR's men's dining hall, for example, the firm's female employees dined at tables seating eight.[28] The company decorated the women's dining room with potted plants and vines hanging from the rafters.[29] H. J. Heinz assigned its 600 women picklers and bottlers to tables seating twelve. As they ate lunch, these workingwomen could listen to piano music or study one of the 100 fine paintings and drawings that adorned the walls.[30] Linen table cloths, silver service, and china dishes were not uncommon, even in some factories.[31]

Dining rooms were not the only spaces that employers set aside for the comfort and enlightenment of their corporate families. Depending on his commitment and his employees' assumed maturity, an employer might furnish locker rooms, washrooms, women's restrooms, men's smoking rooms, reading rooms, gymnasiums, and clubrooms. Well over half of the firms included in the Bureau of Labor Statistics' 1916 study reported one or more of these facilities.[32] As with lunchrooms, welfare advocates believed that rest and recreation rooms would serve a dual purpose. Retirement to a restroom or gymnasium would offer relief from the grime, fast pace, or monotony of work. After a brief respite, employees would return to work invigorated, more attentive, and willing to work hard for their kindly employer.

The benefits expected from this type of welfare work did not arise solely from their capacity to foster gratitude or to grant short-term relief from physical labor. Welfare advocates claimed that workers who used rest and recreation rooms would *want* to be more efficient and loyal. Enjoyment of these facilities would help them acquire middle-class habits and values. Among the middle class, such functionally separate spaces helped to shape behavior and define a person's character. For example, dressing rooms, which had their counterpart in company locker rooms and restrooms, were private spaces for personal care or quiet contemplation. Men's and women's clubs, which welfare workers tried to duplicate with company clubrooms, promoted camaraderie based on their members' gender identity. Gymnasiums, provided most frequently for male employees, reflected a middle-class interest in health and vigor and a rejection of vice and lethargy. Even more so than with lunchrooms, the decision to establish a rest or recreation room reflected a clear intention to mold employees in the same way that the well-appointed Victorian home molded its occupants. Over time, workers would shed old habits and values that employers believed lay at the root of their labor problems.

Welfare advocates placed great importance on creating rest and recreation spaces that separated their workforces by gender, in accordance with middle-class standards of sexual propriety. They hoped that these work-place examples would prompt employees to adopt similar standards in their private lives. Separate locker rooms and washrooms for each sex were the logical beginning. Numerous firms staggered arrival and departure times as well as break and lunch schedules to ensure that male and female employees would come into contact with one another as little as possible. When the construction of new plants allowed for it, welfare advocates argued for completely separate entrances and stairways.[33]

Limiting unseemly contact between young men and women was only one of the motives behind this aspect of corporate welfare work. As with lunchrooms, welfare workers took full advantage of the isolation of men and women to instruct their charges in the finer points of Victorian masculinity and femininity. They invited male workers to spend rest periods and leisure time in company-furnished smoking or game rooms, clubrooms, or gymnasiums. These facilities encouraged workmen to develop a middle-class sense of male camaraderie and to release their competitive spirits in a controlled environment. In accordance with assumptions about men's nature, their smoking rooms and clubrooms were furnished with an eye to practicality and durability.[34]

While workmen were provided with "smoking rooms," welfare workers furnished and staffed "restrooms" for female workers.[35] They carefully designed women's restrooms to promote genteel behavior and to develop women's aesthetic sensibilities. The middle-class parlor often served as their model. For example, John Wanamaker furnished his department store's restroom with couches, easy chairs, and a piano. The women's restrooms reproduced for readers of the Bureau of Labor Statistics' 1916 report included stuffed sofas, easy chairs, and rockers set out in small, conversational arrangements. Carpeted floors, curtained windows, plants, and lamps created a pleasing and relaxing atmosphere—akin to the one these women were expected to create in their own homes. The addition of pianos, Victrolas, and carefully selected reading material reflected assumptions that women were the guardians of culture and refinement.[36]

Welfare advocates knew that the example of ideal working conditions would not, alone, reform working people. While they hoped that lunchrooms, locker rooms, or restrooms would entice employees to develop middle-class interests and standards, welfare workers did not simply leave workers to use these facilities as they pleased. This was particularly true with regard to restrooms, clubhouses, and other spaces that employees might use during rest periods or after work.

Leisure was a carefully defined concept in the middle-class lexicon, one which welfare workers hoped to teach to their firm's employees.

Middle-class spokesmen in the late nineteenth century praised leisure as both the well-deserved reward for hard work and as a time to reinvigorate and improve oneself.[37] In order to produce these benefits, however, the time had to be spent constructively, not whiled away in idleness. The Victorian sense of discipline, frugality, and industry permeated play as well as work.

With this understanding of leisure in mind, welfare workers organized a wide variety of classes, clubs, and special programs to redirect workers' free time away from amusements that they defined as wasteful or immoral. In their place, welfare workers offered educational, recreational, and social programs that would elevate their workers by instilling manly character and a sense of duty in their male employees and teaching womanly arts to their female employees.

Welfare workers advocated such activities for their male employees primarily as a way to discourage drinking, gambling, and union activities. These "unwholesome" recreations were particularly troublesome as they represented the very vices that Victorian men needed to tame in order to achieve success. In place of these "unwholesome" recreations, welfare workers wanted to encourage a camaraderie and sense of achievement that would tie the workman more closely to his employer. They frequently introduced gardening programs and team sports to accomplish these ends.

Factory gardens, boys' garden clubs, and garden contests were most commonly organized among immigrants and young boys. Welfare advocates assumed that the immigrants' peasant backgrounds predisposed them to be interested in gardening. They hoped that once this initial interest attracted workmen, the gardening itself, pursued in a scientific manner, would help to cultivate an entirely new outlook on life. The desire to reap a good harvest (and the lure of cash prizes from his employer) would help him develop steady habits. He would be less inclined to go off on a drinking spree or mid-summer "vacation" and "leave two hundred dollars worth of vegetables to weeds and thieves."[38] In addition, his efforts would transform the yard into a healthy place for family recreation. Welfare workers hoped that gardening would stimulate workmen to spend more time in the bosom of their families, fulfilling their manly duty as role model to their children.[39]

Welfare workers argued that team sports could produce similar results. Company-sponsored sports were part of the turn-of-the-century physical culture movement. Middle-class enthusiasts, who imposed their own sense of discipline and order on boisterous working-class sport, argued that team sports bred manly virtues, including "steadiness of nerve, quickness of apprehension and endurance against hunger and fatigue and physical distress." Perhaps even more appealing to welfare advocates, re-formers believed that teamwork would develop "social, cooperative, and even submissive virtues" that would help to curb selfishness and impul-sive actions. As one commentator explained, team sports bred "heroic subordination of self to the group," a combination of vigor and deference that would please any employer.[40]

Thus, in addition to individual body building in gymnasiums and pools, companies sponsored a wide variety of sports ranging from baseball and basketball to bowling and track and field. In a typical example, the Plymouth Cordage Company regained control of local baseball teams in 1913 by offering to pay for coaches, equipment, and uniforms. W. E. C. Nazro, the welfare manager who lobbied for this expenditure, argued that company control would ensure that workmen would be trained "scientif-ically," learning discipline and order along with batting and fielding. At the same time, Nazro believed that company control would place baseball "in the same class as college athletics," where it could generate the same kind of enthusiasm and loyalty for the Plymouth Cordage Company that the middle and upper classes reserved for their alma maters.[41] Loyalty to the team and to the Plymouth Cordage Company would become inextri-cably linked.

When they were not cheering their husbands and brothers at baseball, the Cordage Company's female workers (and female members of workers' families) could attend girls' clubs for gymnastics and dancing.[42] By the turn of the century, athleticism and physical fitness had become part of the ideal of the New Woman. However, recreational programs designed for women differed significantly from those offered to male employees. In contrast to the team sports promoted among men, women's recreational activities emphasized a feminine standard of "physical culture." Physical culture programs for women combined lessons in sociability and beauty along with instruction in physical fitness.

Roof gardens and carriage rides were typical of the more restrained forms of recreation encouraged among women. In cities, or where space was limited, welfare workers furnished roof gardens with potted plants and park benches. They encouraged employees to visit with one another as they strolled about in the fresh air. H. J. Heinz equipped such a garden for his picklers and bottlers with rustic benches, awnings, a fountain, bloom-ing plants, and a conservatory. During the summer months, Heinz women periodically shed their company-issued aprons, donned fancy hats, and spent the morning or afternoon being driven elegantly through city parks and the downtown area in a fancy "wagonnette" (with no loss of pay).

Dancing became one of the most common forms of recreation encouraged among women workers. In contrast to the aggressive, competitive nature of men's team sports, dancing represented a more controlled and less exhausting type of physical activity. Welfare workers also promoted dancing as a vehicle for teaching middle-class standards of sexual propriety and behavior. They chaperoned all company dances to ensure that employees and their guests followed these rules. Firms with large numbers of female workers often organized women-only dances. The Metropolitan Life Insurance Company, for example, introduced noon-hour dancing for its female clerks in 1911. The company's welfare manager felt that dancing reinvigorated the clerks for the long afternoon at their desks and, as the workforce grew, helped to control congestion in the hallways and restrooms.[43] Yet physical activity and crowd control were not the only reasons for sponsoring noontime dancing. For the young clerks socializing with their female partners, dancing in Metropolitan Life's sedate Assembly Hall under the watchful eye of the company's welfare workers was a vastly different experience than spending an evening at one of the city's commercial dance halls.

Although welfare advocates believed that physical recreation was necessary, they expended much more time and effort on filling women's leisure time with educational activities. Many firms offered educational classes and maintained libraries to prepare women, as they did men, for better jobs within the company. However, this was not the primary goal of company-sponsored education for women. Welfare workers expected that women's greatest contribution to solving the labor problem would be in fulfilling their roles as housewives and mothers. Yet they worried that workingwomen seemed woefully unprepared for these most important roles. "It is astonishing," lamented Elizabeth Wheeler, "to see how many women do not know how to sew. The girls are the same way. They marry and don't know anything about housekeeping."[44]

Employers were not shy about blaming their labor problems on the shortcomings of workmen's wives. Dr. Corwin, welfare manager at Colorado Fuel and Iron, told a reporter: "To a hungry man a home's attractiveness begins at the table. But if he come[s] home to a supper of tasteless, indigestible food, served without any attempt to make it inviting or the table attractive, is there any wonder that he seeks the saloon for stimulants?"[45] It was this concern that led an International Harvester welfare manager to express a widely shared view that "welfare work among women should be along the line of domestic science."[46]

Women's lunchrooms began the educational process in domestic science. However, most welfare workers believed that the subtle influence of lunchrooms and restrooms needed to be supplemented with more direct instruction. With few exceptions, welfare workers applied their feminine skills to organizing classes in sewing and cooking. Many added classes in basketry and millinery to encourage other traditional skills that were fast disappearing from American households.[47] Welfare workers and nurses regularly visited employees' homes and offered advice on everything from how and when to bathe infants to proper methods of cooking and house-cleaning. They often organized similar classes for employees' sisters or daughters, hoping to shape their characters while the girls were still young, as well as to introduce new ideas into workmen's homes through the children. The prevalence of these activities reflects the extent to which the corporate welfare system identified the workman's home as both the source of and solution to the labor problem.

At the same time welfare workers were promoting domestic skills among women, they were managing financial benefit programs to help men meet their responsibilities as family breadwinners. Welfare advocates assumed that the laboring man, like his middle-class brother, should define personal success in economic terms. In order to achieve this standard of masculine success a man had to be disciplined, thrifty, and industrious. Yet employers complained that their workmen possessed few of these qualities and demonstrated little regard for their economic responsibilities. They spent too much on drink, gambling, poor diets, and extravagant weddings and funerals. They neglected to save for the future. As a consequence, they and their families suffered from insecurity and poverty, often finding themselves at the mercy of loan sharks. Such employees performed poorly. In a misguided effort to escape from poverty, they joined labor unions and demanded higher wages.

Welfare advocates chose a variety of financial benefit programs to teach their workmen lessons in thrift, personal responsibility, and the advantages of industrial partnership. Profit-sharing, stock-purchase, and bonus plans cast employee participants as part-owners of the business. Welfare advocates designed these programs to appeal to workmen's presumed desire to become independent entrepreneurs. Enlightened employers claimed to be meeting their employees' needs by offering them modern versions of entrepreneurship. As with an independent entrepreneur whose financial security depended on the success of his business, these benefit plans promised rewards to employee-entrepreneurs only to the extent that their steady and industrious labor created profits for the partnership.

Executives of the DuPont Company, for example, which initiated a bonus plan in 1903, spent the next twenty years debating and revising the plan's eligibility requirements, trying to extract the greatest cooperation possible from their employees.[48] The committee's persistence, and almost yearly revisions, belied a deeply held belief that if it could just get it right, a properly constructed plan would entice workmen to fulfill their responsibilities within the industrial partnership. One official expressed this view succinctly when he noted that the bonus plan had been of "incalculable value to the company (and to the employees as well), in that it supplied incentive, calculated to grip the mind and harness the energy of the general run of employees."[49]

As at DuPont, many employers introduced financial benefit plans as the centerpiece of their efforts to forge a new partnership with their workmen. They claimed that such plans exemplified the new, cooperative relationship at work. Workers received direct financial rewards and a vested interest in the business in exchange for loyalty and efficiency on the job. Employers gained peaceful labor relations and greater profits, which they willingly shared with their employee-partners (at a rate and under conditions that they alone controlled).

Yet, welfare advocates argued that employees would not be enticed into this relationship until they developed a better sense of financial responsibility and acquired the "saving habit." Workingmen, in particular, would value industrial partnership only to the extent that they attempted to fully discharge their duties as the family breadwinner. The key, then, to achieving industrial partnership through financial welfare work was to persuade workmen to be responsible husbands and fathers.

Employers sponsored a variety of savings and loan plans to help their workmen fulfill their familial obligations. Despite differences in details, these benefit plans shared a number of features. First, they offered the greatest rewards to those employees who saved on a regular and continuous basis. Welfare advocates hoped that these provisions would help their workmen develop the saving habit. The savings plan at the Crompton and Knowles Loom Works was typical. The plan was open only to those who authorized weekly deductions from their pay envelopes. Once they had signed on, the men were never tempted (or able) to forgo a week's deposit, as the company automatically deposited their funds in a local bank. Workmen had to request withdrawals from the company paymaster, who kept their passbooks, rather than from the local bank that held their money.[50] Many firms supplemented workers' savings accounts both as an encouragement to regular savings and as a reminder that the fastest way to financial security lay in cooperation on the job. As one welfare manager explained it, "Workers who save some portion of their earnings are the most valuable ones to keep, as being careful of their own goods, and having learned the value of economy they are apt to be also more careful of their employers materials and time, than the improvident or those who save nothing."[51]

In addition to encouraging regular saving, employers and welfare workers tried to use financial benefit plans to influence employees' borrowing and spending habits. They assumed that workmen who recognized their duty to provide secure homes, good food, and healthy recreation for their families would work more diligently to protect their standard of living. Thus, employers who granted bonuses or merit pay as a reward for loyalty and efficiency rarely felt any compulsion about instructing their employees in the proper use of these extra wages. When George Eastman distributed wage dividend checks to Kodak employees, he advised them "not to consider this current income . . . put it aside for a rainy day or your old age."[52] In 1915, a DuPont superintendent recommended discontinuing a new merit pay plan, in part because his workmen persisted in referring to their merit pay as "whiskey checks."[53]

Loan programs served as a more direct way to influence workmen's spending habits. Again, the thrust of these programs was to support workmen in their duties as the family breadwinner—for example, to provide financial security and stability during periods of illness or death, or to finance the purchase or construction of a home. Loans were generally available only to those employees who could prove they were responsible and would use the money for the benefit of their families. The Greenhut-Siegel-Cooper Company, for example, investigated each loan applicant "both as to the worthiness of the applicant and the object of the loan."[54] Mary Gilson of the Clothescraft Shops of Cleveland, Ohio reported drawing the line on one loan request when she discovered that the employee's father intended to use it to "make an impression" during an upcoming visit to his hometown in Czechoslovakia.[55] Similarly, when the Massey-Harris Company organized the Mutual Benefit Society for its employees in 1890, it provided for a special committee to visit all claimants to determine whether their sickness was caused by "drunkenness, gross carelessness or immoral conduct."[56]

The Massey-Harris Benefit Society was typical not only in passing judgment on what constituted acceptable personal behavior, but also in the ways in which its benefit structure sanctioned different standards of behavior and financial responsibilities for its male and female employees. Male employees who demonstrated an appropriate regard for morality were accorded benefits that would sustain them in their obligations as the family breadwinner. The company did not recognize any similar financial responsibilities with respect to its female employees. In fact, the regulations of the Mutual Benefit Society carefully differentiated between women as wage-earners and women in their domestic roles. Benefits were not allowed for sicknesses arising from "female complaints, confinements or any cause arising therefrom."[57]

Other financial plans offered similarly unequal benefits to male and female workers. While welfare advocates hoped that financial benefit plans would teach habits of thrift and encourage workers to stay on the job, the structure of these plans clearly reflected a sense that such benefits should appeal more to men, who bore responsibilities as the family breadwinner, than to women, whose financial needs were less consistent. Savings plans designed to promote long-term savings, for example, benefitted working-men much more than workingwomen. They also favored skilled workmen over semiskilled and unskilled workers.

The most common long-term savings plans included pension and bonus plans. Typically, employees could receive benefits from such plans only after a minimum period of employment, and those benefits increased in direct proportion to their wages and length of continuous service. Most pension plans, for example, granted benefits to men at age sixty to sixty-five, after twenty-five to thirty years of continuous employment, and in an amount equal to 1 percent of their average pay over the last ten years. While few workingmen were able to satisfy these conditions, employers recognized that most men would be in the labor force on a fairly continuous basis for the required twenty-five to thirty years. They hoped that the lure of a pension in old age would persuade workers, especially skilled workers who were the most difficult and costly to replace, to spend those years laboring faithfully for their firm.

Pension plans generally set women's retirement age and length of required employment five to ten years earlier than men's. Despite these apparently generous provisions, even the most loyal and hard-working women could expect little from such plans. Their segmentation into more seasonal jobs, combined with women's shorter and more sporadic participation in the labor force, made it unlikely that many would ever fulfill the twenty to twenty-five years of continuous service required to receive pension benefits.[58]

American Telephone and Telegraph, which employed many more women than men, could only have had its male employees in mind when it decided to include a pension plan in its mix of welfare work. Female telephone operators averaged only three years on the job.[59] The Metropolitan Life Insurance Company, another enthusiastic supporter of welfare work, similarly designed its most generous financial benefit plan more for its male employees than for the mass of its female office force. In 1914, the company's bonus plan granted bonuses of $150 after three years of em-

ployment, $300 after six years, and $500 after nine years, with annual increases each year thereafter. Executives knew that very few of Metropolitan Life's clerks would be on the job past the first stage of the bonus plan.

While employers designed long-term plans, such as pensions and
bonuses, to stimulate stability and loyalty by appealing to workmen's responsibilities as breadwinners, they often favored short-term savings plans
for female employees. Welfare workers frequently promoted savings among
women by organizing Christmas or vacation savings funds. As these
names suggest, such plans recognized women's shorter working lives and
reflected assumptions that their wages could be spent for personal, rather
than family, needs.

All the same, employers and welfare workers did not sanction frivolous
or immoral expenditures by their female employees any more readily than
they did by their male employees. Elizabeth Wheeler defined part of her
responsibilities at the Shephard Company as teaching "practical economy" to her female charges. This included persuading working girls not
to spend their savings on nicer dresses or an evening out, or even on a better boarding house. Wheeler expected her girls to learn that the thrifty
person did not spend her income as quickly as it came in, but instead
saved it for a "rainy day." While that "rainy day" might be her annual vacation while unmarried, Wheeler believed that lessons learned by forgo-
ing daily improvements in her standard of living would translate into better management of her family's finances after marriage.

John Wanamaker's desire to impress the same lesson on his female
clerks led him to abandon a profit-sharing plan after only two years. His
decision reflected the ways in which efforts to foster middle-class habits
were inseparable from efforts to create harmonious relations between
labor and management. As usual, Wanamaker expected his profit-sharing
plan to stimulate his clerks to work more loyally and efficiently. The fact
that some clerks earned profit-sharing checks suggests that they met his
expectations at least with regard to work habits. However, they failed to
abide by his standards regarding their personal behavior. When he discovered that one girl had used her profit-sharing check to buy a silk dress,
and another to purchase a piano, he "was not satisfied that they knew how
to handle the money" and decided "he would have to discontinue the
plan."[60]

Welfare advocates' faith that they could solve the labor problem by reforming personal habits received its clearest expression in the attention
they devoted to workers' private lives. They were concerned, as one advocate phrased it, with the "Total Situation."[61] The Total Situation en-

compassed not only the workplace but also the physical and emotional conditions of workers' personal lives. "Happiness," asserted Gertrude Beeks, "often is brought through attention on the part of the employer to family life."[62] To this end, welfare workers included home visiting and personal counseling as routine and essential functions of the welfare program. They used such personal contact to pursue the complex agenda inherent in Beeks's statement, which associated happiness on the job with a satisfactory family life. Welfare workers argued that attention to workers' private lives would help them to become better acquainted with individual needs, demonstrate the employer's sympathy and concern for his employees, and, as a consequence, promote the confidence and trust between employers and employees that was fast disappearing in modern industrial society.

At many firms, this formed one of the earliest and most basic parts of the welfare program. Female welfare managers in particular undertook home visits and friendly conversations with employees as a strategy to overcome initial distrust and to gain workers' confidence. They then went on to formalize policies that required home visits in all cases of illness and unexcused absences or private consultations in cases of unsatisfactory job performance.[63] While the welfare worker used home and office visits to express sympathy for the absent or disgruntled worker, she also took advantage of each visit to carefully inventory the physical condition of the home, the health and appearance of each family member, and their relations with one another.

Based on these inspections, she offered advice, solicited or not, that she believed would prevent further absences, illnesses, or unsatisfactory job performance. While such advice frequently addressed shortcomings in basic hygiene and sanitation, it often shaded indiscriminately into instruction in middle-class styles of child rearing, home decorating, and food preparation. In their efforts to reform employees into better workers, welfare advocates tended to assume that cultural differences, rather than class differences, set financially insecure working people apart from the economically secure middle class.

Laura Ray, welfare secretary at the Greenhut-Siegel-Cooper Company, clearly had the Total Situation in mind when she established her firm's policy for visiting sick employees. If the company merely sent ill employees home, she argued, it would "lose their time and be handicapped." Yet Greenhut-Siegel-Cooper's efforts to return sick workers to the job as soon as possible entailed home visits rather than paid visits to the doctor. Ray attributed illness to multiple problems in the employee's home. Thus, when girls are home sick and report that they are ill, we investigate the situation, the second day. The welfare worker, if she does not send a trained nurse, must see what the cause of disease is in the home and *must try to teach cleanliness as well as godliness*. We often find that the icebox is not clean, the bed not right . . . in fact, all sorts of things that go with the hygiene of the home, and in a friendly way we are able to make little suggestions . . . I simply go and make a friendly call, during which I have my eyes open, and if I do not say anything just then, I have a chance usually to see the people afterward, when I make suggestions.[64]

When they felt that the situation warranted it, welfare workers invited themselves into the family council and spoke up on behalf of their female or male charges. Elizabeth Briscoe, for example, brought the authority of the Bancroft and Sons Company to bear on one family that wanted to pull their daughter out of school before Briscoe thought it wise. In another case, she admonished a workman for his excessive drinking sprees and reminded him that he, and not his wife, bore complete responsibility for his family's troubles.[65] In one unusual case, Mary Gilson, a rare feminist among the ranks of welfare workers, persuaded an indolent workman to become the family housekeeper and allow his "slattern wife" to work in the factory. Gilson was satisfied with the new arrangement; "he enjoyed 'keeping the house.' His wife was happy [and] the children . . . were certainly far cleaner."[66]

Welfare workers intervened most often in the personal lives of young workingwomen, who they presumed were vulnerable "women adrift." "There are times," wrote one supporter of welfare work, "when wise advice and a little financial aid, as a loan in some form, will tide a girl over a crises which otherwise might prove a temptation to irreparable disaster."[67] Female welfare workers in particular adopted the role of protective and nurturing mothers as they tried to discourage behaviors that they found immoral by middle-class standards. They advised their young female charges in everything from romance to dress and hairstyles, the selection of respectable lodgings, and family relationships. They attempted to dissuade them from purposeless flirting, associating with disreputable companions, and frivolous spending. Instead, they encouraged these women to be dutiful daughters and to seek romance with responsible young men with stable jobs.

Considering the methods they adopted, welfare advocates were partially right when they denied that the corporate welfare system was paternalistic. They had no intention of creating a system that forced working people into abject dependency or conditioned their security on their employer's personal largesse and benevolence. Such a system was no system at all, leaving many workers discontented and resistant to management control and exposing business in general to public criticism and government regulation. Instead, welfare advocates promised a new kind of partnership and independence to workers. They claimed that the corporate welfare system would allow working people to provide for their own welfare, peacefully and in cooperation with their employer.

This approach, which located the root causes of the labor problem in the shortcomings of workers themselves, contrasted sharply with arguments by organized labor that poor living and working conditions and economic insecurity stemmed from employers' unwillingness to share the profits of labor's hard work. While progressive employers who adopted welfare work often stated publicly that they were not opposed to labor unions, they invariably resisted any efforts by their own workers to organize. Some of this apparent hypocrisy may have been due to this very different, and self-serving, understanding of the causes of working-class instability and poverty.[68]

Although this was not paternalism in the tradition of an earlier era, the welfare system certainly cast the employer in a paternal role. He, and the corporate family he managed, had a duty to ensure the welfare of employees by providing a healthy and uplifting environment and by instilling in them the habits that welfare advocates believed would help employees to manage their personal affairs more responsibly. By helping his workers build a more secure and healthy home life, welfare advocates argued, a businessman would be removing many of the daily frustrations and worries that workers often blamed on their employer. The result would be a happier, more productive, and loyal workforce. Thus, the idea of the harmonious family permeated all aspects of the corporate welfare system—from locating the causes of the labor problem in improper training and workers' inability to use their wages and leisure wisely, to defining a solution to the problem in the form of a cooperative and compassionate corporate family, to developing a strategy to achieve this partnership by teaching workers to care for their families and charging the corporation with responsibility for the welfare of its employee-children. Despite their concerted efforts, however, welfare managers were able neither to reform their corporate children nor to transform the corporation into a harmonious family.

Shop-floor safety was a cornerstone of welfare work. Welfare advocates believed that simple machine guards would demonstrate employers' concerns for the welfare of their corporate family. Above: Gears of lathe without safety guard. Below: Gears of lathe with safety guard. (International Harvester Collection, State Historical Society of Wisconsin)

Functionality, not elegance, marked this retro-fitted water fountain. Seemingly out of place on the factory floor, this isolated fountain might yield large returns. Provision of clean drinking water addressed real health problems linked to communal water buckets. At the same time, it encouraged workmen to quench their thirst with water instead of beer. (International Harvester Collection, State His-. torical Society of Wisconsin)

One of the more elaborate company hospitals, this facility boasted a laboratory, surgical apparatus, and "every appliance known to the best hospitals for the handling of emergency cases." Whereas some welfare managers did double duty as company nurses, Sears employed two physicians and several nurses to staff this hospital. (Employees Hospital, Sears, Roebuck & Co., ca. 1908. Reprinted by arrangement with Sears, Roebuck & Co.)

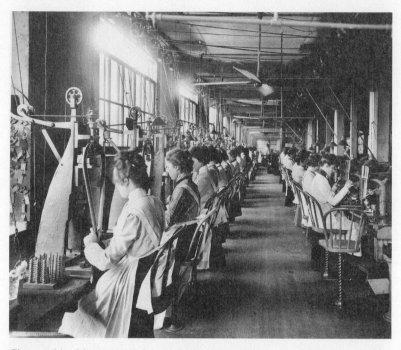

Clean and healthy workspaces were intended to raise productivity and transform employees' personal standards at the same time. These dual lessons are incorporated in the bright light and fresh air from the large windows and circulating fans, in the cleanliness of swept floors and protective work aprons, and in the comfort of stools with back rests. The domestic implications are captured in the small cup of flowers (only partly visible in the lower left corner) at the end of the workbench. (Lock and Drill Department, National Cash Register Company, ca. 1902. Library of Congress, Prints and Photographs Division, Detroit Publishing Company Collection)

These landscaped lawns were intended to teach by example. The company expected employees to gain such an appreciation of order and tranquility on their daily trip past these manicured grounds that they would seek to reproduce the same effect in their own yards. (Main Building, National Cash Register Company, ca. 1902. Library of Congress, Prints and Photographs Division, Detroit Publishing Company Collection)

Above: By all appearances, the employees in these homes learned the welfare lesson well. They have duplicated in their private surroundings the sense of order and tranquility demonstrated by the landscaped grounds at the corporate "house" that looms behind. Flowering vines and tall foliage lend a bucolic atmosphere, perhaps covering physical deterioration as well. Women caring for home and children represent the family ideal in action. (Employees Residences, National Cash Register Company, ca. 1902. Library of Congress, Prints and Photographs Division, Detroit Publishing Company Collection)

Facing page: Serving wholesome food was only part of the mission of company dining rooms. Top: In this quiet setting, workingwomen might become so accustomed to linen cloths, china place settings, and the aesthetics of fine dining that they would seek to reproduce these in their own homes. (National Cash Register Company, ca. 1902. Library of Congress, Prints and Photographs Division, Detroit Publishing Company Collection) Bottom: Welfare managers added touches of refinement even in this stark underground setting. The small table groupings encouraged family-like conversations. Simple place settings, scattered pictures, and music from the Victrola might suggest the refinements possible even on a workman's budget. (International Harvester Collection, State Historical Society of Wisconsin)

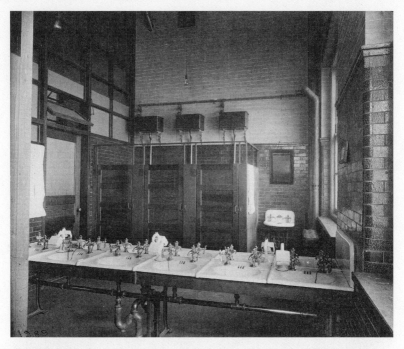

Above: Designed to accommodate at least a dozen employees, this lighted and ventilated restroom invited workmen to clean up before meals or departing for home. Although it lacked the large mirrors and benches commonly provided in women's washrooms, the fastidious workman could avail himself of a semiprivate sink and mirror. The experimental countertop soap dispensers are a good example of welfare managers' persistent search for efficiency and cleanliness. (Washroom and Toilets, International Harvester Company, State Historical Society of Wisconsin)

Facing page: Most company-sponsored leisure activities were segregated and gender-specific. Top: Pool tables and spittoons invited manly competition, tempered, perhaps, by the strategically seated referees. Water from an insulated water dispenser would, presumably, satisfy the men's thirst without need for recourse to the local saloon. (International Harvester Collection, State Historical Society of Wisconsin) Bottom: Women's resting rooms encouraged more sedate pursuits. This rough factory space is softened by shielding curtains, paintings, potted plants, rocking chairs, and table cozies. Reading or listening to music in this parlor-like space might influence young women to manage their home parlors in a similar manner. (International Harvester Collection, State Historical Society of Wisconsin)

napshots *at one of our* nnual ield eets

Field Days encouraged camaraderie and healthy exercise. At the same time, these company-sponsored events channeled employees' competitive spirit into disciplined paths. Frequently combined with an all-day picnic, field days drew men and women, employees and their families, into the fold of the corporate family. (Annual Field Meet, Sears, Roebuck & Co., ca. 1908. Reprinted by arrangement with Sears, Roebuck & Co.)

Less prevalent than other recreational programs, employee gyms offered facilities beyond the financial reach of most workingmen. Gymnasiums appealed to workingmen's valuation of physical strength. At the same time, regular workouts, like team sports, taught self-discipline that might be carried onto the shop floor. The seats above suggest that gymnastics might also be a spectator sport. Welfare advocates clearly hoped to divert workingmen from less productive recreations. (International Harvester Collection, State Historical Society of Wisconsin)

Employees could enjoy fresh air, get light exercise, and forget the "trials and troubles of the morning" in this block-long garden. The well-ordered gardens encouraged similarly disciplined behavior on the part of employees as they wended their way around fountains, flower beds, and vine-filled urns, all within sight of the main building. (Fountain and Gardens, Sears, Roebuck & Co., ca. 1908. Reprinted by arrangement with Sears, Roebuck & Co.)

Chapter Four

Welfare Workers:
Mothers and Managers

Welfare advocates drew their vision of the corporation as a harmonious partnership, as well as specific policy ideas, from Victorian notions of family. It was this grounding in the Victorian family that bound a confusing array of welfare programs into a coherent labor relations system. Any hope for success depended upon the willingness and ability of all the players to fulfill their prescribed roles. To a certain extent, they did so. Welfare managers, like good mothers, attempted to teach proper values and habits to their corporate children. Businessmen discharged their fatherly responsibilities by sponsoring welfare programs and by appointing sympathetic welfare workers. Employees of such firms seemed more disciplined, productive, and faithful than workers in companies without welfare programs.

However, the Victorian model was never more than an ideal. Despite the rhetoric, the modern corporation was not a family. It did, after all, create the problems that made welfare work necessary. While the modern corporation might attempt to build a sense of community and security for its workers, employers, welfare workers, and wage-earners could never conceive of themselves simply as fathers, mothers, or children in a corporate family.

Employers and wage-earners had long faced each other as antagonists, believing that one party's gains signified the other's loss. Both groups approached welfare work determined not to be the losers. Further complicating the situation, employers were also espousing the principles of systematic management.[1] Claiming only a dispassionate adherence to scientific methods, they increasingly explained their purposes, and measured their successes, in terms of efficiency and productivity. Fatherly duties would have to be consistent with these new business standards.

Welfare workers seemed to be the only ones not burdened by conflicting agendas. Historical neglect has exacerbated the impression that they served only as passive administrators for their innovative employers.[2] This was not so. Welfare workers thought of themselves as independent actors with a serious job to perform. They wanted to serve as the bridge uniting employers and employees. Yet welfare workers faced daunting obstacles as they attempted to do this. First, they had to negotiate their maternal mission amidst the mutual antagonisms between employers and workers. At the same time, the new systematic management movement was promoting business practices that widened the gap even further.[3] Equally challenging, welfare workers needed to create a legitimate place for themselves and their maternal approach among businessmen who fiercely defended their prerogatives and scorned anything effeminate.

The ideal of Victorian motherhood offered no specific guidelines for addressing these kinds of problems. As welfare workers met these challenges, they began to construct a version of corporate motherhood in which certain feminine skills became business assets. What eventually emerged was much more than a simple re-creation of Victorian motherhood in the business community; it was a new definition of the professional business manager.

DURING THE 1890s and early 1900s, when welfare workers were beginning from scratch, they frequently looked to the example of their contemporaries in the social housekeeping movements for a ready-to-hand model of motherhood in the public domain. Many welfare workers, as already noted, came to this new field from the settlements, charity aid organizations, and home missions. Familiarity with this female style of reform influenced the ways in which welfare workers constructed their own version of corporate motherhood.

Welfare workers, for example, shared the social housekeepers' focus on constructing an uplifting environment for their clients.[4] It was public sector reformers who pioneered such staples of corporate welfare work as lunchrooms, workingmen's and girls' clubs, vacation cottages in the country, medical clinics, educational classes, and friendly visiting. By the time Gertrude Beeks began her work at International Harvester, for example, Chicago reformers had built boarding houses for single workingwomen and were operating lunchrooms, workingwomen's social clubs, and vacation homes in the country.[5] Beeks herself had managed an independent lunchroom before taking up her duties at International Harvester, where one of her first acts was to open a lunchroom for female employees.[6]

Welfare workers also followed the lead of their public sector counterparts by claiming that certain feminine qualities, such as compassion, nurturing, and self-sacrifice, were indispensable to their work. In fact, welfare workers attributed their qualifications more to their personal character than to any practical experience. According to one contemporary advocate, "the man or woman who would be a social secretary must necessarily be . . . imbued with a purpose higher than the mere earning of a salary . . . and the possessor of those qualities of soul, mind and behavior that are an ever present influence, a stimulant in time of discouragement."[7]

Isabelle Nye, speaking before a class on welfare work, included compassion, tact, patience, and the ability to inspire and encourage others among the necessary requirements for good welfare work. Others emphasized the value of sympathy, love, delicacy, morality, honesty, and perseverance.[8] The welfare worker needed these qualities to gain the trust and friendship of her charges, to persuade them of her sincere interest in their welfare, and to induce them to participate in the many uplifting activities he or she planned. They believed that these qualities, in combination with a certain domestic sensibility, helped them select just the right mix of welfare features—from better factory lighting, to coffee service on the shop floor, to home visiting—that would be most beneficial to the welfare of their workers.[9]

Not only were feminine virtues required for good welfare work, but certain masculine ones were clearly unacceptable. Serving others, not controlling them or earning a high salary, had to be paramount. "Aggression," noted one writer, "is out of the question."[10] "The personal and human factor must come in to supplement the relatively rough and clumsy provisions of law and of male management," explained another.[11] The corporate welfare system was premised on the belief that workers could not be bullied into greater loyalty or productivity.

The prevalence of women in these positions reinforced welfare work (and by implication the new corporate responsibility for labor relations) as a distinctly maternal task. Employers often favored women for these positions, particularly in the early years when they had only vague ideas of how they should go about improving relations with their employees. Sharing a widespread belief that men and women were inherently different, they assumed that women naturally possessed the nurturing skills and qualities that they, as men, lacked. Thus, John Bancroft chose Elizabeth Briscoe to be his firm's first welfare secretary because of her teaching skills and her sympathetic personality. Department store owners Lincoln Filene and B. J. Greenhut also hired women to create their welfare programs. They gave these women (Diana Hirschler and Isabelle Nye) only the vaguest of instructions, expecting them to draw on their feminine intuition and domestic skills to develop their firms' welfare policies.

To a certain extent, this reflected employers' assumptions that female welfare workers would better serve their female workers. In a number of cases, women worked primarily with female employees. Yet the preference for women went far beyond this. Many women managed programs for male workers. Some, like Beeks, began by serving women and then expanded their work to include their firm's male employees as well. Others, like Briscoe, began serving both men and women; Bancroft's workforce was still 75 percent male a decade after Briscoe began her work there.

Despite the importance of feminine virtues and the large proportion of women engaged in this work, welfare work did not become a predominantly female preserve, as did social housekeeping. As noted earlier, as many as half of all welfare workers may have been men. In fact, the presence of men had a profound effect on the construction of this new occupation.[12] Male welfare managers undertook this new work in the midst of the late-nineteenth-century redefinition of Victorian masculinity. Scholars generally attribute this "crisis of manhood" to the growth of big business, which severely limited opportunities to achieve manly autonomy through individual proprietorship. In place of personal autonomy, the new Victorian man aspired to a different kind of independence—the leadership and mastery over others that came with corporate management. Success in this arena required personal qualities, new manly virtues, that an earlier generation had ascribed exclusively to women. Most importantly, success within the corporate hierarchy required that the new man replace personal ambition with an ambition to serve others. In order to do this, he must become a team player and develop the interpersonal skills needed to cooperate with and influence the actions of others. Judging by their activities, male welfare managers were early adherents to these new standards of manhood. They were ardent proponents of teamwork, engaged in manly social service, and they unabashedly incorporated a kind of masculine domesticity into their work.[13]

Like many of the women, the men who took up welfare work were often inspired by the Social Gospel movement. In addition to helping to legitimize a new public role for women, the Social Gospel movement helped to legitimize public service for men. In the process, it contributed to a redefinition of Victorian masculinity. As a number of scholars have demonstrated, Social Gospel leaders made an effeminate Christianity appealing and relevant to middle-class men by recasting Jesus as a more virile and active character. In contrast to a Victorian masculinity expressed through individual ambition and self-reliance, Social Gospelers in the late Victorian era posited a "new man" who, like Jesus, expressed his masculinity through service to others, self-sacrifice, and teamwork.[14]

This standard clearly had relevance to those engaged in welfare work. In a telling exchange, the chairman of an NCF conference appealed to this new image of Jesus to settle a debate on the philanthropic tendencies of welfare work. Those who considered welfare work a form of philanthropy must "break away from the old philosophy," he asserted, and recall Jesus, who "is to us the personification of service to others."[15] Rather than sentimental coddling, he argued, welfare work was a virile form of service that helped others to help themselves. Men who lived up to this manly standard of service infused welfare work with many of the same qualities that their female colleagues brought to this endeavor; they, too, demonstrated qualities of service, sacrifice, honesty, fairness, patience, and compassion.

This new masculinity entailed a kind of feminization of manhood. More specifically, as a number of historians have argued, the workplace became feminized during this era.[16] While this is certainly an accurate representation, the consequences for welfare work (and labor-management relations more broadly), I think, went beyond this one-way transmission. By claiming these previously feminine qualities as essential business skills, male welfare managers helped to "masculinize" an inherently feminine endeavor. At the same time, they retained certain masculine qualities, such as rationality, initiative, and strength, which were considered vital in the world of business.[17] This interchange led to the construction of an androgynous welfare personality as welfare workers shed the excesses of both female sentimentality and male competitiveness.

The example of W. E. C. Nazro, welfare manager at the Plymouth Cordage Company for almost twenty years, suggests the ways in which male welfare workers integrated a manly standard of service into the maternal mission of welfare work.[18] While he devoted a great deal of time to safety and health projects inside the plant, Nazro explained this work in terms of serving his firm's employees and helping them to become better citizens.[19] He focused his attention on workers' families, applying his professional skill as an architect to designing and constructing more sanitary and cheerful homes. Under his leadership, the welfare program at the Plymouth Cordage Company addressed its workers' domestic shortcomings with classes in cooking, sewing, and basketry. For children, he arranged kindergartens, story hours, Boy Scouts, and book selections at the company library. Among the litany of achievements included in his 1913 annual report, Nazro proudly noted that sewing classes for young girls had also taught lessons in manners and hygiene; as a result, two-thirds of the students who began the course sleeping in their clothes were persuaded to make or purchase nightdresses.[20]

Nazro was not atypical. His early leadership of the movement suggests that despite its similarities to social housekeeping, welfare work reflected more than an effort to carve out a new public arena for female domesticity.[21] Welfare workers, female as well as male, carefully avoided defining their new positions as inherently feminine or welfare work as a female occupation. Gertrude Beeks, for example, never claimed that women were uniquely or better qualified than men. She was more likely to warn against tendencies to infuse welfare work with the "sentimentalism of women" than to suggest that women were particularly well suited for this type of work.[22] The qualities Beeks most frequently identified with good welfare workers—"tact, common sense and executive ability"—reflected her belief that welfare work could not succeed as a simple extension of women's maternal activities.[23]

Rather, the importance that Beeks and others placed on such characteristics should be understood as part of their effort to translate a task traditionally assigned to women within the home into an arena that was decidedly not like a home. While welfare workers needed to employ feminine compassion and intuition in their work, these qualities alone would prove inadequate to the task of transforming labor-management relations. Most importantly, welfare workers needed to prove that they were disciplined, efficient, and systematic managers, that they could control workers as well as service workers' needs, and that they shared their employers' goals of higher profits and productivity. As Beeks characterized it, they needed to demonstrate "executive ability."

In order to accomplish this, welfare workers defined themselves not simply as mothers, but also as mediators between powerful and antagonistic parties. "It is not unusual," noted one reporter, for welfare managers hired for some specific work to "discover that the very nature of their calling forces upon them the role of intermediary."[24] Diana Hirschler, at Filene's Department Store, came to a similar conclusion. As with others, her original contract did not contemplate such a role. Yet Hirschler's interest in the conditions of work led her to "realize that I was really in a judicial position."[25] Thus, welfare advocates included not only sympathy and patience among the essential qualifications of a welfare manager, but also common sense and a judicial attitude. These entailed the ability to discern facts from fancy and to analyze and weigh those facts in proper relation to the situation at hand.[26] In effect, they needed to satisfy workers without violating employers' sense of fairness.

Welfare workers also needed a degree of assurance and initiative sufficient to "steer so straight a course between sympathy [for employees] and fear [of employers]" that both would acknowledge their authority to resolve disputes.[27] In the competitive marketplace, a logical, pragmatic, and firm temperament, not emotionalism or moralizing, served the welfare worker best. Although such qualities were indispensable to a successful housewife, these were characteristics more traditionally associated with men.

Whereas male welfare workers demonstrated sympathy and certain domestic skills, female welfare workers displayed these more masculine traits. Responding to a referral made by Gertrude Beeks, one executive inquired whether the woman recommended had "a sufficiently masculine manner" to control his workingmen. Recognizing that the welfare worker brought a nurturing personality into the workplace, this executive explained his concern further: "No great ferocity is needed for this, but at the same time somewhat of a firm hand is necessary." Beeks reaffirmed her initial recommendation, asserting that the woman in question was "very prepossessing and, while not in the least masculine, she has the appearance of one who might be firm."[28]

As they adjusted to the corporate setting and sorted through the various personal qualities, feminine and masculine, that best suited their day-to-day needs, welfare workers increasingly departed from the kind of public motherhood being constructed by social housekeepers. In fact, welfare workers quickly jettisoned the very foundation of social housekeepers' claim to a public role—female moral authority. For their part, social housekeepers recognized a clear separation between the public and private spheres. They argued that it was their duty to introduce domestic values into the public sphere. They legitimized their reform efforts by pointing to Victorian women's monopoly of morality. Social housekeepers claimed that both the domineering upper class and the suffering lower class needed their impartial moral guidance.

Welfare advocates, on the other hand, grounded the corporate welfare system on a different construction of the intersection of public and private spheres. Rather than expanding domestic standards beyond the home, the welfare system pretended to shift the corporation out of the public sphere and into the realm of the private sphere. By doing so, it denied any need for a public-spirited, impartial third party. Welfare workers did not position themselves as outsiders carving out an institutional foothold in the public arena, but rather as members of the corporate family itself.

This difference was clearly evident in the structure and operations of the National Civic Federation, the leading institutional exponent of welfare work. The NCF personified reform based on the idea of a public-business-labor triad, with the NCF acting as the impartial third party. The NCF Welfare Department, however, very purposefully rejected such a public role for itself. Unlike other departments within the NCF, Welfare Department membership was open to employers exclusively, and Welfare Department employees served employers exclusively.[29]

Welfare workers believed that they were a part of, not intruders into, the competitive marketplace. Unwilling to claim the imprimatur of female moral authority, welfare workers built their authority on a different foundation. They clearly understood that power within the modern corporation depended upon one's position within the managerial bureaucracy. To this end, welfare workers offered themselves as business executives, and they used the maternalism of their new occupation to solidify their place within the managerial hierarchy.[30] By defining the new corporate responsibility for labor relations in domestic terms and by asserting the need for traditionally feminine virtues, welfare workers set themselves apart from others involved in the supervision of labor. Their nurturing role clearly bore little resemblance to the methods employed by most foremen and plant or office managers. Welfare workers often explained their special contributions by contrasting their maternal care of workers to the greed and callousness of foremen and superintendents, which they believed contributed to workers' disloyalty and inefficiency.

A correspondent for the American Institute of Social Service explained this unique role of the welfare worker by recounting one situation in which a tyrannical forelady badgered her girls to the "verge of hysteria and nervous breakdown." Without the protection of a sympathetic welfare worker, these girls had no recourse; one brave girl even lost her job for reporting the problem to an insensitive superintendent. The lesson was clear: "All this would have properly fallen within the province of the Social Secretary to investigate and judiciously rearrange."[31]

Welfare workers also asserted their femininity as a strategy to gain the support of employees. Charles Carpenter, who began his welfare career at the National Cash Register Company, thought it "better for a woman to introduce this work than a man as the [workmen] are less apt to be suspicious of anything offered by a woman."[32] Others in the field shared this view. As an early pioneer in welfare work, Gertrude Beeks had initially rejected this idea, believing that differences between men's and women's nature precluded one sex ministering to the needs of the other. However, in her new position as secretary of the NCF Welfare Department, Beeks began to promote the femininity of welfare work as a managerial strategy. Like Carpenter, Beeks argued that assumptions about women's caring nature would make workmen more accepting of new welfare policies.[33]

Equally important, welfare workers found that the same feminine skills that helped them befriend workers could be used to enhance their power in relations with fellow managers and corporate executives. Despite the fact that they had been hired to improve workplace relations, welfare workers often received only tenuous support from company executives, and they frequently faced open hostility from foremen. In addition, welfare workers, unlike most involved in business management, were not directly engaged in production, and they did not have the power to force others to do their bidding. Instead, they helped to pioneer a new strata in business management, the staff position, which was advisory by nature. As staff managers, welfare workers provided information, advice, and services to line managers who were directly responsible for production or selling.[34] Success depended on their ability to persuade executives and line managers, as well as wage-earners, to accept their advice and services.

Welfare workers called on their reserves of patience and tact, and on their commitment to serve others, to cajole recalcitrant managers and company executives into adopting their welfare proposals. When executives at the Westinghouse Lamp Company hired Dr. Lucy Bannister in 1908, for example, their only intention was to provide medical care for the firm's growing female workforce. Bannister, however, had a broader view of employee welfare, which included healthy homes and congenial leisure activities. She advocated this broader view to company executives year after year, patiently repeating her explanations of the relationship between productivity and employee happiness. As a result of her persistence, Bannister gradually transformed her medical department into the nucleus of a more comprehensive welfare program, with factory safety, recreational, and educational activities. While company executives proudly directed both public and employee attention to this evidence of their goodwill, Bannister understood that her role in these developments demanded tact and self-effacement. In 1911, she admitted to an audience of welfare workers that the Westinghouse Lamp Company "would be very much surprised if they thought they had a welfare worker. They think they have a physician in charge of a medical department."[35]

Although welfare workers like Bannister understood their responsibilities in maternal terms and depended on certain feminine skills to enhance their authority, they rarely limited their ambitions to mastering the intricacies of corporate motherhood. Bannister, for example, was frustrated that company officials failed to recognize her expertise in raising productivity. Most welfare workers shared her ambition to succeed as a business executive.

Whether they moved into this new occupation from public sector reform, the shop floor, teaching, or some other occupation, those who entered welfare work were looking for a career that would support them in middle-class comfort and accord them a degree of responsibility and prestige. While some of their contemporaries viewed big business as exploitative and corrupting, they tended to see it as the source of opportunity for themselves and others. Having thrown their lot with those who argued that the benefits of big business outweighed the costs, welfare workers were eager to demonstrate that they could serve the needs of business. They took pride in their ability to apply modern business principles of efficiency, systematization, and rationalization to the task of reforming labor-management relations.[36]

An early indication that welfare workers would not be content to remain as reformers on the periphery of regular business operations, but would demand official positions within the business hierarchy, can be seen in their efforts to dignify this new occupation with an appropriately businesslike title. Growing out of its close affinity with philanthropic reform, welfare work was initially referred to as betterment work, industrial service, or social service. Those engaged in welfare work were frequently called betterment workers or social secretaries. However, many welfare workers became dissatisfied with the philanthropic connotations of such titles. Diana Hirschler, social secretary at Filene's Department Store in Boston, voiced this concern early. In 1903, she wrote to a handful of fellow welfare workers, proposing that they organize a convention of social secretaries. The purpose would be to dignify their new profession and increase employer demand for welfare workers. Hirschler suggested that the convention could also provide an important forum for welfare workers to discuss practical ideas for solving the labor problem. In response to her proposal, the National Civic Federation organized the first Convention on Welfare Work, held in March 1904.[37]

The "scientific welfare workers" who attended the convention took up the task of finding a title that would more clearly distinguish them from charity workers and other sentimental reformers. They also hoped to dispel notions that they were merely social activities directors.[38] After considerable deliberation, the convention adopted the term "Welfare Manager."[39] Although the title of "Welfare Manager" never came into universal usage, "Betterment Worker" virtually disappeared after this point, and the designation "Social Secretary" was joined by a range of new titles more suggestive of a business position.

More was at issue here than the choice of a new name. After 1904 welfare titles referred as much to the supervision of subordinates (Manager, Director, Chair, or Supervisor), as they did to the service or reform purposes of such work. As they set about defining the scope of their responsibilities, welfare workers began to demand that all labor matters be centralized under the supervision of a specially designated department. While the division of various managerial functions into separate corporate bureaucracies was becoming more common in the early twentieth century, the centralization of responsibility for labor relations was not a foregone conclusion. Welfare workers made this a central part of their own agenda and pursued this goal aggressively.

Summarizing opinions expressed at the 1904 Conference on Welfare Work Gertrude Beeks wrote that the "successful prosecution of welfare work requires concentration of responsibility. All of its branches must be under the supervision of one person, or efforts in different directions may conflict, or special and, perhaps, pressing needs may escape attention."[40] Almost from the beginning of her tenure at the National Civic Federation, Beeks committed the NCF Welfare Department to promoting centralization as a key element of welfare work. For welfare workers, centralization meant both a centralized administrative structure (with an executive delegating specific duties to a subordinate staff) and a centralized operational structure (to ensure systematic enforcement of labor policies). Centralization was an important part of the process by which welfare workers' maternal tasks were translated into the corporate setting.

Initially, most employers and early welfare workers gave scant attention to organizational issues. As they introduced new features, welfare workers either administered these themselves or sought approval to hire someone to help them do so. It did not take long for these early welfare workers to find themselves trying to coordinate a number of disparate activities and assistants. Laura Ray began her work at the Greenhut-Siegel Department Store in this way. Hired with a broad mandate to keep in personal touch with employees and take care of their needs, Ray soon established a wide variety of programs to do this. In addition to personally visiting absent employees in their homes and listening to complaints in her office, Ray acquired responsibility for an emergency hospital, lunchroom, restroom, reading room, and a staff that numbered at least a half dozen. Although she enjoyed her work, NCF investigators found her duties "overwhelming and . . . a great tax upon her."[41]

Faced with growing responsibilities, welfare workers turned their attention to creating more efficient administrative structures. Ray acquired an office girl to help with the phones and paperwork; still, NCF investigators reported that a lack of employer support left her department woefully understaffed. Similar strains at Filene's resulted in "a nervous breakdown or two" before management acceded to the necessity of reorganizing the Welfare Department in 1906. As a result, the various duties that "formerly had devolved on everybody and nobody" were carefully divided between the welfare manager and her small office staff, newly hired with an eye toward their ability to fulfill specifically assigned tasks.[42]

Although welfare managers continued to conduct welfare work personally, they increasingly became the "Managers" envisioned by those gathered at the NCF's 1904 conference. By 1912, for example, W. E. C. Nazro was supervising a staff of seventeen assistants at the Plymouth Cordage Company, each of whom was hired to perform a specific task. The chairman of the NCF Welfare Department clearly delineated this managerial role to students in the first training course for welfare workers: "It is not to be expected that you will equip yourselves to perform the service along all special lines, but that you will have the opportunity of securing expert service to help you install any part of welfare work. . . . It is for you as an executive to learn to draw into your service such specialists as may be necessary, either temporarily or permanently."[43]

These students, like others entering welfare work during the second decade of the century, were entering a fairly well-developed field. Unlike the first generation of welfare workers, they often paid as much attention to organizational aspects of their duties as they did to their goals of service and education. Marguerite Walker Jordan, welfare worker for a West Virginia coal company, reported that she gave "particular attention to accounts of corporate welfare departmental organization" during a month spent in New York in 1915.[44] Mary Hamson, welfare worker at the Solvay Process Company, made a similar visit a few years later. She came away convinced that Solvay could improve its welfare program by creating a more systematically organized welfare department headed by a welfare manager.[45] Hamson's recommendations are indicative of the extent to which centralization had become an essential component of good welfare work. The National Civic Federation had featured the Solvay Process Company as an example of advanced welfare work at its 1904 conference. Solvay qualified for this honor because of the large number of special programs and benefits offered to its employees. A dozen years later, Solvay's expanding welfare program had not kept pace with the field. Hamson's careful survey of practices in 1917 led her to conclude that a better organized department, not new welfare features, were the key to upgrading her company's welfare program.

As part of their effort to centralize responsibility for labor policies, welfare workers supported decisions to charge all expenditures for employee welfare to a single welfare account. This accounting practice reinforced the specialized function of welfare departments, helping to solidify their place in the emerging corporate bureaucracy. At the same time, it also forced employers and welfare workers to more carefully define the scope of this new field. There was little dispute that some features, such as libraries and company bands, should be charged to welfare work. However, features that touched production phases of a firm's operations could generate controversy. While welfare workers placed better lighting, ventilation, and clean drinking water high on their list of priorities, these often required structural improvements that were traditionally charged to production departments. Production managers naturally had little interest in seeing welfare managers make decisions that affected their departmental costs. Welfare workers, on the other hand, recognized that if such costs were included in their own budgets, they would have greater control over employee welfare, as well as preclude some of the opposition from line managers.

This connection between budgeting and centralization is evident in the way Gertrude Beeks presented the first budget for the International Harvester Welfare Department. Noting that in the first year she had appealed for funding for each welfare feature separately, Beeks prefaced her budget proposal with a litany of the inconsistencies and inefficiencies that had resulted. In the preceding year, the costs of the Twine Mill lunchroom had been charged to Beeks's account, but those of the McCormick Works lunchroom had not. The cost to install toilet facilities was charged to welfare work, but not the cost of operating those facilities. Expenditures for relief were charged to the separate departments in which the men and women worked. Beeks included all these costs in her budget proposal. Toilet and drinking water facilities, as well as other welfare operations, Beeks argued, "would be more successfully operated if one person were held responsible . . . and that person given plenty of support."[46] To provide such support, executives would need to insist that foremen recognize the Welfare Department's authority and comply with its efforts to provide the same benefits to all employees.

While centralizing responsibility for labor policies would increase the power of welfare managers, this was not their only objective. According to welfare workers, a thoroughly organized welfare department would serve workers and management more efficiently. "The greater the care and system," wrote one welfare worker, "the surer will it be that all will be done well and economically."[47] Efficiency in welfare work would produce a happier and healthier workforce, a workforce that would, in turn, be more efficient and productive.

Welfare workers systematized their work on a number of fronts. On an administrative level, they established record-keeping and reporting systems to keep both themselves and their employers informed of the work being done.[48] One of the first changes made by Mary Goss when she became welfare manager at International Harvester in 1907 was to require monthly reports from the six matrons employed at the company's plants. At the Plymouth Cordage Company, W. E. C. Nazro began issuing annual reports (with budget proposals) in 1912. These reports were more than descriptive window-dressing. Goss, for example, intended to use the monthly reports to enforce more consistency between the work at different plants. Nazro clearly hoped that annual reports would create better informed company officers who would then give more systematic attention to the welfare needs of their workers.

Welfare departments conducted extensive data-gathering operations. Most welfare workers kept track of the numbers of employees who patronized various activities, ranging from sewing classes, to lunchrooms, to libraries. They depended on this careful record keeping to evaluate the success of their work and to identify new areas of need. Company librarians, for example, collected data on the people visiting their reading rooms and on the numbers and types of books checked out. (Despite the careful selection of reading material, such records were often disappointing; workers preferred popular to fine literature.) Welfare workers gathered data in medical emergency rooms to help them identify the need for better safety programs, special food programs for malnourished employees, or tuberculosis treatment. They conducted interviews with discharged employees, which served as systematic checks on the behavior of foremen and led to the creation of employment files.

Efficiency and system were equally important when it came to operational aspects of welfare work. Some systems clearly worked better than others, and welfare workers carefully investigated the costs and details of each new welfare feature before making recommendations to their own firm. They frequently visited or corresponded with others before establishing a lunchroom, washroom, drinking water system, or savings plan. Tours, like the one made by Gertrude Beeks in 1901, became fairly common. Those without the time or financial support to undertake such a tour could more easily consult a growing number of sources that provided the same kind of information.[49] Correspondents with the NCF Welfare Department commonly asked for information on setting up a lunchroom, company savings plan, or some other welfare feature. The NCF Welfare Department encouraged these kinds of inquiries (and systematically gathered the information needed to answer them) as part of its effort to centralize and systematize corporate welfare work.

The federal Bureau of Labor Statistics undertook its national survey in 1916 in response to demands for a systematic evaluation of "what is practicable and easily administered, and popular versus those which are costly to install and maintain and which prove less satisfactory."[50] Readers of the bureau's report could learn the most efficient way to store emergency medical equipment, the best way to position drinking fountain splash-guards for the greatest hygienic effect, and what style of lockers worked best for drying wet outer garments or preventing the spread of lice. The variety of washroom sinks, lockers, lunchroom serving systems, and so on suggests that welfare workers experimented widely as they searched for more efficient ways to meet employees' needs.[51]

Ironically, as welfare managers institutionalized their positions and systematized their departments, it became less and less likely that welfare work would fulfill its maternal mission of humanizing the business system. As noted earlier, welfare advocates argued that more harmonious labor relations depended on reestablishing the personal intimacy between employer and employee that had been lost with the rapid expansion of business enterprises. Yet wage-earners were not working in an entirely impersonal environment. Although they rarely saw top executives, they had daily and intimate contact with their immediate supervisors. The task confronting welfare workers was not so much to bring intimacy back into the workplace as it was to replace the kind of intimacy that already existed. In place of the insensitive foreman, who managed by force and favoritism, the welfare worker was committed to demonstrating her employer's compassion to all, equally. Welfare workers referred to this as "fair dealing." With workforces numbering in the hundreds and thousands, this could be accomplished only with a centralized, well-organized department that conducted its work efficiently and systematically. However, efficiency and system were not necessarily conducive to intimacy and nurturing.

Beeks unwittingly recorded this dilemma as early as 1901. Reporting on her tour of the Westinghouse Electric Company, she noted that its welfare program sought "to get at a man personally, that is the individual man . . . [to] impress men with feeling of confidence as having an interest in them." Beeks went on to note (approvingly) that Westinghouse accomplished this with "a method that is entirely independent of personality of office management but rather a part of the system which they know will find them if they do well and also if they do wrong."[52] "A certain sense of detachment must be present or the work is a failure," summarized one welfare advocate, who recommended that welfare workers would be most successful if they maintained a "disinterestedness and impersonality" in the pursuit of their goals.[53]

As welfare workers pursued their goal of systematically transforming the corporation into a compassionate family, they created a welfare system that tacked unpredictably between personal intimacy and impersonal bureaucracy. Suggestion systems, designed to reestablish personal lines of communication between employers and their workers, demonstrate the uneasy fit between these two aspects of welfare work.

John Patterson initiated one of the first formal suggestion systems at the National Cash Register Company. Beginning with suggestion boxes scattered randomly throughout the factory, NCR officials made the system increasingly efficient (and impersonal). In place of the workman's scribbled notes, the company began furnishing official suggestion forms, which had to be filled out on site. Each form had a carbon copy that was automatically retained in the suggestion register. Patterson soon transferred responsibility for a suggestion contest, designed to foster interest and enthusiasm, from the welfare manager to a special Suggestion Department comprised of department heads. They were to classify each suggestion by subject, assign it contest points based on an elaborate grading system, remove the suggester's name, and submit it anonymously to the appropriate department for formal investigation. NCR certainly benefitted from the suggestions its employees offered. Patterson bragged that he saved as much as $15,000 per year from just a fraction of the suggestions made in a single six-month period.[54] However, it is less certain that this elaborate system, designed to bypass parochial foremen, did anything to bring the workers closer to Patterson or other company officers.

Suggestion systems at other firms often followed the pattern set at NCR. Rather than breaking through the bureaucratic barriers, suggestion systems became part of the bureaucratic maze that separated employers and employees. The welfare manager at the Curtis Publishing Company reviewed all suggestions before submitting "good" ones to the firm's welfare advisory committee. Those deemed worthy of further consideration were acted on directly by the welfare manager or, if warranted, were passed on to the firm's general manager.[55] The DuPont Company developed a suggestion system reminiscent of that at NCR—with an official suggestion form, administrative and record-keeping guidelines, and an annual report

to the company president summarizing awards granted, names of benefi-
ciaries, and the value of company savings to be realized.[56] There is no evidence that welfare workers or corporate executives took any special interest in the workingmen and -women who made suggestions. Clearly,
concerns for efficiency and productivity came to outweigh those for personal relations.

The extent to which efforts to systematically personalize the workplace
could become entangled in impersonal bureaucracy is suggested by the
situation at the Plymouth Cordage Company. By the early 1920s, Plymouth had one of the oldest, most elaborate programs in the country. The
new welfare manager, Charles Marshall, proudly reported that the "very
nature of our community keeps the work from being formal or professional . . . [because] we are all neighbors."[57] Yet his own reports belie the
informality and neighborliness of the Cordage Company family. Marshall's predecessor, W. E. C. Nazro, had purposefully sought to formalize
and professionalize this work, requesting assistants to help him manage
the welfare office more efficiently and traveling the country as a consultant
for the National Civic Federation. Marshall inherited a filing system that
catalogued every worker and his family, listing those who took advantage
of various welfare features. Marshall not only maintained this system, but
added the town's out-of-work families as well. Rather than using his files
to promote an inclusive vision of the Cordage Company family, however,
Marshall proposed using the files to exclude people from company benefits. Employees would formally apply for welfare privileges, with approval
dependent on verification of their employment status. Two decades after
the Cordage Company established its welfare program, Marshall reported
that welfare work "has helped in an indirect way to make us more familiar with the men and their families . . . [but] we do not know the people
well enough."[58]

While early welfare workers would have been proud of such an elaborate record-keeping system, they would have been chagrined at the results. Yet such results should not have been entirely unexpected. Welfare
workers had had to reconcile the contradictions inherent in the ideal of
Victorian motherhood with the demands of managing workers and employers in the modern corporation. By the 1910s, they had created a system that promised to personalize the workplace by centralizing and systematizing labor policies.

Welfare workers wedded these two aspects of their work into a unique
professional identity. First and foremost, welfare workers claimed a place
as specialized managers within the corporate bureaucracy. Like their fellow managers, welfare workers strongly supported more efficient and sys-

tematic business methods. Yet their particular area of responsibility, labor relations, set them apart from other managers. They had to nurture workers, they argued, in order to make them more efficient. They had to mediate between company officials and employees in order to foster a harmonious partnership. Most managers did not possess the combination of skills needed to accomplish these tasks. Welfare workers did; they were compassionate, self-sacrificing, patient, tactful, judicious, and pragmatic. Translated into the business world, these were no longer maternal qualities. Instead, welfare workers defined them as essential business skills. Welfare workers even claimed that these skills made them better qualified to increase profits and productivity than most managers. They were team players who channeled personal ambition into their company's search for higher profits.

Welfare workers called on all businessmen to do the same. The timing of this call is significant. Entering the business world in the 1890s, welfare workers were among the first managers who had no direct power on the shop floor. Those in marketing, public relations, accounting, and research faced a similar situation. In an environment where power flowed from one's control over others, managers in these new staff positions had to find a way to persuade line managers to heed their advice. Although fellow managers often resisted that advice, welfare workers insisted on their right to give it. They grounded this right in a new concept of team management, and they argued that the very qualities that made them good team players would make others team players, as well. Thus, at the same time that they actively shaped their own professional identity, welfare workers challenged businessmen to adopt their standard of professional business management.[59]

Chapter Five

The Corporate Family in Conflict:
Welfare Workers and Employers

W elfare workers offered themselves as models of a new type of business manager, one capable of fostering peace and cooperation between employers and employees. They would accomplish this, in large part, by teaching employers to honor their obligations as heads of the corporate household. This task, however, proved more difficult than they imagined. The role of the Victorian father was no easier to transfer to the business world than was that of the Victorian mother.

Ideally, employers, like their fatherly model, should have submitted willingly to the advice and gentle discipline of their welfare workers. They should have recognized the welfare workers' special ability to harmonize the corporate household. However, the family metaphor was not a good fit. The same Victorian system that assigned a degree of power to women in the home assigned complete power to men in the business world. Employers (and shop-floor managers) could not exercise their authority as men in the world of business and simultaneously concede that authority to welfare workers posing as corporate mothers. This dilemma became particularly acute when welfare workers challenged decisions and prerogatives traditionally monopolized by business executives and managers.

Despite their willingness to experiment with welfare work, employers never fully committed themselves to the corporate welfare system. They remained more interested in controlling their workers than in drawing them into a cooperative partnership. They supported welfare work because it promised a more disciplined workforce. Their reforming zeal fell short when welfare workers called on them to make the substantive reforms (particularly in wages and hours) needed to build real cooperation.

Conflicts between welfare workers and employers have received little attention because both contemporaries and historians have assumed that welfare workers acted simply as surrogates for their busy employers. In a framework that has long explained shop-floor relations as a polarized contest between labor and management, welfare workers clearly fell on the management side. The fact that employers were among the most prominent advocates of the welfare system has further reinforced assumptions that businessmen and welfare workers acted in unison. Progressive employers seemed to confirm these perceptions when they joined welfare workers in publicly admonishing fellow businessmen to change their managerial practices.

Assumptions about the affinity between employers and welfare workers are, to a large extent, accurate. However, the actual practice of welfare work quickly exposed the very different interpretations each had of the other's responsibilities. As welfare workers developed their maternal role to better fit both the corporate setting and their own ambitions, they recast themselves as indispensable members of the managerial bureaucracy. Employers, however, rarely accepted them on these terms. Although they expected significant economic benefits from their welfare programs, few employers accorded labor relations the same importance as their production, or even accounting, departments. In their own minds they appointed welfare workers to pursue essentially maternal, not business, tasks: to establish personal relations with employees, teach good work habits, and foster company loyalty. While this might require skills that they and their shop-floor managers did not possess, employers rarely thought of these as business skills. These differences between welfare workers and employers contributed their own dynamic to the welfare system and, ultimately, inhibited its potential to restructure labor-management relations.

AS DISCUSSED EARLIER, welfare workers supported a holistic vision in which employee welfare rested on both economic security and moral education. Employers were generally enthusiastic about welfare features designed to educate employees in the values and habits of the middle-class work ethic. Public attention focused on these nurturing activities, and employers had these features in mind when they decided to introduce welfare work. This type of activity seemed to promise a quick and easy return in worker loyalty and productivity. With few exceptions, this side of welfare work introduced entirely new features into the corporate world, so conflicts with existing practices were minimal. Furthermore, given their relatively low cost, businessmen felt satisfied that welfare work did "pay."[1]

However, employers proved much less enthusiastic when welfare workers called on them to provide for the economic security of their corporate families (with higher wages, shorter hours, or better shop-floor management). Although they might acknowledge that a harmonious partnership entailed economic security for all, even the most progressive employers possessed a business mentality in which their economic security depended on controlling labor costs.

Most welfare workers understood this and judiciously focused their energies on less controversial welfare policies. "My sole aim," declared one department store welfare worker, "is to increase wages of the employees." Yet she never approached her employer on this point, and he apparently ignored her suggestions for changes in managerial practices. Instead, this welfare worker devoted herself to improving the store's lighting, ventilation, and heating systems and to promoting "voice training." Under these improved conditions, she claimed, the clerks would earn higher wages because they would be more efficient.[2]

Elizabeth Briscoe, who had the courage to confront her employer over issues of economic security, came away frustrated. Bancroft and Sons Company had been an early leader in welfare work and had shown considerable confidence in her abilities as a welfare manager. In some cases, the firm allowed Briscoe to introduce welfare features on her own authority; they conceded her point when she argued against the ill effects of an experiment with scientific management; and in 1912, they financed her on a tour of welfare programs in Europe. Yet Briscoe encountered a brick wall when she recommended a standard nine-hour workday for all employees and a factory closing time of 5:00 P.M.[3] (Briscoe also lobbied for a nine-hour law in the Delaware legislature.) Although she remained secure in her job while she aggressively pursued this issue, she clearly understood the limits of executive tolerance. After this incident, Briscoe carefully restrained herself. "I do not ask for too many things," she told a welfare class in 1913, noting that her most recent addition to the Bancroft welfare program was the installation of the sanitary drinking cup.[4]

Like Briscoe, other experts found their advice ignored or rejected when they weighed in on issues of economic security. Despite the tens of thousands of dollars invested by the McCormicks at the behest of Gertrude Beeks, they ignored her repeated entreaties to publish a simplified and uniform wage schedule and to reform their policies for fining employees. "I have talked of this matter for a year," she complained to Stanley McCormick when she resigned in 1902.[5] The following year, strikers at the newly merged Deering Plant demanded the same welfare benefits enjoyed by International Harvester employees at the McCormick Works. Harvester executives turned to Beeks for professional advice. Having been consulted as an expert, Beeks aggressively pursued her agenda of fair wage scales and wage rates. "It will be of little use to install comforts and conveniences recommended," she wrote to the general manager, "unless the [wages] question is properly taken up."[6] It was not.

Few people pursued this aspect of welfare work with such determination. Those who did often had to settle for much less than they believed was adequate, or they left in frustration. At Filene's Department Store, Diana Hirschler, like so many others, became a "consultant" on wages and promotions, but had little real power to affect wage levels.[7] Elizabeth Wheeler, who touted the economic benefits of welfare work and the progressive nature of Shephard Company management at the 1902 Minneapolis Conference, also voiced frustration with her firm's employment of children. Apparently, the company ignored her advice. She proved much less enthusiastic in public statements in 1904. The following year, Wheeler resigned and took up welfare work on the West Coast.[8]

While many employers acknowledged that economic security was an essential foundation of a harmonious partnership, few conceded much of real substance on this issue. In some cases, they raised wages, shortened hours, or reined in autocratic foremen. However, these changes often did little more than make a firm more competitive in the labor market. They did not provide employees with real economic security.[9]

In large part, this reflected employers' inability to reconceptualize their relationship to their employees. For example, when Augustus Loring, president of the Plymouth Cordage Company, evaluated his firm's welfare program, he readily admitted that it raised productivity and generated higher profits. Yet he pointedly criticized his management consultant for assuming that welfare work constituted part of the cost of labor. Management alone decided how much to expend on welfare work, Loring asserted. As a consequence, it charged the cost of welfare work to company profits, which belonged to stockholders, not to labor. By the same reasoning, any return on the investment in welfare work also belonged to stockholders, not to workers. His employees' greater productivity did not entitle them to a greater share of the economic pie.[10]

As at the Plymouth Cordage Company, control over wages served as a measure of employers' authority and power. Increasing wages or shortening hours would have signified an unacceptable change in their relationship to their workers. Yet businessmen did not completely neglect their obligation to provide for the economic security of their employees. Rather, like welfare workers, they developed a version of corporate fatherhood that reconciled their paternal responsibilities with their business interests.[11]

This fatherly role melded particular features of Victorian masculinity with late-nineteenth-century Social Darwinism. Social Darwinism, of course, served a variety of interests. Some employers used it to justify repressive labor practices, claiming that such practices were legitimate weapons of the "most fit." Welfare employers applied Social Darwinism in a different way. The welfare system presumed that employer and employee were partners, rather than antagonists, in the competitive struggle for survival. As employers sought to draw workers into partnership, they tried to foster the qualities that they believed contributed to their own success in that struggle.

Business leaders clearly attributed their own success to their adherence to the values of self-made manhood. Whereas male welfare managers began to incorporate new masculine identities into the definition of professional business management, corporate owners and top executives seem to have retained older Victorian notions of masculinity. They were less affected by the turn-of-the-century "crises in masculinity."[12] Having matured and prospered during the heyday of the era of self-made manhood, business leaders had, perhaps, less incentive to experiment with new masculinities. In this respect, we might think of corporate fatherhood as one point on a turn-of-the-century continuum of masculine gender constructions.

Various studies suggest that leading American businessmen linked their own, and their families', upward mobility to hard work. In 1883, for example, a Brooklyn clergyman asked 500 businessmen to explain their success. Seventy-five percent attributed their success to work habits they cultivated in their youths. Two decades later, Russell Sage, whose wife established the Russell Sage Foundation with his fortune, expressed similar sentiments. Sage wrote that he had imbibed the habit of work so fully that it was "the chief, and, you might say, the only source of pleasure in my life . . . it has become the strongest habit that I have and the only habit that I would find it impossible to break."[13]

When businessmen spoke of work habits, they meant more than a willingness to work hard at a given task. Their work habit incorporated a belief that work was a means to an end, a stepping stone to something higher, where "up" meant the greater independence and larger financial return that came with occupational mobility. Thus, one should look for the rewards of hard work in the future, not in the present. John D. Rockefeller advised one audience that those with ambition must be prepared to work their way up: "Always obey instructions . . . you must learn to obey orders before you can hope to give them."[14] While Victorian manliness prescribed independence, that independence might need to be earned through a period of temporary subordination during which one "proved" oneself worthy.

Along with temporary subordination to others, the path to upward mobility required deferred rewards. University of Wisconsin-Madison president, Charles Van Hise, advised the graduating class of 1907 that, to succeed, "Each of you should appreciate that the only possible way in which promotion can come to you is *by earning more than you are receiving*. . . . All who are worthy of the places they occupy, whether janitors or heads of divisions, are earning more than they are receiving."[15] One executive who began his career at Eastman Kodak recalled that George Eastman, like all the major executives he knew, often worked excessively long hours, and typically six-day weeks.[16]

As they reflected on their own pasts, business leaders might reasonably believe that the rewards for temporary subordination were worth the sacrifices along the way. Studying over 7,000 leading businessmen at the end of the 1920s, Harvard professors F. W. Taussig and C. S. Joslyn discovered significant histories of upward mobility. Their studies show that 66.7 percent of those surveyed whose grandfathers had begun their working careers as unskilled or semiskilled laborers had fathers who began their working careers at a higher level on the occupational ladder (most as skilled laborers or small business owners). And 60 percent of those whose grandfathers began their working careers as salesmen or clerks had fathers who began their working careers at a higher occupational level. Even 40 percent of those whose grandfathers already owned a small business had fathers who enjoyed upward mobility, beginning their working careers as major executives, as owners of a large business, or as professionals.[17] The success literature generated by business leaders at the turn of the century, as discussed earlier, supplied strong anecdotal evidence that such mobility was the reward for hard work.[18]

Welfare employers drew on this kind of evidence to focus their fatherly energies on welfare activities that promoted deferred rewards. They supported welfare benefits that they believed would build ambition and manly independence in the long run (or womanly subordination as wives of independent workmen). In place of improving wages and hours, employers took the lead in establishing the pension, bonus, profit-sharing, and other financial benefit plans that became a standard part of the welfare system. Their preference for financial benefit plans reveals the particular way in which employers defined their duties within the corporate household. They preferred to teach self-reliance rather than provide economic security to their corporate families. They preferred to stimulate the work ethic by rewarding industriousness over the long run rather than rewarding hard work in the short run. Employers claimed that financial benefit plans, which promised income for the uncertainties of old age and invalidism, helped workers to become economically independent.

Despite the obviously self-serving nature of such plans, this did constitute an admission that low wages contributed to working-class poverty and that management bore some responsibility to alleviate that poverty. Yet employers attempted to deflect blame by wrapping themselves in the mantle of corporate fatherhood; financial benefit plans proved that employers were part of the solution, not part of the problem. Thus, Augustus Loring attributed his workers' poverty directly to low wages, without assuming any responsibility for their poverty: "There is no doubt that the wages of the lower paid operative is insufficient to support himself and bring up his family, and make adequate provision for old age or invalidism;—either present living conditions must be cut below a healthy basis, or provision for the future must be neglected."[19] Employers who framed the problem this way could believe that financial benefit plans would make a difference; their employees would no longer need to trade off present living conditions for future security. Financial benefit plans would ensure future security so that workers could use wages to support their families in the present. This begged the question, of course, whether wages were sufficient even for this.

Financial benefit plans promoted employers' particular understanding of reciprocity within the new corporate partnership. Such plans established mutual obligations between employers and employees, and promised mutual rewards. At the same time, they reinforced, rather than challenged, existing inequalities between these corporate partners. When employers linked eligibility for financial benefits to length of service or to payroll deductions, they restricted economic partnership to those who met their standards of loyalty and productivity. In addition, employers decided the size of bonuses and pensions, chose the level at which they would match employee savings, and so on. In this respect, they limited the rewards that employees might earn from partnership, without restricting their own benefits. Employers even reserved the right to discontinue financial benefit plans at will, making it possible for them to avoid their obligations altogether.[20] This construction of corporate fatherhood meant that employers retained control of the purse strings, a power reserved to them both as businessmen and as heads of the corporate household.

Although welfare workers would have preferred a broader vision of economic security, they wholeheartedly supported financial benefit plans.

They also recognized that firms with welfare programs tended to pay higher wages and require shorter hours of labor than did firms without welfare programs.[21] Drawing on their reserves of patience and tact, welfare workers accentuated these positive, if small, steps in the right direction. They held out hope that more would follow.

Despite their public optimism, however, welfare workers knew that their differences with employers went much deeper than matters of economic security. Welfare workers argued that peaceful labor relations depended on systematizing labor policies within a functionally specialized department. Yet neither employers nor fellow managers were willing to relinquish authority over labor matters entirely to welfare managers. The functional separation of financial benefit programs from other aspects of welfare work and employers' monopoly of the development of these programs were only two examples of this. Many employers aggravated the situation further by refusing to commit to the welfare system as their only strategy for managing labor relations. Employers tolerated contradictions in their handling of labor matters much more readily than did their welfare workers. As a consequence, welfare workers continually struggled to define and defend their responsibilities within each company.

Although they employed a variety of strategies to enhance their authority, welfare workers were often dissatisfied with the results. Dr. Luci Bannister's complaint that she engaged in the same arguments with executives at the Westinghouse Lamp Company year after year suggests the pattern of confrontations that preceded success at many firms. A manager at the National Biscuit Company faced a similar uphill battle. After explaining his plans for a complete welfare program to an NCF gathering, he asked Beeks to keep his comments anonymous since "my position here is somewhat peculiar in that the gentlemen in authority in our company are not fully in accord with my views." Despite such resistance, and the need to "be careful," this manager made it clear that he would continue to push his vision of labor relations.[22]

Even those who managed elaborate welfare programs expressed dissatisfaction with the scope of their authority. At the Plymouth Cordage Company, W. E. C. Nazro seems to have persuaded a scientific management consultant, H. K. Hathaway, to lobby on his behalf with company executives. Referring to his conversations with Nazro, Hathaway recommended that the firm's officers cooperate with Nazro more actively, and he proposed that Nazro sit on a board of directors for welfare work. President Loring vehemently rejected Hathaway's suggestions. From Loring's perspective, Hathaway and Nazro misunderstood the welfare manager's position. Although company officers had "profited by [Nazro's] suggestions," Loring wrote, they had "never delegated their powers to him."[23]

Although appropriately loyal in their public statements, welfare workers rarely enjoyed harmonious relations with their employers. They further aggravated the problem when they challenged the methods and authority of foremen or forewomen and plant superintendents. Gertrude Beeks's experience at International Harvester typified that of many others. Being as tactful as possible, Beeks noted with deep regret that plant superintendents had prevented her from maintaining the close contact with workers that she thought necessary.[24] Laura Ray, at Greenhut-Siegel Department Store, suffered similarly. Floor managers apparently refused her access to various parts of the store.[25] Louise Hynson, the welfare worker whom Beeks recommended as having a firm but not masculine manner, lost such a contest at the Wanamaker Store in less than a year. Although John Wanamaker praised her relations with subordinates within the Welfare Department and with store clerks, he noted that she ran into considerable trouble with those in "equal positions of authority who [had] occasion . . . to cross her path."[26] (Wanamaker apparently felt no compulsion to come to her defense.)

Part of these difficulties can be attributed to the uniqueness of the position that welfare workers were creating. Although labor relations developed into a staff function, not a responsibility of production managers, this trend was not entirely predictable. In fact, welfare workers were carving out their niche in the managerial bureaucracy at the same time that American companies were working out the duties of staff and line managers. They did not fit easily into either of these categories. Welfare workers thought of the shop floor as their real workspace. They felt sympathy for the plight of wage workers and they wanted to engage them on a personal level. Like Beeks and Ray, most early welfare workers assumed that it was their duty to mingle with employees during the workday. Many located their offices adjacent to the shop floor and left their doors open. They believed that familiarity with industrial machinery and the work process were just as essential to their work as the ability to give personal advice or to organize a lunchroom. Not surprisingly, foremen and superintendents showed little enthusiasm for this invasion of their domain. They resisted welfare workers' advice as unwarranted interference, and they resented welfare workers' ability to appeal over their heads to top corporate officers.

The struggle to establish their authority over labor relations often contributed to high turnover among welfare workers. Events at International

Harvester serve as a good example. After frustrations over these issues led to Beeks's departure in 1902, the chair of the company's new Recreation Committee, S. M. Darling, continued the struggle for a centralized and systematic welfare program. Darling actively lobbied the McCormicks to make the Recreation Committee the nucleus of a fully developed Sociological Department. He envisioned subdepartments in each Harvester plant, with a full range of educational, social, athletic, and economic programs. The broad scope and aggressive nature of Darling's plan proved his downfall.[27] In addition to antagonizing Cyrus McCormick Jr. and plant superintendents, he became involved in a struggle with a fellow welfare worker, Henry Bruere, over which man would be appointed to head this work. By early 1905 McCormick had disbanded the newly created Sociological Department, relieving Darling and Bruere of their duties.

Neither Beeks on the outside nor various welfare workers on the inside were willing to let the matter rest. Under constant pressure, McCormick commissioned internal studies in 1905 and again in 1907 to develop an appropriate administrative structure for the firm's welfare activities.[28] By 1909, Harvester executives had settled on a semiformal "Advisory Committee on Welfare." The Advisory Committee, chaired by a company executive with production responsibilities, satisfied McCormick but not his welfare workers. Throughout this period, a number of strong-willed welfare workers engaged in a series of confrontations with plant superintendents and company executives over what constituted labor policy and who had authority in this area.

One such confrontation, at the Twine Mill, lasted over a year. It eventually involved not only the mill's welfare manager, Mary Thaon, and her immediate superior, the assistant superintendent, but also the mill superintendent, executives at company headquarters, and Gertrude Beeks. Thaon charged that the assistant superintendent treated her with disrespect and was "too much interested in the details of welfare work and wished to be matron himself." Thaon wanted more autonomy in managing the plant's welfare program and greater authority to intervene in shop-floor disputes. When the mill superintendent and home office executives failed to meet her demands, Thaon recruited Gertrude Beeks to lobby Cyrus McCormick Jr. on her behalf. Beeks's intervention brought the conflict to a head, resulting in reprimands and restructuring at the Twine Mill, but little satisfaction for Thaon. She soon resigned.[29]

Thaon's replacement, Catherine Brannick, moved to International Harvester after one year at the Curtis Publishing Company. Shortly before her departure from Curtis, Brannick had run into stiff opposition from the superintendent of the Curtis mechanical department. Her early days at International Harvester seem to have been equally fraught with conflict. Antagonism from plant foremen and workers there led her to consider leaving welfare work altogether.[30]

The evidence suggests that turnover rates among welfare workers may have declined as their positions became more clearly defined. At a number of firms the first welfare workers left after one to two years, whereas their successors remained on the job for five to ten years. After seven years of internal turmoil and rapid turnover at International Harvester, for example, Mary Goss assumed many of the daily responsibilities for welfare work and retained her position for at least a decade. At the Curtis Publishing Company, Catherine Pfeiffer, who replaced Brannick, stayed for two years, twice Brannick's tenure. Pfeiffer's replacement, Helen Snow, began her work five years after the company first established the position of welfare manager. Unlike her three predecessors, who served for one to two years each, Snow managed the Curtis Welfare Department for five years, from 1909 to 1914.

Declining rates of turnover do not necessarily signify complete harmony between welfare workers and their employers. Rather, they suggest that both employers and welfare workers may have developed a mutual understanding of the parameters within which they could pursue conflicting agendas. The experience of welfare managers at the Greenhut-Siegel Department Store was probably shared by many. The first two welfare managers, Isabelle Nye and Mrs. Joseph Spencer, spent only a year each at Greenhut-Siegel. Laura Ray, who took up welfare work after Spencer's departure in 1906, remained with the firm for at least seven years. Yet, Ray did not enjoy peaceful relations with B. J. Greenhut or with lower-level supervisors during her long tenure. After interviewing Ray extensively and observing the Greenhut-Siegel welfare program, National Civic Federation investigators severely criticized the store's management: managers failed to listen to Ray's advice, executives did not support her in confrontations with floor managers, and they refused to staff her department adequately.[31]

Women probably suffered from this contest for authority more acutely than did men. Welfare workers entered a business world in which men held virtually all positions of power and women seemed out of place. In addition, it appears that men were more likely than women to have held positions of authority prior to entering welfare work. Nazro, for example, was Superintendent of Grounds when he assumed responsibility for welfare activities at the Plymouth Cordage Company. The company's officers had already recognized his expertise and placed him in a managerial position before they tapped him to add welfare work to his other duties.

While he desired more authority than he had, company officers seem to have given Nazro free rein to administer his department once they approved his annual budget request. The National Biscuit Company manager who asked Beeks to keep his comments anonymous was, perhaps, even more secure. While he needed to proceed cautiously, he happened to be the plant's general manager, as well as its welfare manager.

Like those tapped from within, men who entered corporate welfare work from the outside often commanded a level of respect not readily available to women. Many had established themselves as respected professionals in other fields. A considerable number were doctors. The American Smelting Company placed its welfare program in the hands of Dr. Charles Neill, a former U.S. Commissioner of Labor. AT&T hired Dr. Alvah Doty, former quarantine officer for New York.[32] Not all physicians brought this level of prestige, but employers could hardly ignore their expertise. Lee Frankel, who assumed responsibility for the welfare of the entire Metropolitan Life family (employees and policyholders), came as a trained chemist, former director of the United Hebrew Charities, and prominent researcher for the Russell Sage Foundation. After a 1908 speech piqued the interest of company executives, Frankel negotiated his entry into the private sector with the director of the Russell Sage Foundation at his side.

Others, like Frank Bolles, the welfare manager at Allis-Chalmers in 1914, established their business credentials before entering welfare work. Bolles had apparently gained experience in welfare work prior to his employment at Allis-Chalmers. Although he hoped to engage in welfare work at Allis-Chalmers, he did not seek such a position initially. Instead, Bolles gained employment as a commercial engineer; he spent his first months producing sales reports, courting company executives, and generally trying to demonstrate his worth to the company. Bolles also used that time to improve his knowledge of welfare work, with an eye toward his real goal. Within a few years Bolles's careful planning was rewarded; Allis-Chalmers officials appointed him as the firm's welfare manager.[33]

The men could also look forward to career opportunities that were not available to the women. Lee Frankel, who began his career at the Metropolitan Life Insurance Company in 1909 as Director of the Welfare Division, rose within seven years to become sixth vice-president and then third vice-president. Charles Carpenter had been a plant superintendent at the National Cash Register Company when he moved into welfare work following the 1901 strike. Carpenter became so dissatisfied with president John Patterson's labor policies that he left the firm within two years. After being refused by International Harvester (perhaps because he would have been a stronger personality than the McCormicks desired), Carpenter continued his climb in the business world. Within five years, he was president of the Herring-Hall-Marvin Safe Company.[34]

Women, on the other hand, rarely entered welfare work with the kind of status enjoyed by their male counterparts. In addition to establishing themselves as business managers with special expertise in labor relations, women found it necessary to prove that they were business-minded. "It must not be supposed that a woman in this line can ever have a path of roses to travel," advised Gertrude Beeks. That path could be particularly rough if a woman chose to address economic issues "simply because the Superintendent who is striving to keep down the manufacturing expenses, will consider that she is interfering in a line about which she knows nothing." Beeks recommended that women be prepared with facts to refute charges that they did not understand the business situation.[35]

Businessmen often chose women from service-related careers because these experiences seemed to qualify them for the maternal role of corporate mother. They were less willing, however, to presume that these women had also acquired business skills. When B. J. Greenhut decided to introduce welfare work at his department store, for example, he chose a widow, Isabelle Nye, specifically because of her charity aid background and her maternal experience. He deferred to her feminine skills to develop the work as she saw fit. After Nye's departure, Greenhut hired welfare managers who, like Nye, were widows with real experience as mothers. Yet his initial enthusiasm waned when they began making recommendations to improve the store's efficiency with more systematic methods of labor management. Although their weaker positions do not seem to have prevented women from trying to assert their authority, it did make them more vulnerable.

As their skills, or frustrations, grew, women could not count on the same kinds of career options as men. Very few had an independent profession to which they might return, nor could they look forward to moving up the corporate ladder. Ella Haas's career, while strikingly similar to Carpenter's in many ways, suggests the differences. After serving as head forewoman at NCR for thirteen years, Haas moved into the firm's Welfare Department about the time of Carpenter's departure. By 1907, she, like Carpenter, had become frustrated with NCR executives and began seeking employment elsewhere. Gertrude Beeks recommended her, as she had Carpenter, to International Harvester. Although it is unclear whether Haas spent time at International Harvester, her welfare experience created opportunities that kept her off the shop floor. Haas, however, faced a more limited range of opportunities than Carpenter. While he climbed the ladder to a corporate presidency, Haas, in 1909, was serving a stint as a factory inspector for the state of Ohio. By 1916, she was back in welfare work at Commonwealth Steel.

Despite the frustrations and conflicts that frequently led welfare workers to seek new positions, there is little evidence that they questioned either the goals or the methods of corporate welfare work. As both educators and mediators, welfare workers placed themselves at the nexus of conflict between employers and employees. They never expected a path of roses or instant success. Yet, relations with executives and fellow managers proved to be unexpectedly difficult. Many expressed skepticism that their employers were willing to make "fair dealing" part of a new business ethic. Employers gave them plenty of reasons for skepticism. Despite their support for innovative welfare activities, employers failed to act on issues of economic security or to give welfare workers real control over labor policies. Under these circumstances, welfare workers found themselves in an untenable position. Without these fundamental building blocks, they did not have the tools they needed to persuade employees to join the promised business partnership.

Chapter Six

The Corporate Family in Conflict:
Welfare Workers and Employees

Although employers made the task extraordinarily difficult, welfare workers dedicated themselves to transforming wage earners into responsible members of the corporate family. While welfare workers foresaw some initial hesitancy, they expected employees to submit willingly to their authority. They did not need to walk the fine line between submission and control with workers as they did with employers. Instead, their assumption that workers were merely unenlightened children pointed to a much simpler relationship. This optimism, however, was misplaced. Whereas welfare workers believed that their work represented a new style of business management, one that would pay dividends to both employer and employee, workers often believed that it was another instance of exploitation intended to reap dividends for employers only.

Wage-earners' greatest objection to welfare work grew out of their very different notions of reciprocity. They rejected welfare workers' and employers' assumption that a mutually beneficial exchange could occur between two such unequal partners. In fact, working people did not believe that an employer's decision to offer clean drinking water, a lunchroom, or a savings plan obligated them to reciprocate in any way. To the consternation of many employers, their workers reaped the benefits of welfare work, but did not reciprocate with either greater loyalty or productivity. The president of one firm complained that the management "never had any expression of appreciation . . . and believe a fraction of a dollar per week offered by another concern would take a majority of our men away."[1]

Employers' complaints reflect the different meanings that reciprocity held for each. The welfare partnership presumed that employers and employees had mutual, but different, obligations toward one another and that each would receive mutual, but different, rewards. American workingmen and -women, on the other hand, had forged cultures that valued a form of reciprocity that entailed equal obligations and equal rewards. Working-class women relied on friends and family to assist at weddings and births, provide child care, nurse the sick, offer gifts of food and clothing in times of need, and even provide protection from abusive husbands or turn tricks on unsuspecting pick-ups.[2] In exchange, they expected the same kinds of support when they were in need. Failure to reciprocate could mean ostracism and a loss both of help in times of need and of camaraderie.

While working-class women's sense of reciprocity centered on assistance in daily survival and domestic duties, working-class men built egalitarian reciprocity into their leisure-time pursuits. Working-class saloon culture centered on the tradition of treating; each man bought a round of drinks for his comrades, and each of them, in turn, returned the favor. Treating extended men's leisure time. It also validated a belief in egalitarianism and symbolized rejection of the commodification of modern life that underpinned the welfare system's construction of reciprocity. In the saloon, noted Jack London, "Money no longer counted. It was comradeship that counted." Another observer of workingmen's custom of treating commented that "the 'treat' goes round, the poor vanity of the free-hearted meets its reward, the mean man is scorned."[3] Judged according to this working-class standard, the employer who refused to reciprocate in kind earned scorn, not loyalty and productivity.

From the perspective of wage-earners, the reward for loyalty and productivity should have been higher wages. When employers offered welfare programs instead, employees logically concluded that those programs were financed with monies that rightfully belonged to them. As Charles Eliot, president of Harvard, noted in reference to the disparity between the workingman's wage of $2.00–3.00 per day and the executive's salary of $300 per day: "[The workingman] will never believe that any man can fairly earn such a salary. He will never admit that the salary of a manager should be proportionate to the agglomerated bulk of the business he manages, while the workman's wages remain proportionate only to his own individual daily productiveness."[4]

Rather than accepting employers' claims that welfare work was managements' contribution to the corporate partnership and thus a charge against company profits, workers believed it was simply a new strategy for coercing their labor and thus a charge against them. They complained that the money spent on welfare work, and on welfare workers' salaries, should have been used to increase their wages. At the National Cash Register Company, workmen assumed that the firm must have been "rolling in money" if it could afford welfare work. One man bravely told John Patterson that he "did not care a damn for flowers, grass, etc. [and] would rather have that money divided among the people."[5] An anonymous "faithful servant" at the Eastman Kodak Company advised George Eastman that "there is too much *fluff* with positions of [this] kind. . . . It is a great mistake how the company falls for such bull . . . the people in charge can do very well without [Mrs. Armstrong] and *divide her salary among the real workers*."[6] When employers refused to make concessions on wages or hours, they reinforced workers' sense that the costs of welfare work came directly out of the workingman's pockets. One Iowa manufacturer cut wages on the same day he opened a lunchroom. His employees, needless to say, refused to go near it.[7]

Employers' decisions to substitute financial benefits for higher wages often added to workers' disgruntlement. Financial benefit plans further exposed the deep material and ideological differences between employers and employees. Aside from the obvious failure to meet workers' real economic needs in the present, these plans pretended that working people could, with the right incentives and opportunities, build a secure economic future for themselves. Employers offered these plans with much fanfare, promising that they would turn workmen into business partners and self-reliant men. Although the ideal of the self-made man was an article of faith in Victorian culture, by the turn of the century it had little basis in reality even for the middle class and none for the working class.

What mattered most to the workingman, observed Whiting Williams, reformer turned undercover workingman, was the daily job.[8] Workingmen's masculinity depended on that daily job and the wages tied to it. As with Victorian manhood, work was at the core of working-class masculinity. However, working-class men measured their performance at work differently from their middle- and upper-class brothers. In a highly unstable economy, having a job at all was the first, indispensable mark of manhood. All men labored, and, if not employed, they looked for work. Once on the job, Victorian men measured their manhood according to their positions and incomes; upward mobility and wealth signified manly character. Working-class men could not count on either of these rewards. Instead, working-class masculinity called for qualities that were measurable in the "here and now," in daily job performance: skill at the assigned task, physical strength and stamina, and a cooperative ethos. Highly skilled work naturally commanded more respect and bestowed a greater sense of manhood than did less skilled work. Yet even unskilled workingmen could take pride in a job well done. Whiting Williams, for example, earned a grudging "You all right" from the boss of his four-man rolling mill crew only after he learned to loosen the metal sheets and put them on the skids in rhythm with the pace set by the roller boss.[9]

Since job performance often depended as much on hard physical labor as it did on skill, workingmen also learned to judge the quality of their work according to their endurance and physical strength. Combined with masculine competitiveness (a quality shared with Victorian manhood), the glorification of hard labor could drive men to destruction. Employers often tried to capitalize on this competitive spirit with production contests. Yet, like Victorian masculinity, working-class masculinity prescribed limits to manly competition. A cooperative ethos, most evident in adherence to the stint and in the creation of labor unions, promised respect for physical labor at the same time it protected men from working themselves into an early grave. While the stint is most commonly associated with skilled workers' defense of manly independence, less skilled workers practiced the stint as well. One workman expressed the mixture of pride in hard labor with respect for the cooperative ethos in this way: "I like work and I'm not afraid of it, but I ain't goin' to be none of your hogs for it." Whiting Williams was introduced to the stint during his first day as an undercover laborer. As he shoveled bricks out of a dismantled open-hearth furnace, fellow workers repeatedly berated him for working too fast, warning him that he would wear himself out at such a pace.[10] Union demands for shorter workdays are another clear example of the intersection of the cooperative ethos and workingmen's respect for hard physical labor. Long workdays wore a man out, exposing weakness where he should be strong and forcing him to limit his exertions for self-preservation. Shorter workdays would allow him to labor hard like a man without endangering his long-term health.[11]

Ultimately, men's skill and stamina translated into wages. Wages, the immediate reward for the workingman, determined his status as a breadwinner. The level and regularity of wages affected how he lived and, most importantly, whether and at what types of jobs his wife and children labored. Working-class men's success as breadwinners undergirded a definition of manly independence quite different from that of middle- and upper-class men. Whereas the latter groups defined independence in terms of positions that gave them mastery over others on the job (as managers or owners), working-class men found independence in their ability to determine whether wives and children went out to work. The manly breadwinner could choose to send family members into the labor force rather than it being forced upon him by looming destitution. In order to achieve this kind of independence, workingmen had to earn enough to save for the inevitable "rainy day" (injury, illness, layoff, or strike) and to purchase minimal comforts in an increasingly commercialized world.

To the extent that his income was insufficient to meet these needs, other family members had to assist him in the breadwinner role. When this happened, the workingman had to admit failure in his most basic duty as family breadwinner. In this sense, workingmen's achievement of manly independence depended much more on wages than it did for middle- and upper-class men. Employers missed the mark when they refused to discuss wages and hours and instead offered bonus or pension plans. Workingmen's sense of reciprocity led them to expect something different in return for their loyalty and productivity. Employers' claims that the future rewards of financial benefit plans would bestow manly independence did not convince workingmen, for whom manly independence rested on steady work at a family wage with sufficient leisure time to restore their energy.

Employees of the Plymouth Cordage Company, for example, described their company's profit-sharing plan as "a very stupid idea. . . . [We] are not asking for such as you call it a Bonus. [No!] But we are asking for a better condition in wages and . . . hours."[12] The problems they faced were not, as President Loring had asserted, in choosing between present and future security, but rather in finding some way to survive the poverty of wage labor. Security was certainly an issue. Laboring people, however, did not have the luxury of divorcing present from future security. Real independence meant the security of wages sufficient to provide for the present and the future at the same time.

In fact, contrary to employers' pretensions, financial benefit plans included their own elements of uncertainty as companies regularly revised or canceled such plans at will. In a number of cases, employees enthusiastically invested money in new company savings plans only to discover that they had misplaced their confidence. Workers who made deposits to the Greenhut-Siegel Savings Bank discovered this when the company declared the plan bankrupt and all their savings lost. Similar failures by other companies caused minor scandals and generated calls for government intervention.[13] The state of California banned company savings plans altogether as a result of such scandals.

Bonus and profit-sharing plans, whose award amounts depended more on broader market conditions and distribution structures than on employee productivity, likewise proved to be an uncertain source of income. DuPont workers who referred to their merit pay as "whiskey checks" were not only choosing their own kind of recreation, but also recognizing the unreliable nature of this form of wages. The DuPont Company changed award amounts, the distribution structure, and eligibility requirements almost annually between 1903 and 1920. Sometimes the company made payments in cash, and other times in stock. Sometimes it paid a higher proportion to managerial staff, and at other times it distributed more to lower-wage workers. DuPont continually revised eligibility requirements for employees laid off or transferred.[14]

Wage-earners seem to have had few illusions about the purposes or benefits of financial plans. They enrolled in such plans only sporadically and only to the extent that they expected to reap real economic returns. The DuPont Company, for example, persuaded less than 600 employees to open accounts in a new savings plan established in 1911. When more than half of these closed their accounts in the first two years, the company decided to discontinue the plan. A later offer to establish an Employee Building and Loan Association fared no better. Employees returned less than 20 percent of the 3,500 questionnaires distributed by the company. This group showed so little interest (only 111 out of 682 respondents indicated that they would use the fund in the near future) that the company dropped the idea entirely.[15]

Even in those cases where employees appeared more enthusiastic about financial benefit plans, their participation did not necessarily indicate that they had become loyal business partners. Executives at International Harvester, for example, believed that they had earned their workmen's loyalty in 1903 with an eleventh-hour announcement of a stock gift, averting a threatened strike at the McCormick Works. However, the ongoing labor crises at International Harvester suggest that workers understood this as only one more battle in the labor war, not the beginning of a more cooperative partnership. Before accepting this "gift," workers used the leverage of the strike call to force company executives to increase the size and broaden the distribution of the stock offer.

Although the company soon became a leader in developing financial benefit plans, its workmen continued to reject these entreaties to cooperation. Instead, they evaluated each plan according to their own standards of reciprocity and economic security. Thus, when executives offered a profit-sharing plan in 1909, workmen accurately concluded that it would yield more benefit to the company (through better public relations) than it would to them (with its limited discounts on stock purchases and dividend restrictions). Few men enrolled. Six years later, a revised plan, with more favorable terms, attracted over 60 percent of the company's workmen. Contrary to management's hopes, however, workers demonstrated no willingness to reciprocate with the desired loyalty. Workmen struck the following year. When the economic benefits of the new profit-sharing plan proved illusory, most of the men dropped out (barely 5 percent remained in 1921.)[16]

Suspicion of the corporate welfare system was directed not only at employers, as they acted out this version of corporate fatherhood, but also at welfare workers, as they performed their duties as corporate mothers. As the most visible symbol of the new welfare system, welfare workers sometimes bore the brunt of workers' animosity. The fact that many reported directly to company owners or executive officers did nothing to allay workers' suspicions. In what was probably a fairly common reaction, Bancroft and Sons employees initially referred to Elizabeth Briscoe as the "lady detective." Employees at a Maine manufacturing plant greeted their new welfare manager, Jean Hoskins, with suspicious glares and the unfriendly title of "Sanitary Jane."[17]

Some welfare workers were more successful than others at overcoming this kind of resistance. Briscoe's sympathetic manner and successful interventions on behalf of individual workers apparently inspired enough confidence that employees stopped calling her the lady detective and began referring to her in less hostile terms as the "lady nurse" or the "manager of the mills." Sanitary Jane was apparently less successful. Months after her arrival a group of workers marched into her office and informed her that they were as clean as she and had no intention of submitting to her inspections.

Even if they were able to overcome personal animosity, however, welfare workers found it nearly impossible to persuade employees to accept them as moral guardians and teachers. Understandably, most working people did not believe that they needed moral guardians or teachers. They were, after all, adults with their own well-developed sense of family responsibility. They did not attribute the labor problem to any defects in their character. Nor were they persuaded by welfare workers' arguments that they could solve their problems by cultivating middle-class habits.

In fact, working-class culture frequently valued qualities directly at odds with the welfare system's moral lessons. Workingwomen, who were often subjected to the most intense forms of moral instruction, developed their own particular grievances against the welfare system. Unlike working-class manhood, working-class womanhood did not center on paid labor. Instead, wage-earning women acquired status by fulfilling familial responsibilities. However, the generation of young women most likely to experience welfare work were in a unique stage of their lives; care of household and children were not paramount. Most were suspended between subordination within their parental families and the responsibilities of marriage and motherhood to come.

These women's identity was connected to the pursuit of both independence and a femininity that would ultimately attract a husband. The independent workingwoman earned enough and spent her earnings wisely enough to support herself. This gave her leverage to escape intense parental supervision (whether that meant living on her own or simply more freedom to spend leisure time unsupervised). She often used her new-found independence to enhance her femininity, a femininity that she defined in terms of an expressive heterosocial sexuality.[18] In contrast to welfare workers' presumptions that Victorian femininity entailed circumscribed contact with men, self-denial, passivity, and domestic skills, working-class femininity found full expression in women's open contact with men and their boisterous participation in the night life of the streets, dance halls, theaters, and amusement parks. When welfare workers sent matrons after women in restrooms or stationed chaperones at company dances, they imposed the kind of parental oversight that most working girls struggled so hard to escape.[19] When welfare workers taught classes in domestic skills or promoted "good books," they offered lessons largely irrelevant to working-class femininity.

Thus, workers frequently ignored carefully crafted lessons in personal hygiene, domestic skills, or uplifting recreation. Adverse reactions, like those directed at Sanitary Jane's hygiene program, were not unusual. It often took strong incentives or coercion to convince workers to use newly built washrooms and baths. The National Biscuit Company finally persuaded some of its working girls to use newly installed baths by allowing them to bathe during working hours. With this enticement, as many as 15 percent of the girls took baths on hot days.[20] One company found it necessary to impose a penalty for using wash buckets on the shop floor before its workmen began to use the new washrooms. Pressure of these kinds was fairly common not only with regard to hygiene features but also with regard to use of dining facilities and, in some cases, enrollment in savings and benefit plans.

Scattered evidence suggests that working people showed no more enthusiasm for educational and social activities than they did for hygiene programs. Sewing, cooking, and other domestic classes typically drew twenty to thirty students from female workforces numbering in the hundreds. Rather than try to interest store clerks in a formal sewing class, Greenhut-Siegel's first welfare secretary demonstrated sewing skills at the store's vacation cottage, where she had a captive audience. Other educational ventures, such as libraries, suffered from neglect as well. A trustee of Ludlow Manufacturing Associates reported that out of a community of 5,000, only twenty to twenty-five people per day used his company's well-equipped library. Records of the Metropolitan Life Insurance Company suggest that in 1914 only two employees out of its heavily female, and literate, home office staff visited the company reading room each day. That same year the Metropolitan Life Glee Club attracted fifty members, from a home office force of close to 5,000. The Natural Food Company, with 500 employees, found it necessary to draw from the outside community to fill out its thirty-piece "company" band.[21] Working people were clearly not the eager students that welfare workers hoped they would be.

On the contrary, in the face of welfare workers' efforts to raise them out of an assumed immaturity, workers strongly asserted their right to conduct their own affairs as they saw fit. They did this not simply by ignoring welfare work, but also by negotiating the terms on which they would participate. The fact that workers refused to use washrooms, or had to be coerced to use them, for example, tells only part of the story. The ways in which workers used these facilities is equally important. Although female bottlers and picklers at the H. J. Heinz Company welcomed a decision to install washrooms, they drew the line at the company's plan to have them share towels and soap. The women insisted on supplying their own towels and soap rather than let the company violate their sense of privacy and dictate their standards of hygiene.[22]

Telephone operators in Cleveland felt highly insulted when the company installed a bath but required that the door be left open to allow a matron to supervise its use. Similarly to the workingwomen at Heinz, these telephone operators resisted this violation of their independence. They refused to use the bath for over a year, relenting only when they discovered that it could enhance their independence in other ways. The first operator to use the bath did so to avoid returning home before going out with friends. The company bath, she discovered, made it easier for her to escape parental oversight. Once they decided that the bath could be an advantage, the women no longer avoided it. Within a short time, demand became so great that the company installed a second bath.[23]

Patronage of dining rooms depended on similar evaluations of personal needs and assertions of independence. Although welfare workers would have preferred to serve free meals so that employees could not escape their carefully designed lessons in nutrition and meal planning, most workers refused to accept free meals. They believed that this would constitute an unacceptable admission of dependence. Most could be persuaded to use lunchrooms only if they paid for their food. Workers not only escaped the onus of charity by paying for their own meals; they also gained the right to choose what they would and would not eat. At the Metropolitan Life Insurance Company, which made free meals a cornerstone of its educational mission, office clerks rebelled against efforts to control their eating habits. Whenever possible, they rushed past the nutritionally labelled meats and vegetables and filled their plates with ice cream and cakes; this prompted the company to post a watcher at the end of the line to prevent such unbalanced selections. Others, like the independent women at Heinz, deigned to purchase only coffee and bread, preferring to bring the balance of their meals from home. Most men went home or, if there was a local saloon, joined fellow workers for a free buffet. On the other hand, single men were among the most frequent customers in company lunchrooms. Without a wife to prepare their meals or a nearby saloon, the company lunchroom might be the only option.

In similar ways, enrollment in sewing classes, visits to company reading rooms, and participation in other educational and social features often signified self-interested opportunism rather than a judgment on the corporate welfare system itself. In 1913, Joseph Feiss and Company noted that the twenty-five women enrolled in its sewing class were primarily interested in the class as a way to supplement their wages. With the skills learned in class, women were able to attract orders for tablecloths, sheets, pillowcases, and other articles.[24] These working-class women clearly had a different sense of the value of domesticity than did their welfare managers. Welfare advocates promoted domesticity as a way to move working girls into the dependence of marriage and motherhood. In contrast, these working girls valued domestic skills because the income they earned on sales enhanced their independence.

When Gertrude Beeks stocked the new reading room at the International Harvester Twine Mill with both popular magazines and "Good Books to Read," the young Twine Mill women went "simply wild with delight" over copies of the *Ladies' Home Journal*. They wanted an education, and they left little doubt about the kind of knowledge they desired. Instead of seeking the gentility that Beeks hoped to instill, these working girls recognized in the *Ladies' Home Journal* a resource that would help them learn about the heterosexual femininity that was most important to them. The women were so happy with the magazines that they appropriated the copies for their private use. Beeks could not get them back once they had been checked out.[25]

As at International Harvester, employees at other firms often forced welfare workers and employers to accommodate their preferences. Had they not done so, participation rates would have been considerably lower.

The National Biscuit Company's decision to allow baths during working hours is an example of this type of accommodation. Numerous other firms adopted similar policies. Heinz Company picklers and bottlers enjoyed summer carriage rides through the park without loss of pay. Students in Bancroft and Sons cooking classes learned these domestic skills on company time, and applicants to the company's baseball team received special time off each week for practice. When foremen refused to allow women to attend the cooking class during work hours, Briscoe was unable to interest enough women to maintain the classes.[26]

Companies also offered cash prizes to entice employees to participate in welfare activities. This strategy was commonly used to stimulate interest in suggestion systems, home beautification programs, and company picnics. Like many others, Henry Heinz discovered that his employees would not take an interest in the company's annual outing unless it included contests, with prizes. Those prizes ranged from candy, to cash, to such practical necessities as shoes and belts.[27] In addition to the material rewards, such contests certainly appealed to a working class for whom leisure meant boisterous games and play.

Welfare workers also accommodated their employees' interests by offering a multitude of welfare activities. Welfare workers generally explained the variety of welfare features in two ways. First, it helped them to expose wage-earners to many facets of the middle-class work ethic and lifestyle. In addition, it allowed them to respond to the particular needs of their company's workers. The wide array of welfare activities also made it possible to reach more workers. While a sewing class or company band might attract only a few dozen employees, when welfare workers supplemented these with a range of other activities, they were able to draw many hundreds of workers into the welfare system.

Thus, the Solvay Process Company began its welfare work around 1900 with a small sewing class for young girls. By 1904, the company offered a wide variety of programs to its 2,500 employees and their families. The sewing school had grown to 275 students; new dance classes attracted over 150 boys and girls, while older employees took part in senior gymnastics; the library registered 1,000 cardholders; the formal dining room served almost 200 people each day, and an informal lunch house served another 600; and a generous mutual benefit association enrolled almost 90 percent of the firm's male employees.[28]

Other firms that established similarly broad programs experienced the same kind of success. By the early 1920s, two-thirds of the employees at the Plymouth Cordage Company were active in one or another of that firm's welfare activities. About 500, mostly single men, dined in the company lunchroom each day; scores of families sent their youngsters to the company kindergarten; and close to 1,000 employees and their older children enrolled in classes ranging from sewing, to physical culture, to the use of simple tools.[29] While it is likely that some employees participated in more than one welfare activity and others in none, companies clearly designed their programs to target different groups of workers: single men used the lunchroom, young women attended cooking classes, and older employees enrolled their children in the kindergarten classes.

Employers and welfare workers offered prizes, time off work, and a multitude of activities because they believed that their carefully designed programs would transform their employees into cooperative business partners. Were they correct? Did those who became involved in welfare work adopt the middle-class work ethic and become more loyal and productive employees? Did labor-management relations become more peaceful as a result of welfare work? The record is somewhat ambiguous. Understandably, because they were the ones who created the system, employers and welfare workers expressed much more satisfaction than their workers. The fact that so many companies invested thousands of dollars in their welfare programs, year after year for over two decades, suggests that they considered these neither a passing craze nor a failed experiment. Although some employers expressed frustration at their workers' ingratitude, many more went on record to praise the effects of their welfare programs. The conclusion of an officer of the Acme White Lead and Color Works was fairly representative: "We think the first feeling of 'uncertainty' among our employes, due to the radical feature of the new policy, has been largely overcome, and we are feeling the benefit of co-operative work all along the line."[30]

Even those who saw no change in their employees, like the manager who felt his employees would leave for slightly higher wages elsewhere, expressed their determination to continue their welfare programs. They believed that their employees, like those at Acme White Lead, would eventually be brought into the fold. As welfare advocates studied the effects of welfare work, they found much evidence to support these expectations. A National Civic Federation investigator found that Filene Department Store employees who participated the most in welfare activities were also the most enthusiastic and interested. They had, she concluded, been "educated up to it." The welfare manager at the Plymouth Cordage Company was similarly encouraged when an internal investigation revealed that the employees who were least likely to participate in welfare activities were also the most recently hired. He noted with satisfaction that even this generally reluctant group, primarily recent Portuguese immigrants, was beginning to send its children to the company kindergarten.[31]

Welfare advocates found ample evidence to confirm their expectations that welfare work would foster more genteel personal habits and more industrious work habits. From the working girls who began wearing nightdresses to bed to the workmen who graduated from oilcloth to linen tablecloths in their dining rooms, it appeared that working people were learning their lessons well. In addition, many firms noted with satisfaction that turnover and absenteeism rates declined after they established their welfare programs. Perhaps more importantly, employers believed that workers were less inclined to join unions or to go on strike.

Despite these positive signs, employees saw the picture very differently. Certainly welfare work introduced millions of wage-earners to the comforts and habits of middle-class life. Some most certainly strove to apply those lessons to their daily lives. Yet even if some workers were earnest converts, not simply affecting interest for their own reasons, they did not necessarily become more cooperative and loyal on the job.

Whiting Williams's conversations with workmen during his months as an undercover workingman offer some insight into the ambiguous impact of welfare work. During the course of his investigation, Williams worked at firms that offered welfare amenities and at firms that did not. He noted a marked difference between the employees at the two types of companies. He concluded that employee attitudes were generally much better at firms where welfare programs existed. At a rolling mill where welfare work included clean drinking water, an employee restaurant, well-swept floors, and landscaped grounds, the workmen agreed that company pay, hours, and plant conditions were generally satisfactory. A number of his fellow workers had enrolled in the company stock plan, and Williams frequently heard them asking one another "How is she [the stock price] to-day?"[32] Workingmen showed little interest in unions, and Williams felt that few unions could offer better conditions.

Nevertheless, the welfare firms where Williams worked had entirely failed to convince employees that they were partners in a cooperative enterprise. The average workman did not develop a sense of "mutual respect and confidence" in his employer because the employer (or his representatives) made little effort to find out "what the other fellow's got in his head and heart." Contact with the employer was limited to daily interaction with foremen, who were notoriously unsympathetic when workmen did state their mind by lodging a grievance. Further, the nature of the work itself, increasingly unskilled or low-skilled, offered no "opportunity to find a satisfactory sense of manliness."[33]

Not surprisingly, the failure to address the wage issue seems to have been the greatest barrier to welfare partnership. Discontent over wages emerged on a number of fronts. At the rolling mill where Williams worked as a helper, employees enjoyed a wide range of amenities. Yet piece rates and other wage practices militated against full cooperation, pitting workers not only against their employer, but against each other as well. Helpers, for example, earned a straight hourly wage, whereas the roller bosses earned piece rates. The faster the crew completed the day's jobs, the more the roller boss made, and the less the helper made. Wage problems similarly prevented welfare work from building partnership at a coal mine where Williams worked. One fifteen-year veteran, while admitting that the firm provided a range of benefits (including company housing, a baseball team, and a company band), evidenced no respect or loyalty toward his employer. Instead, he expressed deep-seated distrust, accusing the company of endemic dishonesty in weighing the coal. Even where the size of the pay envelope was not an issue, workmen took offense at their employer's attitude about paying wages at all. Many firms instituted pay rules that seemed designed primarily to prevent the workman from receiving his due. Paymasters were famous for their nasty temperaments and tough enforcement of these petty rules. "The effect of a lot of nice welfare near-luxuries," commented Williams, "can be canceled in an instant by one growly paymaster; for he hands out the necessity of life."[34] Failure to address what one welfare advocate referred to as the "supreme economic question" in the workman's life, made it virtually impossible to convince workers that they were family partners.

While some employers enjoyed peaceful labor relations, others did not. Strikes and union organizing, the most obvious signs of disloyalty, shook many companies with well-established welfare programs (including the National Cash Register Company, International Harvester, Bancroft and Sons, the Plymouth Cordage Company, and Filene's Department Store). Many workers, like those at the Endicott-Johnson Company, rarely struck, but engaged in a continuous series of strike threats, slowdowns, and open confrontations with foremen and company officers. A Cleveland merchant summed up the experience of many when he noted that his firm's elaborate welfare program had not lessened labor conflict.[35]

While a number of scholars attribute declining strike activity in the 1920s to the effects of welfare work, the evidence is less than conclusive. Considering the fact that welfare work was fairly widespread by 1910, measurement of its effects on union organizing and strike activity should not be limited to the post–World War I era. In addition to welfare work, a number of other factors contributed to the decline in strikes in the 1920s, including a general rise in wages and a tighter job market. Further, none of these accounts consider the many impediments to union organizing or strike activity among female workers, who made up a large proportion of those subject to welfare work.

The reasons for continued conflict seem fairly clear. Despite improvements in workplace safety and comfort and an array of special educational, social, and financial programs, American businessmen had failed to address the real sources of conflict. They ignored welfare workers who advised that real partnership must include better wages, shorter hours, and stable employment. Further aggravating the situation, most were only half-hearted in their efforts to control autocratic foremen, and some continued to antagonize their workers with onerous labor policies, ranging from indiscriminate fining to repressive anti-unionism. In fact, employers had constructed a version of corporate fatherhood that perpetuated existing inequalities. Under these circumstances, working people were not inclined to consider themselves partners in a common enterprise.

Instead of developing a proprietary interest in the economic fortunes of their employers, working people seem to have developed a proprietary interest in welfare work itself. Although this had not been their intention, employers and welfare workers actually helped to foster this more limited focus. In the name of corporate partnership, employers openly declared their obligation to care for their employees in new ways. While working people cared little for many aspects of the welfare system, they happily allowed themselves to be "educated up" to those aspects that brought improvements in workplace safety and comforts. Gertrude Beeks acknowledged this development a decade after entering welfare work. "The American workman won't get down upon his knees to thank an employer for decent surroundings, but he appreciates them none the less. And he is now developed to the point where *he demands them*."[36]

Beeks had experienced this firsthand as early as 1903, when workers at International Harvester's newly merged Deering Plant demanded factory improvements, including clean drinking water, as part of a strike settlement. By the second decade of the century, the employer's responsibility for providing decent surroundings had become so institutionalized that architects included better lighting, ventilation, clean drinking water, locker and toilet rooms, lunchrooms, and emergency medical facilities as standard features in factory design.[37]

In some cases, working people expected welfare programs to provide more than improvements in workplace safety and comfort. In an effort to foster employee interest and a sense of proprietorship, welfare workers encouraged employees to ask for new benefits. They interpreted such requests as signs that employees were becoming "educated up" to both middle-class habits and to the corporate partnership. From the workmen who wanted an on-site savings bank because they could not go to town during business hours, to those who demanded a shelter to protect them while waiting for the streetcars, to those who looked to company sponsorship as a way to finance new baseball uniforms, workers demonstrated a willingness to take them up on the offer. Some even leveraged their employers' talk of a corporate partnership to demand reforms in shop-floor management and wages policies. Workmen at Bancroft and Sons, for example, regularly appealed to Elizabeth Briscoe to overturn foremen's decisions, while those at Endicott-Johnson traded on their employers' claims of compassion to demand higher wages.

By creating a new set of expectations on the part of workers, the welfare system did alter the relationship between labor and management. However, this was not the kind of transformation that welfare advocates had envisioned. Welfare work was internally flawed as a labor relations system. The model of the Victorian family on which it was based presumed that deference and loyalty were a fair and necessary exchange for economic security. Welfare workers could not persuade either workers or their employers to act on such an assumption. The familial roles prescribed to employers, welfare workers, and wage-earners proved impossible to duplicate within the modern corporation. To the extent that people tried, they often found themselves at odds with one another. Employers could not reconcile their obligations under the welfare system with a competitive ideology that valued lowest-cost production. Instead, they offered a kind of education and protection to which their employees were largely indifferent and, at times, hostile. Welfare workers pursued their maternal duties with a rigor and authority that their employers refused to honor. Wage-earners found the entire concept of the corporate family alien and asserted their independence at every opportunity. As it turned out, it was easier to build the institutional skeleton of the corporate family than it was to breathe life into it.

While the welfare system struggled unsuccessfully to recast the American corporation in the image of the Victorian family, broader social and economic developments began to challenge the Victorian ideal itself. By World War I, it had passed out of favor, replaced by ideas of family that had no relevance in the business world. Over the course of the next fifteen years, employers and a new group of labor relations experts began to experiment with alternative systems for managing labor relations—systems that retained the institutional forms of welfare work, but which invested them with meanings and purposes that reflected the altered social and economic environment.

Chapter Seven

From the Family Ideal to
the Personnel Manager

I n the afterglow of the National Civic Federation's first conference
on welfare work, Gertrude Beeks wrote enthusiastically about the
prospects for a new profession. Although welfare work was still in
its infancy in 1904, Beeks looked forward to a time when employers
would create a "real demand" for professionally trained welfare workers.
This would become, she felt certain, a new career opportunity for women
as well as men. Confidential talks were already underway, according to
Beeks, to introduce welfare work into the curriculum at Harvard University and at a Massachusetts school for domestic science.[1]

Progress in this direction over the next decade should have brought her
a considerable degree of satisfaction. The 1911 conference on welfare
work ended with a call for establishing a journal dealing with the "human
side of industry," one comparable to those already published on the mechanical side. Although Harvard had not incorporated welfare theory into
its curriculum, New York University had begun offering courses in welfare work in 1913 (sponsored by the NCF). The 1914 course, which graduated twenty-nine students, included over twenty lectures given by experts working in the field. The two dozen welfare workers identified by a
reporter in 1906 had mushroomed into the hundreds. National Civic Federation Welfare Department records in 1914 identified almost 200 women
and men with direct responsibility for welfare programs in American corporations. Welfare programs at hundreds, perhaps thousands, of other
firms went unrecorded; many managers added welfare work to their other
duties without changing job titles. Five hundred businessmen claimed
membership in the NCF Welfare Department: paying dues, subscribing to

the *National Civic Federation Review*, and presumably supporting welfare work in their own firms.[2]

Yet a decade later, in 1925, no journal devoted to corporate welfare work had emerged, the New York University course had ceased to exist, and the Welfare Department of the NCF had virtually disappeared (along with the NCF itself). Although scores of new organizations had appeared to advise employers on labor matters, not one advocated the corporate welfare system. Women, who had created and managed a majority of corporate welfare departments, had virtually disappeared from executive rosters. An executive in the field could identify only a handful of women holding such managerial positions in the early 1920s.[3] What had happened? Had businessmen decided that welfare work was too costly? Had worker resistance led employers to abandon their newfound interest in harmonizing the workplace? Had employers rejected welfare work in favor of a new panacea for solving the labor problem?

To answer these questions, we must carefully distinguish between the corporate welfare *system* and specific *features* of corporate welfare work. By the early 1920s, with only a few exceptions, even the most progressive employers had abandoned the effort to forge a harmonious workplace by educating their employees to the family ideal. However, very few had abandoned welfare work itself; workplace safety, locker rooms, lunchrooms, clubs, sports, and other recreations and financial benefits remained integral parts of corporate labor relations long after the corporate welfare system that spawned them had disappeared. Thus, the more pertinent questions are: Why did employers lose interest in transforming their companies into harmonious families? And why did they not discontinue welfare work at the same time?[4]

Arising in the formative years of modern industrial capitalism, the welfare system had looked backward, as well as forward, for its inspiration. Much of its appeal had grown out of its promise to recreate the familiar in the midst of unprecedented change—in particular, to recreate the family-like intimacy of the small shop. Yet at the very moment that employers embraced the welfare system as an innovative solution to the labor problem, the traditional family and business ideals on which it was grounded were rapidly disappearing. Welfare workers, whose efforts to systematize their work suggest that they were responding to these changes, were overwhelmed by voices calling for an entirely new approach. The federal government, employers, and philanthropic reformers offered personnel management and employee representation as alternative strategies to resolve the labor problem.[5] The welfare system's best advocate, the NCF Welfare Department, was ill prepared to meet these challenges to its agenda. With its ideological foundations crumbling and the NCF unable to defend it, the corporate welfare system gave way in an amazingly short period of time. However, the new advocates of personnel management and employee representation were not willing to dispense with welfare work itself. In fact, thriving welfare programs became essential to the success of these new labor relations systems.

EMPLOYER SUPPORT for the welfare system had been somewhat tentative all along. Businessmen often combined forceful rhetoric with limited action. This discrepancy between thought and deed was responsible, in part, for the frictions discussed previously between welfare workers, employers, and employees. Yet broader social and economic changes proved even more difficult to overcome than these ongoing conflicts. The disappearance of the Victorian family ideal, combined with the managerial revolution that occurred at the same time, undercut the foundations of the corporate welfare system.

The Victorian family model that informed the corporate welfare system gave way during the 1910s to the new ideal of the "companionate family."[6] In contrast to the Victorian family, this new family model was entirely incompatible with the modern business world. Rather than prescribing a hierarchical relationship with clear lines of authority, the companionate model called for a degree of equality and even autonomy among family members. Whereas the Victorian family promised economic security to its members, the companionate family promised emotional fulfillment. In place of the Victorian focus on duty and the sexual division of tasks, the companionate ideal emphasized the family's ability to satisfy individual needs and the shared sexuality of men and women. Children, who appeared as subordinate but central figures in the Victorian family, were minor characters in the vast literature on the new family, which focused on the romantic relationship between husbands and wives. The new companionate family clearly offered nothing to employers who had been inclined to legitimize their authority in familial terms.

Nor did it offer a maternal model for the welfare worker. In fact, the new interest in female sexuality that underlay the companionate ideal tended to obscure women's motherly role. Rather than a mother to her children, the married woman of the 1920s was more commonly defined as a wife to her husband. This new focus on romance and sexuality made it difficult to think of women, or men, as "corporate mothers." While female welfare workers shied away from claiming expertise based on their maternal instincts or moral superiority, their prominence in this new occupation clearly reflected these deeper cultural assumptions. Businessmen had been willing to delegate managerial authority to female welfare workers on the assumption that they possessed special qualifications for this work. The new woman of the 1920s, however, seemed to have something more than self-sacrificing service on her mind. Stories about office romances and the persona of the office wife gained popular currency during the 1920s. In this new business environment, it was no longer possible to conceive of welfare workers simply as "mothers" in the corporate family without also considering their relationships with the presumed corporate fathers.

This new female identity affected perceptions of women workers, as well. Late-nineteenth- and early-twentieth-century portrayals of vulnerable women in need of protection gave way, by the 1920s, to images of assertive, opportunistic workingwomen who were more than capable of taking care of themselves.[7] The modern working girl seemed to need less mothering than had her sister two decades earlier.

These perceptual changes, which made female workers seem less childlike, reflected real changes in the American labor force. The number of wage-earning women grew tremendously during the early decades of the century, from 3.5 million in 1890 to almost 8.5 million in 1920.[8] In certain occupations, women comprised a significant majority of the workforce. By the early 1920s, employers had amassed over three decades of experience with women workers. They were no longer a novelty at the workplace. The unusual situation that led the McCormicks to introduce welfare work in 1901, the hiring of their first female factory workers, could not occur again. They, like so many other employers, were now accustomed to female workers and had established labor policies that assumed large numbers of such workers.[9] In this regard, the success of the welfare system contributed to a sense that no (further) special considerations needed to be made.

At the same time, changes in the immigrant population also contributed to a sense that the labor force was more "mature." Instead of first generation immigrants with strange customs, foods and languages, employers now faced an older immigrant labor force that had accommodated to American society and included second- and even third-generation Americans. Again, welfare work accentuated the effects of these demographic changes. Like many other firms, the Edison Electric Company of Boston added an Americanization program to its other welfare work at the outset of World War I. Along with language classes, the company encouraged its immigrant workers to take out citizenship papers. This was followed by an intensive assistance program and company restrictions on hiring immigrants in the 1920s. Before the end of the decade, Edison Electric of Boston, which carried 700 alien immigrants on its payroll in 1916, employed only U.S. citizens or those holding first papers.[10] Thus, the nature of the 1920s labor force made it difficult for employers to maintain the fiction that their employees were like immature children.

Developments within corporate management made it unlikely that they would continue to try. Employers who instituted welfare work generally attributed their labor problems to the loss of personal contact with their workers. They often remembered a time when they worked or roamed the shop floor and knew many of their employees by name. They hoped welfare work would restore that lost intimacy, bringing with it higher productivity and greater loyalty. Despite welfare workers' efforts to bridge this gap, however, the managerial revolution created ever more distance between top executives and the average worker. By 1920, the line and staff structure adopted by many large firms had created institutional barriers not only between workers and top executives, but also between the welfare worker and the executive in whose name she presumably acted.[11] When Bancroft and Sons reorganized in 1911, for example, Elizabeth Briscoe began taking direction from the "Operating and Advisory Committee," which quickly spun off her responsibility for factory safety to a new department (headed by a trained engineer). While still supervising the welfare of Bancroft and Sons' employees, Briscoe's activities now represented the policy decisions of an administrative committee rather than the personal commitment of John Bancroft, an identifiable employer.

At the same time, the growing reliance on professional managers, many with backgrounds in finance and engineering, shifted decision-making power into the hands of executives who had no recollection of a past intimacy with their employees. The chairman of the board of General Electric in the 1920s, for example, was a former lawyer, Owen Young, who entered the firm in 1913 as an executive vice-president, and its president, Gerard Swope, had been trained as an engineer.[12] Even at the DuPont Company, where family members still managed the company, their executive positions depended much more on their professional training as engineers than on personal experience gained working in the plants.[13] While business executives continued to recall a time when employers and employees knew each other personally, such references became less nostalgic in tone as ownership and management became increasingly separate. Rather than a past to which business ought to return, such references identified a past that had been outgrown.

Employer enthusiasm for the welfare system waned with the growth of managerial capitalism and the companionate family ideal. Employers' growing support of welfare activities managed by community-wide organizations was an early indication of their shifting mood. Rather than providing all benefits in-house, they began in the 1910s to support the work of others—sponsoring industrial athletic leagues rather than company teams, buying group life and health insurance plans rather than assuming the risks alone, working with government commissions to develop industry-wide safety standards rather than devising programs entirely on their own.[14]

Without its cultural foundations, the welfare system simply made less sense. Employers' declining interest may also be attributed to the continual frictions between them and their welfare managers as well as to their employees' refusal to yoke themselves to the familial harness. Welfare advocates proved unable to address, much less to overcome, these challenges. Three factors account for this. First, welfare managers never acquired the professional status that, in this age of experts, might have provided them with the authority to raise their voices in corporate counsels. Second, in her pivotal role as Secretary of the NCF Welfare Department, Gertrude Beeks proved more adept at controlling the corporate welfare movement than she did at fostering its development. Finally, welfare advocates were sympathetic to the ideas of personnel management, which replaced the earlier system by the early 1920s.

There had been some early indications that welfare workers might forge a professional identity. The NCF's 1904 conference on welfare work should be understood as a first, rudimentary step in that direction; conferees began to delineate the special activities that characterized welfare work and to grope for some sense of the training that would best prepare one for that work.

Despite this promising beginning, employer control precluded the professionalization of welfare work.[15] Professionalization within business, noted one expert at the time, was fraught with inherent contradictions. The professional ideal required one to elevate service to others over personal gain, whereas business existed to maximize profits.[16] In the interest of maximizing profits, businessmen retained tight control over their labor policies. As we have seen, the welfare program at each company was a joint effort on the part of the employer and his welfare workers, with welfare workers clearly serving as subordinate partners. While most employers expected their welfare workers to present new programs for their approval, they were not averse to doing so themselves. Their control of financial benefit programs, budgets, and facilities restricted the welfare workers' freedom to act as independent experts.

Employer control of the movement was reinforced by the fact that welfare workers had few contacts outside the business community. Philanthropic reformers, who might have been their natural allies, generally held them at arms length. They were skeptical of welfare workers' conciliatory attitude toward business. Children's advocates responded to a NCF study of child labor in 1906 with "great resentment." Mary Van Kleeck and other prominent reformers denounced a later study of department stores as a "whitewash."[17]

Welfare workers, on the other hand, may have been equally suspicious of philanthropic reformers. Beyond a few who joined women's clubs and nursing associations, there is no evidence that welfare workers participated in the powerful networks that linked those reformers to one another. To do so would have placed them in a dangerous position. Welfare workers had no reason to antagonize employers and jeopardize their new positions by associating with reformers who might sympathize with unions or promote government regulation. Gertrude Beeks, who maintained the closest contacts with such reformers, carefully distinguished between what she called the "right kind of settlement work," and that which showed insufficient appreciation for the employers' point of view.[18] Although they may have conversed with public sector reformers, welfare workers, like Beeks, did not affiliate with them. Thus, this avenue of support, independent of employer control, was closed to them.[19]

Instead, they depended on an informal network among themselves, or on the few organizations that included welfare work as part of their broader agendas. The creation of the NCF Welfare Department in 1903 brought that number up to three: the NCF, the YMCA, and the American Institute of Social Service (AISS). (The AISS was a wing of the Social Gospel movement led by Josiah Strong and William Tolman.) In addition, a number of trade associations and chambers of commerce began to promote welfare work. Although strong advocates of corporate welfare work, none of these organizations actually represented welfare workers in the way that organizations of doctors, social workers, or engineers represented those professionals. Virtually all of them, like the NCF, depended on businessmen for their funding, a situation not likely to foster much autonomy on the part of welfare workers. Rather than focusing on the professional needs of welfare workers, these organizations focused on employers, trying to persuade them to embrace this new labor relations strategy.

The only significant attempt made to form an association of professional welfare workers was co-opted by Gertrude Beeks and brought under the umbrella of the employer-controlled NCF. The resulting conference of welfare workers, held in 1904, highlights the contradictory role played by Beeks and the NCF Welfare Department. Beeks hoped that the conference would elevate welfare work to a more professional status, bringing prestige to this new occupation and increasing the demand for skilled welfare workers. At the same time, she designed the conference to place her organization at the center of this growing movement. Beeks purposefully pushed the NCF's two rivals, the YMCA and the AISS, aside in the process.

"The idea of having the YMCA represented at the conference," Beeks wrote shortly afterward, "was to prevent any feeling of antagonism rather than for the purpose of co-operating with the organization."[20] Events at the conference clearly reflected this intention. In a nasty confrontation, which ended only with a hastily called adjournment, Beeks and others charged that the YMCA was involved in evangelical work, not industrial betterment. YMCA men did not "understand the [work]men or their needs" charged one employer.[21] A few months later, Beeks took issue with a proposed article on welfare managers because it implied that the YMCA had developed welfare management. It is "a term coined by our organization," she asserted. No welfare manager could acquire proper professional training through the YMCA.[22]

Beeks's opposition to the YMCA reflected more than her personal belief that welfare work must not be a front for Protestant evangelicism. It also reflected demands made by the employer members of the NCF who wanted to retain tight control over the welfare work movement. When employers discussed the subject at a preconference meeting, they unanimously agreed that the YMCA should not take charge of welfare work at any institution and that the NCF should not join forces with any other organization.[23]

This decision led the NCF to challenge the AISS as well. The AISS had been the leading advocate of welfare work prior to the formation of the NCF Welfare Department. Nevertheless, the AISS proved amenable to the NCF design. Although its *Social Service* magazine devoted a special issue to welfare work just a few months after the NCF conference, it showed little interest in contesting Beeks's aggressive movement into the field.[24] In contrast to the YMCA's demand to be on the agenda, no AISS representative was even listed as having attended the 1904 conference. Contributors to its special issue on welfare work, such as Diana Hirschler of Filene's Department Store, already had strong affiliations with Beeks and the NCF Welfare Department. As the NCF claimed leadership of the welfare movement, the AISS shifted its focus to other fields.[25]

Beeks proved to be an adept spokeswoman for the corporate welfare movement. Rather than the sedentary clearinghouse of information that it might have been, Beeks's Welfare Department aggressively pursued employers and welfare workers, surveying thousands of companies on their labor policies. She wrote to and visited those who showed the slightest interest in welfare work, recommended new features to those already engaged in the work, sent trained consultants around the country, and helped employers find suitable welfare workers. Beeks amassed a vast reservoir of information, replete with slides, exhibits, and blueprints, that she used to educate employers and welfare workers. Through her copious correspondence and frequent meetings, Beeks quickly placed herself at the center of a loose network of welfare workers who looked to her for ideas, moral support, and contacts with others in the field.

It is difficult to assess the impact of all this activity. However, it is clear that many employers recognized Beeks as the expert she claimed to be. They and their welfare workers wrote to her frequently, keeping her apprised of their new initiatives, asking for advice, and acting on her suggestions.[26] Beeks, for her part, made it as easy as possible for businessmen to accept her point of view. She paraded concrete examples of successful welfare work before them, gave them design specifications, and offered "proof" that welfare programs were a sound business investment. "There is no use," she said, "antagonizing an employer who will want to do better, once he is made to understand."[27]

Yet Beeks's aggressive promotion of corporate welfare work proved debilitating to the movement in the long run. Eminently tactful in the presence of those she hoped to persuade, Beeks was intolerant of those who challenged her particular formulation of welfare work or her leadership of the movement. "Don't *give* your employees their lunch, as this firm does," she told a visiting Ohio manufacturer as they toured the Metropolitan Life Insurance Company. "I'm glad the eye clinic is to offer lenses ground at cost, not free." One can well imagine the reaction of the insurance company executive who accompanied them as he endured this public scolding.[28]

As this incident suggests, Beeks's devotion to spreading the gospel of welfare work shared the stage with her desire to control the movement. Although she made her comment before the Metropolitan Life executive and her moves against the YMCA openly, Beeks also engaged in back-room manipulations to maintain her dominance. In 1904, she recommended an associate, N. V. Moore, for welfare work at the National Cash Register Company. National Cash Register officials fired Moore within a matter of days, suspecting her of being a spy for Beeks and the NCF. They were not far off the mark. Moore's long report to Beeks leaves little doubt that Beeks and Patterson saw each other as rivals for leadership of the movement. Beeks's strategy in recommending Moore had been to "influence the policy" at the National Cash Register Company. Since this had failed, Moore suggested that the NCF "persistently point to other genuine work, [so] that the N.C.R. shall be lost sight of."[29]

Beeks proved equally vigilant when the success of the welfare movement sparked interest in organizing special courses of study outside her control or in organizing independent associations of welfare workers. It was probably no coincidence that her formerly cordial relations with S. M. Darling, her replacement at International Harvester, soured around the same time that he tried to organize monthly meetings of Chicago welfare workers. In addition to seeking out fellow welfare workers, Darling was advocating new welfare features of which Beeks disapproved. These features, such as cooperative stores, might have received more approval from residents of the radical Chicago settlements, who Darling also invited to his meetings.[30]

Beeks's contacts also kept her informed when Graham Taylor of Chicago Commons set up a ten-week course in welfare work the following year. Beeks seemed to show no interest in his efforts. Although she later recommended one of Taylor's students for a welfare position, she made no mention of the course when listing the woman's qualifications.[31] Beeks proved similarly uninterested when the Human Welfare League contacted her a few years later seeking information that could be used in another course on welfare work. In this case, she ignored the first request and then instructed her secretary to reply to the second by stating that she felt that her initial reply was sufficient![32] Her action in these cases is particularly noteworthy since Beeks was herself desperately seeking to establish a training program that would raise the standards of welfare work.[33]

Efforts to create independent organizations of welfare workers met a similar response. The welfare secretary at Pilgrim Laundry in Brooklyn, a Miss Klink, attempted to organize a national Welfare Workers Club in 1910. After an employer member of the NCF Welfare Department warned Beeks that the woman might "try to make herself prominent" at the upcoming conference on welfare work, Beeks turned a decidedly cold shoulder to her. She closed Klink off from the conference discussions, agreeing with her informant that the renegade should not be allowed to "capture" the conference.[34] A few years later, another welfare secretary tried to enlist Beeks's aid in establishing a club for welfare workers in New York City. Despite the fact that he recognized her leadership of the movement (by asking her to be honorary president of the new club), Beeks showed no enthusiasm for his proposal.[35]

By the second decade of the century, Beeks had helped to build corporate welfare work into a significant national movement that attracted the interest not only of employers but also of various educators and career-minded reformers. Yet aside from the employer-controlled NCF, no independent organization claimed leadership of this movement. "There is but one legitimate welfare organization . . . in the United States," Beeks replied to an association that had the effrontery to suggest that it might serve as a clearinghouse of information on welfare work.[36] Ironically, at the very time that Beeks exercised her greatest power to direct the movement, she and the NCF began to turn their attention in a different direction—to the denunciation of socialists.

Antisocialism was not a new mission for the National Civic Federation. The NCF and its Welfare Department had been dedicated antisocialists all along. "Welfare work," Beeks argued, "is an antidote to Socialism."[37] Her Welfare Department combatted socialism by demonstrating that the average employer was interested in the welfare of his employees. Working people who understood this would be less likely to become socialists. Beeks's work on behalf of the corporate welfare system comprised one element of the NCF's broader strategy to fight socialism.[38] Other elements of this strategy included mediation of labor disputes and support of government legislation.

World War I, however, changed the way in which the NCF and its Welfare Department countered the socialist threat. Instead of deflecting workers from the socialist appeal through mediation or through advocacy of welfare work and legislation, the NCF increasingly devoted itself to direct attacks on socialists and socialist sympathizers. The *National Civic Federation Review*, which reflected the activities of the various NCF departments, carried only two articles relating to welfare work between December 1918 and its final issue in November 1920. Much more typical of the postwar *National Civic Federation Review* were a denunciation of old-age pensions as "socialistic" and a five-page diatribe against the New School for Social Research.[39]

By the early 1920s, the NCF's new look brought it the endorsement of the National Association of Manufacturers, which the NCF had earlier criticized as a roadblock to industrial peace. It joined forces with those responsible for the eventual publication of the Spider Web Chart.[40] Beeks and her Welfare Department slipped into the shadows. Her active correspondence with employers, welfare workers, and others tapered off considerably during the war and virtually disappeared in the postwar years. Meanwhile, Beeks's vocal opposition to women's suffrage helped to sever her already tenuous links with the prewar reform community. In the 1920s, she decried the League of Women Voters, whose radical program, she believed, constituted "a dire calamity" for the American political system.[41] For a short time, the NCF Welfare Department became the simple clearinghouse of information that it might have been without Beeks's aggressive leadership. Then it disappeared altogether.[42]

The corporate welfare system did not survive the loss of its most vocal advocate. Yet it did not entirely disappear. Instead, rival strategies, which had their origins in the early part of the century, incorporated many elements of the welfare system into their own approaches. Proponents of these alternative systems demanded that labor relations be centralized and systematized, that foremen relinquish much of their power, and that employers provide fair wages and good working conditions. Two aspects of the welfare system, in particular, survived this transition: calls for management reform and welfare work itself.

The most popular of these new strategies, personnel management, began to take shape as early as 1903. At that time, the National Cash Register Company centralized hiring, transfers, and discharges within the nation's first corporate Labor Department. Virtually no one followed the National Cash Register Company's lead. Then, around 1910, reformers from the vocational guidance, industrial education, and systematic management movements began sharing their joint concerns about the costs of labor turnover and other problems associated with monotonous and unrewarding jobs. The responsibility for solving these problems, they all agreed, lay with management. Meeting under the roof of the Taylor Society, these reformers began expounding the benefits (both in terms of productivity and labor peace) that would result from stabilizing production, from systematically hiring, training, and promoting employees, and from offering nonwage incentives.[43]

A number of employer members of the Taylor Society heeded the call for management reform and began acting on these ideas at their own firms; Richard Feiss at Joseph Feiss and Company, Dexter Kimball at the Plimpton Press, and Henry Dennison at the Dennison Manufacturing Company led the way. To varying degrees, they created personnel departments, adopted new employment procedures, conducted audits of their labor needs, and developed job classification and wage schedules. In many respects, these reforms were entirely consistent with the trend toward centralizing and systematizing labor relations that they had introduced with welfare programs in earlier years. None of these employers discontinued, or even restricted, his welfare programs. These new employment techniques, however, constituted the backbone of a new approach to the labor problem—personnel management.[44]

Although it may not have been immediately apparent, personnel management signified an important shift in perspective. Rather than reforming workers, as the welfare system attempted to do, personnel management promised to help the employer find workers who already possessed the requisite values and skills. One text advised its readers that the employment department was analogous to the purchasing department. "Indeed, the actual routine of the two departments has much in common: the requisition, the securing of the materials according to specification and the change when the material secured does not live up to specification."[45]

Personnel management promised to make the employer a wise consumer of labor. This new "art of handling men" entailed matching the right worker to the right job. Men and women who were well suited to their work would be more content and productive employees. Personnel management would accomplish this by centralizing employment procedures, systematically screening applicants (employment forms, skills, and psychological tests, medical exams), maintaining training, transfer, and promotion programs, and keeping extensive records.

Yet this was only half of the new labor relations equation. While the new system promised to transform the employer into a discriminating consumer of labor, it also presumed that the worker was a discriminating seller of that labor. If employers wanted to attract and hold the best labor, they would need to prove themselves worthy as well. Whereas welfare advocates spoke of nurturing and educating workers, advocates of personnel management used the language of the new consumer culture. "Management should deal with its employees in the same manner it deals with people in selling a product," wrote Cyrus Ching, an early pioneer of the new approach. "In labor relations it is so necessary to keep the employees sold."[46] The motivation behind the current interest in personnel management, explained another author, was to keep the employee satisfied: "It pays to serve the customer well; he comes back. It pays to serve the employee well; he stays."[47]

Welfare work was to be the employers' stock in trade. Accordingly, one text advised that "selling the personnel department to the prospective employees really amounts to selling the benefits of the entire organization . . . training, bonuses, working conditions, restaurants, athletic teams, dancing, housing and the like are all selling points."[48] Despite their rejection of the welfare *system*, advocates of personnel management incorporated welfare *work* into their new strategy for solving the labor problem.[49] Thus, students in the University of Rochester's courses for employment managers spent two of their first three days learning about suggestion systems, athletic and social activities, and plant safety.[50] When Robert Clothier, employment manager at Curtis Publishing Company and later a labor relations consultant, divided the field of personnel management into four divisions, two of the four covered traditional welfare work. Like Clothier, educators and practitioners who wrote on the subject always included welfare work among the four or five main divisions of personnel management.[51]

Employers' apparent repudiation of the welfare system, then, did not mean that they dismantled their welfare programs.[52] A 1926 Bureau of Labor Statistics study found that very few companies had discontinued the welfare activities instituted in earlier years. Only sixteen firms out of the 430 surveyed, for example, reported that they stopped luncheon services. More typically, welfare work expanded in the postwar years. A comparison of the 1916 and 1926 Bureau of Labor Statistics surveys, both of which covered the same number of large and middle-sized firms, reveals a growth in welfare activities. This was particularly noteworthy in the areas of medical services (where the proportion of firms with doctors on staff increased from 45 percent to 83 percent), lunchrooms (provided at 50 percent of firms in 1916 and at 70 percent of firms ten years later), group insurance (a new product offered by less than 10 percent of companies in 1916 was offered by over 40 percent of respondents in 1926), and paid vacations for wage laborers (up from 4 percent to 30 percent of reporting companies). Over 70 percent of firms surveyed in 1926 continued to sponsor social and recreational activities for their employees; concerts, dances, clubhouses, and athletics remained especially popular.[53]

A number of other sources confirm the Bureau of Labor Statistics' findings. A National Industrial Conference Board (NICB) study at the end of the decade found that less than 20 percent of those surveyed had dropped any of their industrial relations activities over the previous five years. Similar to the results of the bureau's study, the NICB reported that the greatest growth occurred in the areas of medical care, lunchrooms, clubhouses, recreational activities, and group insurance. Other studies indicated that expenditures for welfare activities remained constant between 1918 and 1929, at 1.5 percent to 2 percent of payroll.[54] This is the same level at which companies funded welfare work during the first decade of the century. Evaluating postwar developments in American department stores, Susan Porter Benson concluded that welfare work "virtually always continued and often expanded in the succeeding decades. If the managers spoke less frequently about welfare work as such, it was not because they had abandoned it as a tactic but because it had become axiomatic, an accepted feature of department store life."[55]

Businessmen who included employee representation plans in their labor relations programs found welfare work doubly attractive. Although significantly less popular than personnel management, employee representation similarly absorbed welfare work into its very different approach to the labor problem.[56] Ideally, employee representation turned each company into a small democracy. Employer and employee representatives met to debate and then jointly resolve disputes, adjust wages and hours, and monitor working conditions. Unlike a political democracy, however, corporate executives retained an absolute veto power over decisions made in these "democratic" forums. In addition, most plans carefully circumscribed the topics open to democratic decision-making. Based on a study of common practices, the National Industrial Conference Board advised its members that works councils should not be allowed to interfere with management prerogatives; those prerogatives included hiring, transfer, promotion, discharge, selection of foremen, production methods, and industrial processes.[57] Employee representatives might discuss these issues, but they had no authority to make policy.

Yet democracies can function only if the minority (employees in this case) is convinced that it has some power to shape affairs. Having removed so much from the table under the heading of management prerogatives, employers felt compelled to recognize employee prerogatives in some other arena. Welfare work was just such an arena. Early employee representation plans set the pattern. Filene's Department Store introduced the first plan in 1898 with the express purpose of making its new Filene's Cooperative Association responsible for the firm's medical, savings, and insurance plans.[58] Following the Ludlow Massacre, John D. Rockefeller Jr. sponsored the most publicized plan in the prewar years at his Colorado Fuel and Iron Company. In addition to its provisions for addressing workplace grievances, the plan encouraged employees to take up questions of safety, sanitation, health, housing, recreation, and education.

Although welfare work was not the primary concern of employee representation plans, it was an area in which management was more likely to acquiesce to employee demands. For this reason, welfare work assumed an importance in employee representation programs that might not have been expected. Whereas the employee representation plan at the Colorado Fuel and Iron Company had virtually no impact on wages and hours policies, even the highly critical Russell Sage Foundation acknowledged that it had brought significant improvements to working and housing conditions.[59] Employee representatives at other firms similarly achieved their greatest successes in overseeing welfare activities; they successfully lobbied for more shower baths and toilet facilities at International Harvester, a new outdoor eating area and automobile shelter at the Dennison Manufacturing Company, a ban on collections for weddings and funerals at Joseph Feiss and Company.[60]

With the encouragement of management representatives, committees devoted a significant portion of their energies to welfare matters. The Standard Oil Company of New Jersey reported that almost 25 percent of the issues discussed during the first fifteen months of its new plan were welfare-related. The Dan River Cotton Mills established committees for recreation and amusements, as well as for factory safety and suggestions. In a typical arrangement, the International Harvester plan created four subcommittees devoted solely to welfare matters; a fifth took up grievance and wage issues.

By the early 1920s, thousands of companies had placed personnel departments or employee representation at the center of their labor programs.[61] In 1920, one-fifth of manufacturing firms with 250 or more employees had a personnel department. By the end of the decade, over one-third of these manufacturers had established personnel departments. The numbers were in fact much higher since large employers in the communications, retail, insurance, and other nonmanufacturing sectors also embraced the new personnel strategies. Not surprisingly, the larger the company, the more likely it was to have a personnel department. According to one estimate, personnel departments existed at over 50 percent of firms employing 5,000 or more workers.[62] Although some personnel departments supported less elaborate programs than others, the creation of such a department did signify a commitment to the principles of personnel management.

Employee representation plans, although never as widespread as personnel departments, also grew dramatically in the 1920s, from less than 150 at the end of World War I to more than 800 by 1924.[63] The medium-sized and large employers who had turned to welfare work in earlier decades were also the most likely to adopt these new methods.

The rapid expansion of these new labor relations strategies was due, in part, to the demise of the corporate welfare system. The welfare system, after all, seemed archaic in the modern world of managerial capitalism. No one remained to defend its presumption that employers ought to educate their employees up to some middle-class ideal.[64] Yet it was not a foregone conclusion that personnel management or employee representation would necessarily replace the welfare system. A few employers had introduced personnel strategies in the early part of the century, but they had generated little enthusiasm.

Government intervention during the first World War, the growth of university business schools, and new employer initiatives changed the tide. The success with which these groups promoted the new methods meant that welfare work would continue, although with a different purpose. It also meant that corporate labor relations would become a male preserve. Women, who had largely pioneered the field, were decisively excluded.

The federal government played a crucial role in this development. The war, which required complete mobilization of the country's economic resources, elevated labor relations to a national priority. The Army, the Labor Department, and various government boards hired hundreds of new staff to stave off industrial conflicts that might hinder war production. A significant minority of these people hailed from the Taylor Society. This opened the door for these advocates of personnel management, who had largely been shut out of corporate labor relations, to gain the government's stamp of approval for their agenda. Rather than speaking to each other or preaching to recalcitrant businessmen, they suddenly had the power to transform their ideas into national policy.

An important element of that national policy was the decision to require all war contractors to employ personnel managers. Originating in the Ordnance Department of the U.S. Army, this policy was designed to ensure that war contractors abided by department standards, which required fair wages and decent working conditions.[65] Taylor Society members working for the Ordnance Department decided that it was necessary to train a corps of personnel managers to implement these new standards. The War Industries Board assumed formal responsibility for establishing a training program, and a number of Ordnance Department staff members were transferred to the War Industries Board for this purpose. Among them was Boyd Fisher, who had organized a fledgling Employment Managers' Association in 1916. Fisher hoped to raise personnel management to professional status.[66]

Fisher and his associates opened the first government-sponsored training program for personnel managers at the University of Rochester in the spring of 1918. The course, which lasted six weeks, included lectures on "the formation of a personnel department, the hiring and assignment of workers, transfer and promotion, wage payment methods, shop discipline, turnover and welfare work." Businessmen and employment managers from local companies gave some of the lectures. Students were given long reading assignments, and they engaged in numerous group discussions. In addition, they spent four nine-hour days in local factories observing personnel work firsthand. The course was so intensive, according to its director, that some of the men lost weight during the first two weeks.[67]

Following the success of this first class, the War Industries Board sponsored courses at a dozen universities. By the time of the armistice, over 360 graduates of these courses were working as employment managers around the country, approximately three-fourths of them in private industry.[68] Within a span of six months, the government had spearheaded the creation of a new type of labor relations expert.

Government promotion of personnel management, moreover, went far beyond training these hundreds of men and urging their employment in war-related production. Those who organized the Rochester school clearly understood that this was a golden opportunity to establish personnel management as an independent profession. Under Boyd Fisher's leadership, they purposefully affiliated the government training program with a nascent movement to create a national association of employment managers. A small number of regional associations had met twice in the previous two years. Both times there had been talk of creating a national organization. At Fisher's urging, they rescheduled their 1918 meeting, originally planned for Cleveland, to coincide with the graduation ceremonies of the first government class in personnel management.

The resulting Employment Managers' Conference, held in Rochester, New York in May 1918, lasted for three days. The conference opened with the commencement exercises for the twenty-four students graduating from the government course. On the final day, conferees chartered a new organization, the National Association of Employment Managers. Throughout the three-day event, a parade of speakers extolled both the economic value of personnel management and the professional qualities of this new occupation. Over a third of the speakers were government representatives, virtually all of them hired for war-related service. The 600 delegates attending the convention (business executives, middle managers, and government officials) could hardly have missed the message. The conference was a celebration, Boyd Fisher told the delegates, "of governmental recognition of the professional status of the employment manager."[69]

Government support of professional personnel management continued after the war ended. Following the armistice, Fisher was placed in charge of a new Federal Board for Vocational Education, which continued to train employment managers for another fourteen months. By the time that postwar demobilization led to the closure of the Federal Board for Vocational Education, the government had trained an additional 600 personnel managers.[70]

Those who organized the wartime training programs used their government positions not only to promote the development of this new profession, but also to control access to it. Organizers of the first Rochester training course set the standard in this regard. They required that all students be sponsored by an employer and that they have practical shop-floor experience. Neither corporate welfare work nor activities with working people off the shop floor (such as settlement work) satisfied their strict criteria. "I don't expect that many women will have as much experience as men," Fisher told delegates at the 1918 Employment Managers' Conference in Rochester. He lamented that several "promising women" had not been able to enter the course because they "had a different kind of industrial training."[71] The men who did take the course averaged thirty-five years of age; two-thirds of them were married. "These are not boys; they are men," Boyd Fisher announced at the graduation ceremonies. "All are practical experienced men."[72]

More than a desire for experienced students lay behind the exclusion of women. Government courses to train personnel managers were already experimental, Fisher argued. It would be too radical a departure to admit women. Further, he did not want to "lower the standards of the course." Fisher and his male associates felt certain that admitting women to this new profession would dilute the prestige and the authority of personnel managers.

The women involved in planning these courses did not take this decision lightly. Mary Gilson, a nationally respected personnel manager at Joseph Feiss and Company in Cleveland before joining the Ordnance Department, repeatedly protested Fisher's decision. Like Mary Van Kleeck and other female reformers engaged in war work, Gilson was an ardent feminist who pursued expanded opportunities for women alongside economic reform. Van Kleeck and Gilson challenged the contention that there were no women qualified to take the government courses. When they could not persuade their male colleagues to admit women to the Rochester course, they worked out a compromise that seemed to promise hope for the future.

Gilson was to plan a special three-month course to provide women with the requisite shop-floor experience, including training on various kinds of factory machinery. Upon completing this preliminary training, the women would enter the six-week courses formerly restricted to men. Gilson insisted that those courses be opened up to women and men alike. By her own account, she received thousands of letters from women interested in enrolling. After weeks of planning, the special training course for women opened in Cleveland in the fall of 1918. Before the women could complete the three-month course, however, the war ended.[73]

As a result, the federal government had not simply supported the development of personnel management, but had fostered it as a profession for men only. If the graduates of Rochester, Harvard, and the other government training courses were a model, personnel managers would be middle-aged men with business training and prior managerial experience.[74]

This development was particularly significant since the fledgling movement had not been exclusively male in the prewar years. In addition to Gilson, some of the most respected personnel managers in the country had been women (including Jane Williams of Plimpton Press and Dr. Millicent Pond of Scoville Manufacturing Company). Although they comprised a small minority, twenty-six of the delegates to the 1918 Employment Managers' Conference in Rochester were women with personnel or welfare responsibilities.[75] Equally striking, Mary Gilson served as associate director of the Rochester school for personnel management. This was not simply an honorary title. Throughout the last six months of the war, Gilson traveled back and forth between Rochester, where she lectured three mornings each week, and Pennsylvania and Ohio, where she supervised munitions plants for the Women's Division of the Ordnance Department.[76] Gilson accepted this arduous schedule because she wanted a hand in shaping this new movement. At the same time, the school needed her; Gilson possessed both expertise and prestige.

The exclusion of women continued as the personnel management movement grew in the immediate postwar years. When Daniel Bloomfield compiled a series of articles on employment management in 1919, he included only one article authored by a woman. Written by an Englishwoman in 1916, the paper focused on women in welfare work, not in personnel management. It argued that labor relations careers for women would be limited in the future to conducting academic research or managing their own companies.[77]

Women who read Bloomfield's primer, or another of the dozen texts published on personnel management between 1916 and 1923, could hardly have missed the assumption that this was a man's job.[78] If personnel managers were to reform current business practices, they must be able to meet fellow executives "on a level." Centralizing labor relations had been most successful, advised one text, when "recognized as of comparable importance with problems of production, finance or sales, and so placed in the hands of a mature executive of vice-president calibre."[79] The personnel manager must also be able to "handle men." This, too, demanded a man of executive stature. "The proposition must be firmly grasped," wrote another personnel advocate, "that handling employees is a serious business. . . . Only big men can handle matters like these."[80]

Nor did the message differ at the various conferences held to unify this new movement. Listing the responsibilities of the personnel manager, one speaker told the 1920 conference of employment managers that "they are the duties of a full-grown man, not to be bestowed upon a weakling or a clerk."[81] Such verbal statements were reinforced by the general absence of women from both the speaker's platform and the topics discussed.

A heated exchange between Mary Gilson and Mark Jones, executive secretary of the Industrial Relations Association of America (IRAA), reveals that this was not an unintended oversight. (In 1920 the National Employment Managers' Association was renamed the Industrial Relations Association of America.) While planning the 1920 convention, the IRAA's Board of Directors decided that "it was only fair to allow the women a session by themselves, wherein they could discuss the things that were of most importance to themselves in industry." Subsequently, Mark Jones invited Mary Gilson to chair a special section on the problems of women in industry. Gilson minced no words in declining the offer: "For years I have strongly maintained the position that what affects men in industry also affects women and that there is entirely too much segregating of the problems concerning women. . . . Why don't you accept women as a perfectly natural and normal part of the industrial situation [and eliminate special sessions for women]."

Gilson's pointed criticism drew a caustic response from Jones, who replied that since Gilson was not interested in a special session devoted to women, the board would "promptly forget about special provisions for ladies, with the result that no woman would appear on the agenda at all."[82] Gilson refused to back down. She finally persuaded the IRAA to place a woman on the agenda. However, they pointedly selected a woman who was not a personnel manager, Mary Van Kleeck. Her assigned topic, "The Future of Women in Industry," signified the IRAA's refusal to integrate women into their vision of personnel management; they would address women only as a special case, discussed in isolation from other aspects of the labor problem.[83]

Although employers did not accept personnel managers as independent professionals, they did favor men over women for these positions.[84] Men seemed to better match the profile of the business manager, especially as the personnel movement redefined labor relations as a masculine occupation.[85] Men also had greater access to the labor relations courses offered by university schools of business. Many of these departments refused to admit women in the early 1920s. Employers who increasingly turned to the colleges to recruit new management personnel in the 1920s were drawing from a pool that was overwhelmingly male. In addition to a college education, men were more likely to have the shop-floor experience that would qualify them in the new art of handling men. Many personnel managers, for example, had prior experience as production supervisors, safety engineers, or even as welfare managers.[86]

At the same time that men seemed increasingly qualified to direct corporate labor relations, women's opportunities in the business world were becoming more limited. An expanding economy and the introduction of systematic management at the turn of the century created an enormous demand for new workers. Women entered the workforce by the millions, gaining entry to positions that had previously been closed to them and becoming the mainstay of entirely new occupations. In certain areas, like welfare management, they tested the limits of the expanding economy.

By the early 1920s, however, women's place in the business world was much less fluid. Women would handle the flow of information that was the lifeblood of the new managerial bureaucracies, but they would not rise into those bureaucracies. The woman in business was largely confined to sales or clerical positions.[87] According to popular images, her sojourn into the workforce was only temporary; the business office was primarily a place for her to meet her future husband. On a practical level, the segmentation of women into these dead-end jobs meant that employers no longer considered them for more advanced positions. One contemporary study concluded that women professionals faced a serious problem because employers thought of women as a "sort of innately secretarial sex."[88] Another study of the professional opportunities open to women in the 1920s observed that "there is, associated with practically every field, a sub-zone of activity, one usually down below the level where the business or profession as such begins, and in which the work is entirely performed by women."[89]

The few women who remained in corporate labor relations in the 1920s found themselves in just such a subzone. The experience of one woman, Anne Armstrong, suggests the difficulties women faced when they attempted to move out of these secondary positions. Armstrong first entered labor relations around 1915 when a Wall Street investment house turned down her application to sell bonds and instead offered her a position in its newly created employment department. Despite being refused admission to a course on employment management, Armstrong quickly gained expertise in the new employment methods. Her skills gained the favor of company executives. Although she served as employment director of the women's division, they gave her wide latitude to shape the firm's general employment program. Within a few years, executives fired the man who directed the employment department and doubled Armstrong's salary. They refused, however, to honor her request to become director of the department with responsibility for both male and female employees. It would be unseemly, they told her, to allow a woman to occupy such an important position.

Armstrong resigned and accepted an offer from the Mohawk Instrument Company, an upstate New York manufacturer. The similarities between her new position and the first are striking. Although her new employer had sought her out, and apparently valued her expertise, she rose no higher than director of employment for women. When the male director of industrial relations was let go, Armstrong was passed over once again. She began looking for a new position, eventually finding one as an assistant in the industrial relations department at the Eastman Kodak Company.[90] By the mid-1920s, Armstrong was an outspoken feminist, calling on women to take their business to female professionals and arguing that businessmen exercised a destructive kind of leadership.

Armstrong's inability to rise to the top rank in her profession reflected the ambiguous legacy of the corporate welfare system. Although women had pioneered the field and had called for the kind of systematization and centralization that was the hallmark of personnel management, their greatest experience lay in welfare work. As welfare work became a subdivision of personnel management, welfare workers became subordinate staff within those departments. In some respects, this meant very little change in the kinds of tasks assigned to women. They continued to serve as corporate librarians, visiting nurses, matrons, educational and recreational directors, and personal counselors. These tasks, however, took on a different meaning within the new system of personnel management. The women who filled them were part of a support network; they were no longer at the center of corporate labor relations.

That center now lay in the employment procedures designed to match the right worker to the right job. Women were assigned distinctly secondary roles in this new endeavor. Consistent with the IRAA's assumption that women comprised a special subgroup of workers, personnel departments commonly included separate women's divisions. Women interested in personnel work then found themselves consigned to those women's divisions. In contrast to the early decades of the century when women directed the majority of welfare departments, they rarely became directors of the new personnel departments. A 1920 survey of 250 factories in New York City, for example, located only two women serving in this capacity, but identified over fifty women working as assistant employment managers or as employment managers for women workers. An additional 195 women worked as nurses, instructors, lunchroom managers, and matrons. Those assistant employment managers earned salaries on a par with college-educated secretaries.[91]

Conclusion

The familial assumptions of the welfare system opened the door for women to enter management at an unprecedented level. Once there, they proved to be adept businesswomen— advocates of the new principles of efficiency and system, good managers, tactful, and ambitious. In concert with male welfare workers, they established labor relations as both a new business responsibility and as a new occupation. On a more personal level, welfare workers hoped to establish themselves as professional labor relations experts. They were not able to do this.

Like other women at the turn of the century, welfare workers faced immense obstacles in their struggle to achieve professional status. Their efforts to solve the labor problem, and particularly to do so from within the corporation itself, directly challenged the sexual division of labor. Men expected to exercise leadership in public and business affairs during this era. They imbued those arenas with a competitive, individualistic spirit. Neither women nor their feminine codes of behavior had a place in those affairs. Welfare workers attempted to resolve this difficulty by redefining the maternal nature of their new occupation to meet the needs of the competitive, efficiency-minded corporate world. They offered themselves as exemplars of a new type of business manager.

Despite this effort, welfare workers did not avoid the difficulties that plagued other female professionals. Like social workers, nurses, and teachers, welfare workers served a clientele that could not pay for their services. They had to rely on others for occupational and financial security. As a consequence, female professionals never enjoyed the autonomy exercised by male professionals in such fields as law and medicine. Unlike men, female professionals functioned within larger institutions where bureaucratic administrators decided the conditions under which they worked.[1]

Welfare workers faced a similar situation. Employers sat at the top of the corporate hierarchy, controlling crucial aspects of their work, from the most fundamental elements of wages and hours policies, to the scope of company welfare programs, to the extent to which labor policies were centralized under their control. Like other female professionals, welfare workers functioned within a negotiated space between their employers and their clients. Yet welfare workers assumed a responsibility that other female professionals did not, which made their efforts to professionalize even more problematic. Welfare workers sought to reform the very institutions that employed them. As we have seen, businessmen resisted these efforts. One consequence of that resistance was that welfare workers lacked the supportive network that sustained other professionals; they never established an independent professional association, professional journal, formal training program, or certification standards. Welfare workers had nowhere to turn for support when advocates of personnel management challenged their positions in corporate labor relations.

Welfare workers' successes contributed to that challenge. Between 1890 and the 1910s, welfare workers carved out *potentially* powerful positions within American corporations, and they helped to transform labor relations into an ongoing business concern. Although they could not achieve their goals, welfare workers defined many of the issues that remained central to corporate labor relations: wages and hours, employment security, controlling foremen's powers, health and safety, and company amenities.

Ignoring their experience, personnel managers successfully argued that labor relations had become too important a responsibility to be left in women's hands. The fact that welfare work was never an exclusively female occupation actually contributed to the ease with which personnel managers pushed women out. Unlike settlement workers or nurses, welfare workers carefully avoided claims that their femininity specially qualified them for their work. They crafted an androgynous professional identity that they hoped would demonstrate their value and secure their positions. When male personnel managers challenged welfare workers for control of labor relations, they emphasized the masculine components of that professional identity. In doing so, they reversed welfare workers' careful synthesis of maternal and business ideals.

In contrast to the seamless web of welfare work, personnel managers purposefully subdivided labor relations, privileging a more masculine component focused on employment management and relegating its feminine side, welfare work, to secondary status. Women like Anne Armstrong might still do important work in corporate labor relations, but only in areas that were now carefully defined as women's preserve. (Few could aspire even to Armstrong's limited executive position.)

This marginalization of female welfare workers paralleled the experiences of women in other professions. Like welfare workers, settlement workers and public health nurses pioneered fields that initially attracted little interest from men. However, men became more interested as women developed the legitimacy and prestige of their new professions. Similar to the situation in labor relations, men reshaped those professions when they entered them, positioning themselves at the top and pushing women into subordinate positions.[2]

Ironically, the men who promoted the new profession of personnel management fared little better than their predecessors in welfare work. Businessmen were no more willing to relinquish power over labor policy to male personnel managers than they were to female welfare workers. While they embraced the new methods of personnel management, employers engaged in a concerted and successful campaign to control the personnel management movement.[3] Leading employers manipulated the new personnel managers associations in a manner reminiscent of their control over the National Civic Federation's Welfare Department.

Mary Gilson's journey through the 1920s reveals the fate of those who attempted to professionalize personnel management, as well as the particular problems faced by women in this male-dominated field. Gilson represented the liberal wing of the personnel management movement that actively promoted professionalization.[4] Her first difficulties, as we have seen, occurred with fellow liberals, who purposefully excluded women from the government training programs so that they could establish personnel management as a more prestigious and authoritative profession.

Shortly thereafter, employer-supported conservatives gained control of the National Employment Managers Association, foiling the liberals' efforts to craft an independent profession. Gilson, who lost her battle with the renamed Industrial Relations Association of America in 1921, discovered that employers controlled other avenues of professional independence, as well. She gave up a short postwar foray into private consulting when her clients refused to follow her recommendations to raise wages and stop employing spies, and her longtime employer, Joseph Feiss and Company, complained about her long absences.[5]

When Gilson lost her job at Joseph Feiss and Company in 1924, she decided to follow another path to professional independence—academic certification. After Harvard refused to admit her to its labor seminar because she was a woman, Gilson enrolled in a doctoral program at Columbia University.[6] At the same time, she undertook consulting work for the Rockefeller-supported Industrial Relations Counselors. Gilson eventually joined the staff of Industrial Relations Counselors, only to leave after three conflict-ridden years; Gilson refused to alter her reports to satisfy the group's conservative agenda. By this time, she had concluded that businessmen needed more training than either workers or foremen. In 1931, Gilson embarked on the final phase of her career, teaching industrial relations at the University of Chicago.[7]

Like Gilson, those who spoke most loudly for creating an independent profession found themselves locked out of corporate boardrooms. Those who persisted did so either as private consultants or as educators. Virtually none of them were women. Few other women had the experience or stamina to stay in the field as long as Gilson.[8] Whether marginalized by the new personnel management movement or excluded by the men who controlled that movement, women lost their leadership positions in corporate labor relations by the mid-1920s. When women moved into executive positions as personnel managers in the 1970s, they were hailed as pathbreakers. Women's pioneering role in corporate labor relations had been largely forgotten.

YET THE CHANGING fortunes of women form only part of the story. The gendered nature of the welfare system laid the groundwork for permanent changes in the American workplace and in employers' relations with their employees. When welfare advocates attempted to transform their companies into surrogate families, they insisted that the workplace become more homelike. The appearance of the modern factory and office owes much to that effort. Lounges, washrooms, locker rooms, and lunchrooms had their origins in Victorian notions that different activities required different spaces. Similarly, welfare advocates' desire to duplicate the health and comfort of home led them to demand better lighting and ventilation, conduct fire safety drills, install drinking fountains, institute rest periods, provide medical care, and much more.

At the same time that they were making the factory more homelike, employers responded to the familial ideal by becoming involved in their employees' personal affairs in new ways. In an effort to reform their workers, progressive employers offered pension, savings, and profit-sharing plans, and sponsored an array of educational, social, and recreational activities. Modern pension, health insurance, and other employee benefits had their origins in these early programs. In later years, these features became identified with either personnel management or with various government and union initiatives.[9] The fact that they were rooted in the familial idea of the turn-of-the-century welfare system has been lost to history.

Also lost was the unique idea that corporations bear any special responsibilities for the personal lives of their employees. Thus, the introduction of day-care centers at the workplace, flex-time, on-site banking, and a variety of other personal services now being offered by a few companies are hailed as unprecedented innovations. Fortunately, these recent experiments lack the moralizing zeal of their predecessors. They are not, however, entirely new. They are, in part, a reaffirmation of the welfare ideal of a century ago, when welfare advocates argued that home and work form part of a continuous fabric.

NOTES

ABBREVIATIONS

DPC E. I. duPont de Nemours and Company Papers,
     Hagley Museum and Library
MLICA Metropolitan Life Insurance Company Archives
NCF National Civic Federation Collection,
     New York Public Library
NFM Nettie Fowler McCormick Papers,
     State Historical Society of Wisconsin
PCC Plymouth Cordage Company Papers, Baker Library

PREFACE

1. Scott, *Gender and the Politics of History*, ch. 2; Kessler-Harris, "A New Agenda for American Labor History: A Gendered Analysis and the Question of Class," 225.

INTRODUCTION

1. Crowther, *John H. Patterson*, 81–82, 125.
2. Ibid., 253.
3. Ibid., 196–97.
4. Ibid., 193.
5. Nelson, "The New Factory System and the Unions."
6. See, for example, Bernstein, *The Lean Years*, 157–75; Brandes, *American Welfare Capitalism*, ch. 14; Brody, *Workers in Industrial America*, ch. 2; Kessler-Harris, *Out to Work*, 162–64, 238–40; Jacoby, *Employing Bureaucracy*, ch. 2; Montgomery, *The Fall of the House of Labor*, 236–40; Nelson, *Managers and Workers*, 101–21.
7. For examples of efforts to define the content of an ideal welfare program, see: Henderson, *Citizens in Industry*; Gertrude Beeks, "Ameliorating the Conditions of Employes," 2–3, Folder: Easley, Gertrude Beeks Early Papers and Speeches, Box 85; and D. C. Lowles of Sherwin-Williams Company, "Stenographic Report of Proceedings of Conference of Welfare Workers . . . January 11, 1911," Box 83, NCF.

8. See, for example, Henderson, *Citizens in Industry*, appendix, which lists 223 firms, and U.S. Bureau of Labor Statistics, *Welfare Work for Employees in Industrial Establishments in the United States*, Bulletin 250, which reports on 431 companies surveyed in 1916. (The Bureau of Labor Statistics report is hereafter referred to as Bulletin 250.)

9. See, for example, Nelson, *Managers and Workers*, 116. Nelson provides the names of forty firms with "extensive welfare programs" between 1905 and 1915. He does not attempt to make the list comprehensive, and he completely excludes important sectors of the economy and the welfare movement (particularly in the retail, communications, and clerical sectors).

10. Gertrude Beeks to Diana Hirschler, April 14, 1904, Folder: Filene Company, Box 78, NCF.

11. U.S. Bureau of Labor Statistics, Bulletin 250; and Berkowitz and McQuaid, *Creating the Welfare State*, 20.

12. Brandes, *American Welfare Capitalism*, 28.

13. Henderson, *Citizens in Industry*, appendix.

14. Nelson, *Managers and Workers*, 115–16; U.S. Bureau of Labor Statistics, Bulletin 250, 119.

15. Bernstein, *The Lean Years*; Brody, *Workers in Industrial America*.

16. Nelson, *Managers and Workers*; Jacoby, *Employing Bureaucracy*.

17. Fones-Wolf, "Industrial Recreation, the Second World War, and the Revival of Welfare Capitalism"; Jacoby, *Modern Manors*.

18. See, for example, Benson, *Counter Cultures*; Grossman, *Land of Hope*; Zahavi, *Workers, Managers, and Welfare Capitalism*; Strom, *Beyond the Typewriter*; Kwolek-Folland, *Engendering Business*.

19. Brandes, *American Welfare Capitalism*; Tone, *The Business of Benevolence*.

20. Gendered analysis offers a critical lens for examining how power was shaped and exercised in various institutions, relationships, and activities. Scott, "Gender: a Useful Category of Historical Analysis," *Gender and the Politics of History*; Baron, "Gender and Labor History," *Work Engendered*; Kessler-Harris, "A New Agenda for American Labor History: A Gendered Analysis and the Question of Class," Moody and Kessler-Harris, *Perspectives on American Labor History*.

21. Numerous scholars have highlighted the need for gendered analysis, which, as Ava Baron notes, "is concerned with how understandings of sexual difference shape institutions, practices, and relationships." Angel Kwolek-Folland found that gendered language "was deeply embedded in the gender concepts of the nineteenth century, and it shaped the development of twentieth century corporate culture." Baron, *Work Engendered*; Kwolek-Folland, *Engendering Business*.

22. There are some indications of this line of inquiry in studies on post–World War II welfare practice. Sanford Jacoby, in *Modern Manors*, suggests that preindustrial, feudal constructions of paternalism informed corporate welfare work in the post–New Deal era. Gerald Zahavi is beginning to examine masculine constructions of labor relations at General Electric in the post–World War II era. Paper presented at the American Historical Association annual meeting, January 2000.

23. Jacoby, *Modern Manors*, 4, 50, 150–51.

24. Andrea Tone's argument that welfare work was an antistatist strategy is a variation on, rather than a departure from, this general approach. In Tone's account, state power is a potential ally of either business or labor, and welfare work represents businessmen's bid to prevent the state from allying with labor.

25. See, for example, Brandes, *American Welfare Capitalism*; Nelson, *Managers and Workers*; Jacoby, *Employing Bureaucracy*; Tone, *The Business of Benevolence*.

CHAPTER ONE

1. Quoted in Brandes, *American Welfare Capitalism*, 2.

2. Tomlins, *The State and the Unions*, 44–67.

3. For the purposes of exposition, repression and benevolent paternalism are presented as distinct strategies for solving the labor problem. In practice, however, employers often combined elements of both.

4. Brandes, *American Welfare Capitalism*, 11.

5. Dublin, *Women at Work*, quote 77.

6. Alberts, *The Good Provider*, 37.

7. Ibid., 62.

8. Zahavi, *Workers, Managers, and Welfare Capitalism*, 23.

9. Ibid., 22–28.

10. "Stenographer's Notes of Lectures by Miss Elizabeth F. Briscoe, Welfare Manager, Joseph Bancroft & Sons Co., . . . April 21, 1913," 3, Subject Files: Lectures, Box 84, NCF.

11. Raff, "Ford Welfare Capitalism in Its Economic Context," Jacoby, *Masters to Managers*.

12. Nelson, *Managers and Workers*, 6–9.

13. Lamoreaux, *The Great Merger Movement in American Business*, 1–2, and Gordon, Edwards, and Reich, *Segmented Work, Divided Workers*, 107.

14. Gertrude Beeks to E. A. S. Clarke, General Manager, Deering Division, June 27, 1905, Box 72, NCF.

15. Nelson, *Managers and Workers*, 34–43, and Nelson, "The New Factory System and the Unions," 163–64.

16. Alfred Chandler analyzes this process fully in *The Visible Hand*. See, for example, 394–95 and 436–37. The U.S. Rubber Company's 1902 organizational chart placed the foreman, plant superintendent, assistant general manager, and general manager between the worker and the company president. A 1907 organizational chart for Armour and Company provided for a similar hierarchy to mediate between workers and the company president.

17. Montgomery, *The Fall of the House of Labor*, 216.

18. Chandler, *The Visible Hand*, 454.

19. Ivy Lee to John D. Rockefeller Jr., August 16, 1914, Folder 200, Box 22, Sub-Series: CFI, Series: Business Interests, Record Group: OMR III2C, Rockefeller Family Collection, Rockefeller Archive Center.

20. Crowther, *John H. Patterson*, 253–54.

21. National Convention of Employers and Employes, *Employers and Employes*, 165.

22. J. A. Ritchie to B. D. Caldwell, July 10, 1919, Folder 87, Box 12, Series: Industrial Questions, Record Group: OMR, Rockefeller Family Collection, Rockefeller Archive Center.

23. Henry Dennison to Luther Conant, April 26, 1921, D411 Case Folder 1921–1922, Mss 49: 1900–1952, Henry S. Dennison Papers, Baker Library.

24. Mitchell, *The Generous Corporation*. Beginning with the premise that all power must be legitimized, Mitchell contends that American business uses both ideology and policy to legitimize its economic power. By the twentieth century, corporate America was in need of both a new ideology and new policies to legitimize its unprecedented concentration of power.

25. Thorstein Veblen excoriated the new leisure class for its conspicuous and unproductive consumption of the nation's wealth. Economist Richard Ely challenged the universal benefits of private property; while large corporations may be economically efficient, Ely argued, they should not necessarily be privately owned.

26. Tone, in *The Business of Benevolence*, argues that businessmen adopted welfare work primarily as a strategy to preclude government regulation.

27. Quoted in Mitchell, *The Generous Corporation*, 109.

28. National Convention of Employers and Employes, *Employers and Employes*, 3, 14.

29. For an example of this attitude, see the statement of the New England Civic Federation in the *National Civic Federation Review* (April 1905): 16.

30. Montgomery, *Beyond Equality*, 382–84, 410–11. While very few firms actually adopted profit-sharing schemes, the debate itself helped to shape an understanding of partnership that differed substantially from labor-farmer conceptualizations.

31. Rodgers, *The Work Ethic in Industrial America*, 30–64. N. O. Nelson, a St. Louis plumbing manufacturer, and the Procter and Gamble Company were two of the most public advocates of this new form of workingmen's proprietorship. In 1892, a number of prominent businessmen and academics organized the American Association for the Promotion of Profit Sharing. According to Rodgers, the publicity and public debate generated by these supporters brought the idea of industrial partnership to the attention of most well-read Americans.

32. Gladden, *Working People and Their Employers*; quote on 138.

33. Crowther, *John H. Patterson*, 194.

34. Endicott Johnson Company, "An E-J Workers First Lesson in the Square Deal," September 1923, Employee Pamphlets Collection, Baker Library.

35. "Remarks of Lee K. Frankel of the Metropolitan Life Insurance Company . . . May 29th, 1916," 2, Box 85, NCF; National Civic Federation, *Conference on Welfare Work*, 162. The New York Factory Investigating Committee found that average wages for women in New York at this time were $7.77 per week, and calculated the minimum living wage at $9.00 per week. Tentler, *Wage-Earning Women*, 18.

36. National Civic Federation, *Conference on Welfare Work*, 38–39.

37. National Convention of Employers and Employes, *Employers and Employes*, 20.

38. "Comments on Mr. Hathaway's Report by the President," February 7, 1912, Case 48, PCC.

39. U.S. Bureau of Labor Statistics, Bulletin 250, 118.

40. "Comments on Mr. Hathaway's Report by the President," February 7, 1912, Case 48, PCC.

41. See, for example, the description of the Procter and Gamble plan in H. F. Brown to Irenee Dupont, appendices, p. 22, October 3, 1919, Folder: Employee Representation, Box 27, Accession 1662, DPC.

42. For an example of this frequently repeated sentiment, see Henderson, *Citizens in Industry*, 170–75.

43. Remarks of B. J. Greenhut, *National Civic Federation Review* (May 15, 1905): 13.

44. Folder: Employee Relations Department: Management Deliberations-Bonus Plan 1902–1923, Box 4, Accession 1615, Series II, Part 2, DPC.

45. Alfred I. DuPont to Executive Committee, July 1, 1910, DPC.

46. S. M. Darling to Gertrude Beeks, November 12, 1903, NCF.

47. National Civic Federation, *Conference on Welfare Work*, 106.

48. "Report of tour of NCR factory, 1900," Folder: 1900–1915, Carton 1, Henry S. Dennison Papers, Baker Library.

49. Quoted in H. F. Brown to Irenee DuPont, October 3, 1919, Folder: Employee Representation, Box 27, Accession 1662, DPC.

50. The specific nature of that "machinery" will be addressed in later chapters. Whereas workers would have pointed to inadequate wages and long hours as the reasons for their inability to care for themselves, the welfare system assumed that other factors contributed to their lack of independence and cooperative spirit.

51. In his study of the Lowell Mills, Dublin demonstrates that the associates expected higher productivity in exchange for paternal care, yet they carefully avoided saying this. Dublin, *Women at Work*, 59, 77.

52. Remarks of Lee K. Frankel, May 29, 1916, Box 85, NCF. The Metropolitan Life Insurance Company continued to offer full-course meals to its employees free of charge until the mid-1990s.

53. "Report of Tour of NCR Factory, 1900," Folder: 1900–1915, Carton 1, Henry S. Dennison Papers, Baker Library.

54. Crowther, *John H. Patterson*, 206.

55. One example of this trend was the widespread introduction of employee manuals after the turn of the century.

56. National Civic Federation, *Conference on Welfare Work*, 1.

CHAPTER TWO

1. Nelson and Campbell, "Taylorism Versus Welfare Work in American Industry," 6–7; Chandler, *The Visible Hand*, 444.

2. Peter B. Petersen, "Elizabeth F. Briscoe: Pioneer in Personnel Management," 35–37. I thank Peter Petersen for his generosity in sharing his essays on Briscoe with me.

3. "Stenographer's Notes of Lecture by Miss Elizabeth F. Briscoe . . . Delivered Before the Welfare Class at New York University . . . April 21, 1913," 3, Box 84, NCF.

4. Ibid., 12. Briscoe was not only manager, but also the only member, of the Welfare Department at this point.

5. Nelson and Campbell, "Taylorism Versus Welfare Work in American Industry," 8.

6. Elizabeth Briscoe to Nellie Santabarbara, April 26, 1906, Briscoe to Mrs. Joseph Zurita, June 25, 1906, Briscoe to Joseph Bond, August 25, 1906, Volume 893, Welfare Department Letterbook, Accession 736, Joseph Bancroft and Sons Company Collection, Hagley Museum and Library.

7. Quoted in Nelson and Campbell, "Taylorism Versus Welfare Work in American Industry," 8.

8. Ryan, *Cradle of the Middle Class*. Ryan argues that the middle class redefined both the functions of the family and the roles of individual family members in response to economic changes. While many families, especially those in the working class, did not ascribe to this Victorian ideal, it did dominate public discussions and served as a model to the middle and upper classes, where most welfare advocates had their roots. Unaware of the irony, welfare advocates turned to the Victorian family ideal, designed to help individuals navigate the rough waters of the business world, to reform the business system itself.

9. Quoted in Kwolek-Folland, *Engendering Business*, 45.

10. Dubbert, *A Man's Place*; Peter G. Filene, *Him/Her/Self*; Carnes and Griffen, *Meanings for Manhood*; May, *Great Expectations*; Pleck and Pleck, *The American Man*; Anthony Rotundo, *American Manhood*; Kwolek-Folland, *Engendering Business*.

11. In addition to the sources in the preceding note, Fass, *The Damned and the Beautiful*; Sklar, *Catharine Beecher*; Lasch, *Haven in a Heartless World*.

12. It was not until the 1910s that academics and popular writers began to fill in the outlines of a new family form to replace the Victorian model. This important shift will be discussed more fully in Chapter 7, as it contributed to the shift away from the welfare system.

13. Woloch, *Women and the American Experience*, 276–86; Cookingham, "Combining Marriage, Motherhood, and Jobs Before World War II."

14. Pascoe, *Relations of Rescue*; Muncy, *Creating a Female Dominion in American Reform*; McCarthy, *Noblesse Oblige*; Rosen, *The Lost Sisterhood*.

15. May, *Great Expectations*, 52–55.

16. Ellen Richards, a founder of professional social work, quoted in Lasch, *Haven in a Heartless World*, 14. Also see May, *Great Expectations*.

17. National Convention of Employers and Employes, *Employers and Employes*, 181. Henderson, *Citizens in Industry*, 185. This was not the first time that reformers sought to develop institutions to fulfill responsibilities that they believed families were not properly meeting. David Rothman, in *The Discovery of the Asylum*, argues that mid-nineteenth-century reformers consciously shaped penitentiaries, insane asylums, and orphan asylums to act as surrogate families to their inmates.

18. Lawrence Lewis, "Uplifting 17,000 Employees," 5939.

19. Wyllie, *The Self-Made Man in America*, ch. 7; Rotundo, *American Manhood.*

20. Wyllie, *The Self-Made Man in America*, 21.

21. Quoted in Wyllie, *The Self-Made Man in America*, 29.

22. See Bender, *Community and Social Change in America*, esp. 7–9, on the ways in which community is frequently conceived in familial terms.

23. Norwood, *Labor's Flaming Youth*, 48.

24. *Opportunity* (January 1923): 20–22.

25. Gilbert and Barker Manufacturing Company, "Information for Employees," n.d., Employer Pamphlet Collection, Baker Library.

26. National Industrial Conference Board, *Employee Magazines in the United States*, appendix; Brandes, *American Welfare Capitalism*, 65; U.S. Bureau of Labor Statistics, Bulletin 250, 12. Most employee magazines chose titles that either reflected the firm's line of business or projected the idea of family or partnership. Sometimes both ideas were conveyed, as in the McLaughlin Textile Corporation's "Home Spun Yarns."

27. Zahavi, *Workers, Managers and Welfare Capitalism*, 43.

28. Cranston, "The Social Secretary," 489.

29. "Welfare Managers–Women," "Welfare Managers–Men," "Special Workers–Women," "Special Workers–Men," "Applicants," Box 88, NCF. Although undated, the names and firms recorded suggest that these lists were compiled during 1912–14.

30. Salary figures are drawn from a wide variety of sources. See, for example: Gertrude Beeks to Diana Hirschler, April 14, 1904, Folder: Filene's, Box 78, NCF; "Remarks of William Willcox, Chairman, Employers' Welfare Department . . . at New York University, February 10, 1913," Box 85, NCF; Cranston, "The Social Secretary," 489.

31. See, for example, Jacoby, *Employing Bureaucracy*, 59. Jacoby asserts a commonly held assumption that welfare workers were well educated and dedicated to public service, with "backgrounds in social and settlement work, municipal reform, and religious activities."

32. Ozanne, *A Century of Labor-Management Relations at McCormick and International Harvester*, 32; Comstock, "A Woman of Achievement," 444–45.

33. Ozanne, *A Century of Labor-Management Relations at McCormick and International Harvester*, 32.

34. Ibid., 49.

35. Jacoby, *Employing Bureaucracy*, 59–60; Mary L. Goss to Cyrus McCormick, March 18, 1907, Box 73, NCF.

36. "Applicants–Women," and Winifred Lyford to Secretary, Welfare Department, August 26, 1909, Box 88, NCF; Gertrude Beeks to Annette Austin, December 23, 1904, and Beeks to Franklin Brewer, April 5, 1904, Box 72, NCF.

37. Gwinn, "Her Soul Goes Marching On"; quotes from 76, 80.

38. Gertrude Beeks to Robert A. Woods, April 13, 1905; Alice L. Higgins to Beeks, April 15, 1905; Alexander Wilson to Beeks, April 18, 1905, Box 72, NCF.

39. Catherine Brannick to Gertrude Beeks, October 18, 1906, Box 72, NCF.

40. "Stenographer's Notes of Lecture by Miss Elizabeth F. Briscoe . . . Deliv-

ered Before the Welfare Class at New York University . . . April 21, 1913," 3, Box 84, NCF.

41. *The Home Office* (September 1926): 1, MLICA.

42. Henderson, *Citizens in Industry*, 69.

43. Gwinn, "Her Soul Goes Marching On," 53.

44. *The Home Office* (December 1919): 8, MLICA. My records indicate that approximately 25 percent of female welfare workers were in fact mothers.

45. National Convention of Employers and Employes, *Employers and Employes*, 188–89.

46. "Address of Miss Gertrude Beeks . . . February 20, 1913," Folder: Welfare Workers' Conference, Box 82, NCF.

47. National Convention of Employers and Employes, *Employers and Employes*, 188–89.

48. Ibid. Welfare managers' attention to shortcomings on the part of management created conflicts between them and their employers. These issues, more than anything else, divided employer advocates of welfare work from the reform advocates they hired to direct their welfare programs. This subject will be taken up more fully in Chapter 5.

49. The movement to control and limit the power of foremen, which is most often associated with the scientific management and personnel management movements, found an early and continuous voice among advocates of the corporate welfare system. Welfare advocates argued that autocratic and unfair foremen created many unnecessary grievances between employers and employees, and they constantly tried to persuade employers to limit the power of foremen over "personnel" issues by transferring those responsibilities to the office of the welfare manager.

50. Gertrude Beeks to Stanley McCormick, December 2, 1902, NFM.

51. "Address of Miss Gertrude Beeks . . . February 20, 1913," Folder: Welfare Workers' Conference, Box 82, NCF.

52. "Stenographer's Notes of Lectures by Miss Elizabeth F. Briscoe . . . April 21, 1913," Box 84, NCF; "Opinions of the Social Secretaries," *Social Service* (July 1904): 10, Folder: American Institute of Social Service, Box 76, NCF.

53. In the years before World War I, individual entrepreneurs or members of the entrepreneurial family managed most American firms. Chandler, *The Visible Hand*, ch. 13. Perhaps because they felt the pressure of personal responsibility and loss of personal contact most keenly, owner-managers frequently agitated the loudest in support of welfare work. John Patterson at NCR, Henry Heinz at H. J. Heinz Company, Henry Dennison of the Dennison Manufacturing Company, Richard Feiss at Joseph and Feiss Company, and Stanley McCormick at International Harvester are just a few of the employers who institutionalized their sense of paternal responsibility in formal welfare programs.

54. Crowther, *John H. Patterson*, 206–7.

55. Kwolek-Folland, "The Business of Gender: The Redefinition of Male and Female and the Modern Business Office in the United States, 1880–1930," 85–86.

56. Weinstein, *The Corporate Ideal in the Liberal State*, 20. While Weinstein identifies Rosenwald's actions as expressions of his "fatherly interest," he does not make the connection between the assumption of the fatherly role and the managerial pursuit of efficiency and control.

57. Zahavi, *Workers, Managers, and Welfare Capitalism*, 44.

58. Ibid.

59. *National Civic Federation Review* (May 15, 1905): 13.

60. Gertrude Beeks, "Welfare Work in Mercantile Houses," (New York: National Civic Federation, 1905), 12, NCF.

61. *Addresses by the President of the Metropolitan Life Insurance Company and the Guests of the Company, at the President's Triennial Conventions, 1910–1928*, October 28, 1916, January 31, 1920, September 4, 1920, MLICA.

62. Elizabeth Briscoe to Albert A. Leroy, November 18, 1909, Volume 893, Accession 736, Joseph Bancroft and Sons Company Collection, Hagley Museum and Library.

63. "Stenographer's Notes of Lecture by Mrs. Laura L. Ray . . . April 7, 1913," Box 85, NCF.

64. Meyerowitz, *Women Adrift*.

65. Ibid. Also see Peiss, *Cheap Amusements*; Pascoe, *Relations of Rescue*.

66. Norwood, *Labor's Flaming Youth*, 4.

67. Ozanne, *A Century of Labor-Management Relations at McCormick and International Harvester*, 31–34.

68. Alberts, *The Good Provider*, ch. 10. A male doctor served the welfare needs of Heinz's male workers.

69. Heinz to Ralph Easley, May 3, 1901, Box 79, NCF.

70. Gertrude Beeks, "Welfare Work in Mercantile Houses" (New York: National Civic Federation, 1905). Other examples come from Bancroft and Sons Co., which hired Elizabeth Briscoe to direct its new welfare efforts to ensure a proper moral atmosphere for its female employees, as well as to preclude strikes; Nelson, *Managers and Workers*, 112ff; Kwolek-Folland, "The Business of Gender: The Redefinition of Male and Female and the Modern Business Office in the United States, 1880–1930."

71. U.S. Bureau of the Census, *Women in Gainful Occupations, 1870–1920*, 91; Woloch, *Women and the American Experience*, 220.

72. U.S. Bureau of Labor Statistics, Bulletin 250; Nelson, *Managers and Workers*, 117.

73. Higham, *Strangers in the Land*, 87–96, 107–23.

74. A vocal segment of the native-born population preferred restricting immigration altogether rather than hoping immigrants would assimilate or forcing them to do so. See Higham, *Strangers in the Land* for a discussion of nativism and the movements for immigration restriction.

75. "Conference on Welfare Work at Chicago Commons . . . Minutes of Second Meeting, April 10," Subject Files, Box 87, NCF.

76. "Report of H. K. Hathaway to the Plymouth Cordage Company," January 6, 1912, 3, Case 48, PCC. Hathaway was an advocate of scientific management.

77. U.S. Bureau of the Census, Monograph No. 7 (Washington, D.C., 1927); Brody, *Workers in Industrial America*, 14–15; Kessner, *The Golden Door*, ch. 3; Zunz, *The Changing Face of Inequality*, chs. 9, 13.

78. U.S. Bureau of Labor Statistics, Bulletin 250.

79. Williamson, *The Crucible of Race*. In addition to tracing the subtle and not-so-subtle changes in American racism between emancipation and the 1920s, Williamson forcefully demonstrates the symbiotic relationship between stereotypes of black men and women and ideas of Victorian manhood and womanhood. See, for example, 24–31 and 306–10.

80. Rikard, "An Experiment in Welfare Capitalism," 107. The sudden employment of black strikebreakers by the Lockhart Iron and Steel Company of McKees Rocks, Pennsylvania, similarly sparked its initial interest in welfare work. As at Tennessee Coal and Iron, the welfare program was later expanded to include the company's white miners. *Opportunity* (January 1924): 15–19.

81. Grossman, *Land of Hope*, 198–207.

82. Ibid.; Cohen, *Making a New Deal*, 165.

83. Disagreements over which class of workers were targeted by welfare work continue to shape the debate over the purposes and successes of this system of labor-management relations. David Brody, in *Steelworkers in America*, argued that welfare work was directed primarily at skilled workers (109). On the other hand, Stuart Brandes, *American Welfare Capitalism*, found that the desire to American-ize the unskilled immigrant prompted the adoption of welfare programs (12). And Daniel Nelson, *Managers and Workers*, variously identifies both native-born skilled workmen and unskilled female workers as the primary object of welfare work (95, 111, 115).

84. "Conference on Welfare Work at Chicago Commons . . . Minutes of Second Meeting, April 10," Subject Files, Box 87, NCF.

85. "Conference on Welfare Work at Chicago Commons . . . Minutes of Seventh Meeting, May 15, 1906," Subject Files, Box 87, NCF.

86. National Convention of Employers and Employes, *Employers and Employes*, 21–23.

87. *National Civic Federation Review* (April 1905): 16.

CHAPTER THREE

1. Henderson, *Citizens in Industry*, 252.

2. D. C. Lowles, "Stenographic Report of Proceedings of Conference on Welfare Workers . . . January 11, 1911," Box 83, NCF.

3. The significance of wage levels and the language of wages is analyzed by Kessler-Harris in *A Woman's Wage*. Kessler-Harris argues that wages represent more than simply an economic return for labor. Wages both perpetuate and reflect gendered behavior and expectations.

4. "The Welfare Work of the Metropolitan Life Insurance Company: Reports for 1914," 19, Folder: V.F. Welfare Division General, 1909–1949, Collection: Subject Files, MLICA.

5. "Stenographic Report of Proceedings of Conference of Welfare Workers . . . January 11, 1911," Box 83, NCF.

6. Gertrude Beeks, "Report of 1901 Factory Tour," Box 27, Subject File 3B, NFM.

7. Jacoby, "Employers and the Welfare State."

8. Policyholders' Service Bureau, *Constructive Policies in Industry which Facilitate an Improved Social Order and Insure Against Social Disturbances* (1926), 58–59, MLICA.

9. Beeks, "Report of 1901 Factory Tour," Box 27, Subject File 3B, NFM.

10. These conflicts will be discussed fully in Chapter 5.

11. There were, of course, limits to the "manhood" workmen were encouraged to achieve. Employers hoped to remake them into more loyal and productive workers. They had no intention of helping their workmen acquire the autonomy to which Victorian gentlemen aspired.

12. National Civic Federation, *Conference on Welfare Work*, xi.

13. Patterson encouraged visitors to tour his factory. As a consequence, NCR gained a worldwide reputation as a model for welfare work.

14. Crowther, *John H. Patterson*, 170.

15. Patterson's rapidly expanding workforce was showing marked signs of discontent and resistance, including the purposeful sabotage of a large shipment of registers sent to Europe. Crowther, *John H. Patterson*, 190.

16. Ibid., 199–200; "Report on Tour of NCR Factory, 1900," Folder 1900–1915, Case 1, Henry S. Dennison Papers, Baker Library.

17. Crowther, *John H. Patterson*, 201.

18. Ibid., 199.

19. Ibid., 200.

20. Ibid.

21. National Civic Federation, *Conference on Welfare Work*, 150.

22. U.S. Bureau of Labor Statistics, Bulletin 250, 54–55. In 1926, the Metropolitan Life Insurance Company reported approximately 4,200 lunchrooms in operation: Policyholders Service Bureau, *Constructive Policies in Industry*, 95, MLICA.

23. Crowther, *John H. Patterson*, 211 facing plate; National Civic Federation, *Conference on Welfare Work*, 153.

24. U.S. Bureau of Labor Statistics, Bulletin 250, 61.

25. National Civic Federation, *Conference on Welfare Work*, 153.

26. "Advantages of a Model Industrial Cafeteria," Folder 2: 1922, Collection: Papers and Speeches, Lee K. Frankel Papers, MLICA; *An Epoch in Insurance*, 249.

27. National Civic Federation, *Conference on Welfare Work*, 163–65.

28. Crowther, *John H. Patterson*, 210 facing plate. The larger male workforce may account for part of the difference in seating arrangements. However, the women's dining room seated 500, a number large enough to warrant the 100-seat tables if low cost and efficiency were the only considerations. The Metropolitan Life Insurance Company, which served over 6,000 meals per day by World War I, arranged tables in long rows but left spaces between them so that the four to six women seated at each table could engage in "intimate" conversation. As further

indication that physical features were fraught with implicit lessons, one firm not only separated its employees by race, class, and gender, but provided only high tables for its black workmen, at which they were required to stand during their meals. U.S. Bureau of Labor Statistics, Bulletin 250, 57–58.

29. "Report on Tour of NCR Factory, 1900," Folder 1900–1915, Case 1, Henry S. Dennison Papers, Baker Library.

30. Alberts, *The Good Provider*, 110, 137.

31. National Civic Federation, *Conference on Welfare Work*, 56, 152. There is a striking parallel here with the teas, dance recitals, and other middle-class activities sponsored by allies within the Women's Trade Union League for the union's working-class members. See, for example, Dye, "Creating a Feminist Alliance."

32. U.S. Bureau of Labor Statistics, Bulletin 250, 42, 70, 73. Exact figures are difficult to determine since some firms provided only one of these spaces, whereas others set aside space for all of these purposes. The estimate of over 50 percent is based on the most conservative interpretation of the data. Almost 95 percent of the companies surveyed provided washrooms and/or locker rooms for their employees.

33. Henderson, *Citizens in Industry*, 78. Henderson was not alone in carefully explaining the need to separate male and female workers. The need to explain this aspect of the corporate welfare system to others suggests that such careful regard for middle-class standards of sexual propriety were not common industrial practice, but rather a specific component of the welfare system of labor-management relations.

34. On the role of fraternal clubs as expressions of Victorian masculinity, see Carnes, *Secret Ritual and Manhood in Victorian America*; Rotundo, *American Manhood*.

35. In accordance with the belief that women's nature was more delicate than men's, 87 percent of the female employees and only 31 percent of the male employees in the firms surveyed by the Bureau of Labor Statistics were allowed rest periods during the workday. U.S. Bureau of Labor Statistics, Bulletin 250, 34–35.

36. U.S. Bureau of Labor Statistics, Bulletin 250, 70–74; National Civic Federation, *Conference on Welfare Work*, 132.

37. Rodgers, *The Work Ethic in Industrial America*, esp. ch. 4. It was this understanding of the benefits of leisure that led many welfare workers to advocate shorter hours for wage laborers.

38. Henderson, *Citizens in Industry*, 178–80.

39. Welfare workers' promotion of home gardening and beautification among workingmen may also have reflected a new value on "masculine domesticity," which Margaret Marsh has linked to the turn-of-the-century transformation in middle-class masculinity. Margaret Marsh, "Suburban Men and Masculine Domesticity, 1870–1915," in Carnes and Griffen, *Meanings for Manhood*, 111–27.

40. A number of scholars have argued that group sports often originated within working-class communities and were then transformed by middle-class enthusiasts to satisfy their own sense of discipline and order. Company sponsorship of team sports represented one way in which the middle class attempted to transfer their habits to the working class. See, for example, Rosenzweig, *Eight Hours for*

What We Will; Pleck and Pleck, *The American Man*; Rotundo, *American Manhood*, quotes on 241.

41. "Report of W. E. C. Nazro, August 1, 1912–August 1, 1913," Folder: Welfare Reports of W. E. C. Nazro, Case 48, PCC.

42. "The Human Side of Industry," Folder: Welfare—Mr. Marshall's Reports, early 1920s, Case 47, PCC. This combination of organizing baseball for men and dancing for women was fairly common. See, for example, Gertrude Beeks, "Welfare Work in Mercantile Houses" (New York: National Civic Federation, 1905), 17–18, NCF.

43. *An Epoch in Insurance*, 251; Marion Brockway to President, May 5, 1923, Folder: House Mother, MLICA.

44. National Civic Federation, *Conference on Welfare Work*, 113.

45. Lawrence Lewis, "Uplifting 17,000 Employees," 5943; The Bancrofts used almost identical language to explain both their workmen's drinking problem and the need to educate women. See "Stenographer's Notes of Lecture by Miss Elizabeth F. Briscoe . . . Delivered Before the Welfare Class at New York University . . . April 21, 1913," 4, Box 84, NCF.

46. "Minutes of Welfare Conference at Chicago Commons, May 15, 1906," 3, Box 87, NCF.

47. Male welfare workers were equally committed to this educational agenda— hiring women to do the actual teaching that female welfare managers often did themselves. It is ironic that many of the same manufacturers whose products were replacing goods traditionally made in the home were so willing to promote the handicraft movement among their female employees.

48. Folder: Employee Relations Department: Management Deliberations, Bonus Plan, 1902–1923, Box 4, Accession 1615, Series II, Part 2, DPC.

49. Ibid.; J. A. Haskell to Executive Committee, February 28, 1910, and A. I. DuPont to Executive Committee, February 24, 1910; "Memos from Purchasing Agents" to Frank Tallman, Folder: DuPont Correspondence, Box 54, Accession 381, Frank G. Tallman Papers, Hagley Museum and Library.

50. Policyholders Service Bureau, *Constructive Policies in Industry*, 140–41, MLICA.

51. Quoted in Ramirez, *When Workers Fight*, 150.

52. Marion B. Folsom interview, 1965, 45–48, Part III, Oral History Collection, Butler Library, Columbia University.

53. "1915 Report of Superintendents Meeting," Folder: Wage Bonus Plan, Merit Pay, Suggestions . . ., 1910–1923, Box 4, Accession 1615, Series II, Part 2, DPC. This superintendent also expressed doubts that his workmen were making any extra effort in times of company need or that they would be more loyal in the event of a strike.

54. *National Civic Federation Review* (May 15, 1905): 13.

55. Gilson, *What's Past is Prologue*, 139.

56. Elizabeth Briscoe to Mrs. George McBride, November 8, 1907, Volume 893, Accession 736, Joseph Bancroft and Sons Company Collection, Hagley Museum and Library; Policyholders Service Bureau, *Constructive Policies in Industry*, 137, MLICA.

57. Ibid.

58. Ibid., 134–36.

59. Norwood, *Labor's Flaming Youth*, 51. In 1905, AT&T was offering insurance policies only to its male employees. *National Civic Federation Review* (April 1905): 11.

60. National Civic Federation, *Conference on Welfare Work*, 129.

61. Gilson, *What's Past is Prologue*, ch. 12.

62. "Address of Miss Gertrude Beeks . . . at Columbia University . . . February 20, 1913," 8, Folder: Welfare Workers' Conference, Box 82, NCF.

63. In some cases, employees received home visits within hours of not reporting for work. At other firms, the welfare worker or visiting nurse looked in on employees only after they had missed a second or third day of work. Male welfare managers often hired female assistants or visiting nurses to perform these tasks.

64. "Stenographer's Notes of Lecture by Mrs. Laura L. Ray . . . April 7, 1913," 1–2, Box 85, NCF. Emphasis added.

65. Elizabeth Briscoe to Mother deSales, December 14, 1906, and Elizabeth Briscoe to Samuel Greer, May 19, 1916, Volume 893, Accession 736, Joseph Bancroft and Sons Company Collection, Hagley Museum and Library. In the first case, Briscoe was unsuccessful in persuading the girl's mother to defy her husband's orders and leave the girl in school.

66. Gilson, *What's Past is Prologue*, 138–39. Gilson would have vehemently opposed this characterization of her as a welfare worker. Her specific contribution to the welfare and personnel management systems of industrial relations will be taken up in Chapter 7.

67. Cranston, "The Social Secretary."

68. See, for example, Alice Kessler-Harris's excellent analysis of the multiple definitions of wages used by different groups during this period, and the assumptions about the relationship between work and family that underlay those different meanings, in *A Woman's Wage*.

CHAPTER FOUR

1. The term "systematic management" refers to both the carefully defined scientific management methods promoted by Frederick Taylor and the broader trend toward better coordination and more informed decision-making in American corporations. For a more complete explanation, see Jacoby, *Employing Bureaucracy*, ch. 2, and Nelson and Campbell, "Taylorism Versus Welfare Work in American Industry."

2. Scholars who approach welfare work as an anti-union strategy focus on the two antagonists, workers and their employers. See Brody, *Workers in Industrial America*, and Bernstein, *The Lean Years*. Those who recognize that welfare workers filled new positions in the corporate bureaucracy focus on them as administrative agents for their employers. See Jacoby, *Employing Bureaucracy*, ch. 2, Nelson, *Managers and Workers*, ch. 6, and Brandes, *American Welfare Capitalism*, ch. 12.

3. Nelson and Campbell, "Taylorism Versus Welfare Work in American Industry."

4. As used here, the term "social housekeepers" encompasses a variety of reformers, including settlement workers, anti–child labor advocates, home missionaries, charity aid workers, anti-prostitution reformers, and temperance advocates. Although there were important differences in the philosophies and reform strategies pursued by the various public sector reform organizations, they shared a general belief that "cultivating character" was essential to improving the lives of the poor. For an analysis of the philosophical links and conflicts between philanthropic reform movements, see Carson, *Settlement Folk*, chs. 2–3, and Ladd-Taylor, *Mother-Work*.

5. Meyerowitz, *Women Adrift*, 46–47. See also Shuey, *Factory People and Their Employers*, 63. Reference to similar efforts by Boston reformers, beginning in the 1880s, can be found in Deutsch, "Learning to Talk More Like a Man," 389–90, 398.

6. Beeks began her employment with the McCormick Reaper Company two years before the merger that created International Harvester. The use of the name International Harvester at this point is meant to signify its predecessor, McCormick Reaper Company, as well.

7. Cranston, "The Social Secretary," 493. The fact that so many welfare workers had never engaged in public sector reform probably encouraged them to deemphasize the importance of such practical experience.

8. Henderson, *Citizens in Industry*, 281; National Civic Federation, *Conference on Welfare Work*, 105–10; "Report on Conditions of Employees and Recommendations for Improvements . . .," Folder: Greenhut, Box 79, NCF; Memoranda from Mr. Filene to Miss A. E. Van deCarr, March 22, 1905, Box 78, NCF.

9. For an example of International Harvester welfare workers' recognition of the need to vary welfare work by plant, see Korman, *Industrialization, Immigrants and Americanizers*, 105.

10. French, "A New Occupation," 67.

11. Henderson, *Citizens in Industry*, 281.

12. Men have suffered disproportionately from the general neglect of welfare workers. Few historians even acknowledge that significant numbers of men served in these positions. (A small number of African-American women and men also found positions as welfare workers, serving African-American workers exclusively. Although their presence does not seem to have had any direct impact on the occupation as a whole, their employment, like that of men, reinforces the conclusion that welfare work was not simply a form of white, middle-class women's social housekeeping.)

13. Marsh, "Suburban Men and Masculine Domesticity, 1870–1915," in Carnes and Griffen, *Meanings for Manhood*, 111–27. Marsh argues that prescriptive success literature and contemporary testimony reveal a new masculine interest in the appearance of homes and gardens that included planning, purchasing, and arranging new decor. She refers to this as "masculine domesticity."

14. Curtis, "The Son of Man and God the Father," in Carnes and Griffen, *Meanings for Manhood*; Pleck and Pleck, *The American Man*; Dubbert, *A Man's Place*.

15. "Stenographic Report of Proceedings of Conference on Welfare Workers . . . January 11, 1911," 110–11, Box 83, NCF.

16. DeVault, *Sons and Daughters of Labor*, Fine, *The Souls of the Skyscraper*, Kwolek-Folland, *Engendering Business*, Strom, *Beyond the Typewriter*, Tone, *The Business of Benevolence*.

17. Men in aspiring professions needed to overcome cultural expectations and forcefully declare their commitment to service. Women, on the other hand, needed to disassociate themselves from sentimental conceptions of womanly service and assert their expertise. Melosh, *"The Physician's Hand,"* 24–25.

18. Nazro was among the handful of welfare managers who presided over well-established programs at the time of the NCF's Conference on Welfare Work in 1904. He spoke as an expert at that conference and later served as an advisor and consultant to NCF member companies.

19. National Civic Federation, *Conference on Welfare Work*, 5.

20. "Reports of W. E. C. Nazro: August 1, 1912–August 1, 1913," Folder: Welfare, Case 48, PCC. For a similar commitment, see the statement by Edgar A. Atkin, Manager of Service Dept., Yale and Towne Manufacturing Co., March 10, 1915, Box 83, NCF.

21. Among female philanthropic reformers, the desire to help working people, the poor, or immigrants was often inextricably combined with a personal search for a meaningful public life and career. While welfare workers probably felt the need for a remunerative career even more strongly than did many women engaged in philanthropic reform, there is scant evidence that they tried to define this new profession in a way that would disproportionately favor women. For an excellent analysis of this process among women moving from the settlements to careers in the federal child welfare bureaucracy, see Muncy, *Creating a Female Dominion in American Reform*.

22. Gertrude Beeks, "Informal Talk to Extension Department American Committee YWCA, August 27, 1902," Subject File: Easley, Gertrude Beeks, Box 85, NCF. Beeks did refer substantially more women than men for positions in welfare work. However, this seems to have been a calculated strategy designed to preserve her (and the NCF's) control over the welfare movement rather than an effort to carve out a new female profession. Beeks's role will be addressed more fully in Chapter 7.

23. Beeks's trilogy, "tact, common sense and executive ability," is very similar to the style of "impressionistic management," described by Angel Kwolek-Folland. However, Beeks and others would probably have balked at separating specialized knowledge and rationality into a different management style, "systematic management," as does Kwolek-Folland. Kwolek-Folland, *Engendering Business*, 72–77.

24. French, "A New Occupation."

25. National Civic Federation, *Conference on Welfare Work*, 29.

26. "Copy of Memoranda which Mr. Filene gave to Miss A. E. Van deCarr," March 22, 1905, Box 78, NCF.

27. Cranston, "The Social Secretary," 490.

28. M. Harding to Gertrude Beeks, August 24, 1903, and Beeks to Harding, August 29, 1903, Box 73, NCF.

29. See, for example, Gertrude Beeks to Ripley Hitchcock, April 28, 1905, Box

73, NCF. Leaders in the social housekeeping movement, particularly child welfare advocates, held welfare work in great contempt primarily because of this open partisanship.

30. The fact that so many welfare workers were men certainly militated against using female moral authority to justify their positions. Unlike men in the social settlements who became subordinates within the female space of the settlement house, the position of male welfare workers was bolstered by the fact that they were functioning within the masculine business world.

31. "Value of the Social Secretary," *Social Service* (July 1904): 9, Folder: American Institute of Social Service, Box 76, NCF.

32. Gertrude Beeks to Stanley McCormick, November 3, 1902, Box 27, Subject Files 3B, NFM.

33. Gertrude Beeks to Edward A. Filene, March 23, 1904, Folder: Filene, Box 78; Beeks to H. W. Hillier, March 1905, Box 73, NCF.

34. Formal definitions of line and staff positions did not fully take shape until the 1920s. Although it was not recognized at the time, labor relations management, in the guise of welfare work, was one of the first staff positions created within the managerial bureaucracy. As such, welfare workers were in a unique position to define the attributes of staff-level managers. For a more thorough discussion of the line and staff relationship, see Chandler, *Strategy and Structure*, 96–98, 139, 154–56.

35. "Stenographic Report of Proceedings of Conference of Welfare Workers . . . January 11, 1911," 21–22, 117, Box 83, NCF.

36. Most historians attribute references to efficiency, profits, and other business principles by welfare workers to their desire to ingratiate themselves with their superiors. While welfare workers certainly recognized the advantages of framing their work in business terms, the evidence suggests that they firmly believed that adherence to such principles was essential to improving both the lives of working people and relations between workers and management. There was no reason for welfare workers to consider these alien or unfamiliar ideas. By the early twentieth century, the nation's fascination with principles of efficiency, system, and rationalization affected not only business, but also government, philanthropies, and churches.

37. Diana Hirschler to Gertrude Beeks, January 5, 1903, Box 73, NCF. Hirschler's proposal of a convention was a common strategy used by other groups during this period that were trying to establish their professional credentials.

38. Gertrude Beeks to S. M. Darling, September 12, 1904, Box 72, NCF.

39. "Remarks of William R. Willcox at formal opening of course of lectures to train welfare workers . . . New York University . . . February 10, 1913," Box 85, NCF.

40. National Civic Federation, *Conference on Welfare Work*, vii.

41. Florence M. Hall and Gertrude Beeks, "Report on Conditions of Employees and Recommendations for Improvements by Employer's Welfare Department, NCF," October–December 1911, Folder: Greenhut, Box 79, NCF.

42. "Welfare Work at the Filene Store . . . December 22, 1906 . . . by Alida Lattimore . . .," Folder: Filene Store, Box 78, NCF.

43. "Remarks of William R. Willcox . . . Course of Lectures to Train Welfare Workers, . . . February 10, 1913," 7, Box 85, NCF.

44. "Report of Interview with Miss Marguerite Walker Jordan . . . June 15, 1915," Box 85, NCF.

45. Mary E. Hamson to M. H. Knapp, January 29, 1917, Box 88, NCF.

46. Gertrude Beeks to F. A. Flather, December 2, 1902, File: 1902—International Harvester Company, Box 30, Subject File 3B, NFM.

47. Shuey, *Factory People and Their Employers*, 27–28.

48. While welfare workers did not become bureaucratic paper shufflers, they apparently did join the broader trend in business management toward systematic use of forms and reports. Jacoby, *Employing Bureaucracy*, 42–43.

49. See, for example, Shuey, *Factory People and Their Employers*, and Boettiger, *Employee Welfare Work*.

50. U.S. Bureau of Labor Statistics, Bulletin No. 250, 7.

51. Also see *System Magazine*, which reported on welfare work regularly throughout the 1910s.

52. Gertrude Beeks, "Report of 1901 Factory Tour," 16, Box 27, Subject File 3B, NFM.

53. French, "A New Occupation," 67.

54. Crowther, *John H. Patterson*, 252–59; National Civic Federation, *Conference on Welfare Work*, 122.

55. National Civic Federation, *Conference on Welfare Work*, 165.

56. "Suggestion Plan," Box 54, DPC.

57. Welfare—Mr. Marshall's Reports, early 1920s, 3–4, Case 47, PCC.

58. Ibid., Marshall to Holmes, December 30, 1921.

59. Welfare managers were in the forefront of developing what became a new standard of professional business management. When Louis Brandeis associated the "profession of business" with "service, cooperation and social responsibility" in 1914, welfare managers were among the most prominent practitioners of the new business professionalism. More recently, historians have begun to explicate the emerging profession of business by analyzing the "feminization" of business management. The workplace struggles of welfare managers are a concrete example of how those new gender roles were translated into the new business standards that spread throughout corporate management. More research will need to be done to determine whether welfare managers pioneered or jointly introduced these new standards of professional business management. Brandeis is quoted in Mitchell, *The Generous Corporation*, 133.

CHAPTER FIVE

1. The Bureau of Labor Statistics concluded that a fairly elaborate welfare program would cost no more than 2 percent of a firm's payroll. U.S. Bureau of Labor Statistics, Bulletin No. 250. For examples of similar figures at individual companies, see Scheinberg, "The Development of Corporation Labor Policy"; H. K. Hathaway, "Report to the Plymouth Cordage Company," Case 48, PCC; *National Civic Federation Review* (March–April 1906): 9–10, and (May 1914): 21.

2. French, "A New Occupation," 63. Although cited anonymously, this was probably Laura Ray. Gertrude Beeks severely criticized her employer, B. J. Greenhut, for his unwillingness to support essential welfare activities and his failure to heed Ray's valuable advice.

3. "Stenographer's Notes of Lectures by Miss Elizabeth F. Briscoe . . . April 21, 1913," Subject File: Lectures, Box 84, NCF.

4. Ibid. The sanitary drinking cup was an individual, usually disposable cup, which replaced the communal cup or jug shared by all.

5. Gertrude Beeks to Stanley McCormick, December 2, 1902, F. A. Flather File, Subject File 3B, Box 30, NFM.

6. Gertrude Beeks to E. A. S. Clarke, June 27, 1903, Box 72, NCF.

7. Diana Hirschler, "The Social Secretary at Work," *Social Service* (July 1904), Folder: American Institute of Social Service, Box 76, NCF.

8. National Civic Federation, *Conference on Welfare Work*, 112–14; Sarah S. Chaffin to Gertrude Beeks, June 28, 1905, Box 72, NCF.

9. The Ford Motor Company's $5.00-per-day wage seemed to be a unique exception to the general neglect of wages. However, Ford offered $5.00 per day as a wage supplement and labeled it "profit-sharing," rather than giving it to workers as the rightful return for their labor. The restrictive eligibility requirements, and extreme measures used by the Ford Company to enforce the $5.00-per-day wage, turned this into a more successful public relations strategy than a promise of real economic security. Only a small percentage of Ford workers ever "earned" $5.00 per day. Daniel M. G. Raff, "Ford Welfare Capitalism in its Economic Context," in Jacoby, *Masters to Managers*.

10. "Comments on Mr. Hathaway's Report by the President," 2–3, 5, 10, Case 48, PCC. Although most firms measured the costs of welfare work as a percentage of their labor costs, like Loring, they separated welfare expenditures from their regular calculations of labor costs.

11. Kathleen McCarthy, in *Noblesse Oblige*, argues that by the end of the nineteenth century, wealthy American men had redefined noblesse oblige to mean promotion of social betterment through financial support of institutions serving the needy rather than through direct personal contact with the needy. This was not understood as a form of paternalism or something that the wealthy *should do*, according to McCarthy, but rather as an imperative or something the wealthy *must do* to prevent the poor from rising up against them. Corporate sponsorship of welfare work was consistent with this new role for wealthy American men.

12. Rotundo, *American Manhood*; Kwolek-Folland, *Engendering Business*.

13. Wyllie, *The Self-Made Man in America*, 43.

14. John D. Rockefeller, "Opportunity in America," *Cosmopolitan* 43 (1907): 369, quoted in ibid., 51.

15. Ibid., 52, emphasis added.

16. Folsom, *Executive Decision Making*, 7.

17. Taussig and Joslyn, *American Business Leaders*, 149.

18. Although such real-life experiences shaped employers' construction of their fatherly role, this did reflect a particularist interpretation of business opportunities. While Taussig and Joslyn documented mobility between their respon-

dents' grandfathers and fathers, for example, they found significantly less mobility between fathers and the current generation of business leaders. They concluded that the leading business class was becoming more and more closed over time. Taussig and Joslyn, *American Business Leaders*, 88, 137, 234–35.

19. "Comments on Mr. Hathaway's Report by the President," 5, Case 48, PCC.

20. This does not deny the public relations motive behind financial benefit plans, which many scholars have noted; however, the inordinate amount of time that corporate officers and boards of directors devoted to developing and revising these plans suggests that they actually believed that they could persuade their employees to accept this kind of exchange.

21. Gertrude Beeks, "Report of 1901 Factory Tour," Box 27, Subject File 3B, NFM; U.S. Bureau of Labor Statistics, Bulletin 250, 8–9, 120.

22. Orrin Goan to Gertrude Beeks, May 3, 1905, Box 73, NCF.

23. "Report to the Plymouth Cordage Company by H. K. Hathaway," January 6, 1912 and "Comments on Mr. Hathaway's Report by the President," February 7, 1912, Case 48, PCC.

24. Gertrude Beeks to Stanley McCormick, December 2, 1902, F. A. Flather 1902 File, International Harvester Company, Box 30, Subject File 3B, NFM.

25. "Report on Conditions of Employees and Recommendations for Improvements by Employer's Welfare Department, NCF," 40, Box 79, NCF.

26. John Wanamaker to Gertrude Beeks, April 8, 1904, Box 72, NCF.

27. S. M. Darling to Gertrude Beeks, November 12, 1903, and April 9, 1904, S. M. Darling to Cyrus McCormick Jr., March 22, 1904, Box 72; and Cyrus McCormick to Beeks, March 20, 1905, Box 73, NCF.

28. Cyrus McCormick Jr. to Gertrude Beeks, March 20, 1905, and Mary Goss to Beeks, April 26, 1907, Box 73, NCF.

29. G. L. Rice to John G. Wood, June 4, 1906, Box 74; Gertrude Beeks to Catherine Brannick, October 12, 1906, Box 72, NCF.

30. Catherine Brannick to Gertrude Beeks, October 18, 1906, Box 72, NCF.

31. "Report on Conditions of Employees and Recommendations for Improvements . . .," Folder: Greenhut, Box 79, NCF.

32. Lee K. Frankel, "Corporate Welfare Work," Folder: Lee K. Frankel #2, Papers and Speeches, MLICA.

33. Frank Bolles to Getrude Beeks, December 29, 1908, Box 74; and "Welfare Managers: Men," Box 88, NCF.

34. Gertrude Beeks to Stanley McCormick, December 2, 1902, F. A. Flather File, Box 30, Subject File 3B, NFM; C. U. Carpenter to Beeks, November 16, 1908, Box 73, NCF.

35. "Informal Talk to Extension Department: American Committee Y.W.C.A. . . . August 27, 1902," Subject File: Easley, Gertrude Beeks—early notes and speeches, Box 85, NCF.

CHAPTER SIX

1. H. Belfield & Company to Ralph Easley, October 22, 1902, Box 72, NCF. Gerald Zahavi finds similarly different notions of reciprocity expressed by work-

ers and owners at the Endicott-Johnson Company. Zahavi, *Workers, Managers, and Welfare Capitalism*, ch. 4.

2. Peiss, *Cheap Amusements*, 25–26, 53; Meyerowitz, *Women Adrift*, ch. 5.

3. Quoted in Rosenzweig, *Eight Hours for What We Will*, 60.

4. Quoted in Lee, *Business Ethics*, 145.

5. Gertrude Beeks, "Report of 1901 Factory Tour," 28–29, Subject File 3B, Box 27, NFM. Although Daniel Nelson has demonstrated that workers struck in 1901 to protest management's anti-unionism, not welfare work, it is probable that their anger was aggravated by this sense that the company was "rolling in money." Nelson, "The New Factory System and the Unions," 163–78.

6. "A Faithful Servant" to George Eastman, February 24, 1920, Box 32, Correspondence, George Eastman Papers, University of Rochester. Emphasis in original.

7. *National Civic Federation Review* (September–October 1905): 14. Workers at the Endicott-Johnson Corporation expressed similar sentiments; they accepted welfare work because they felt that they had earned it and were receiving only what they were owed. Zahavi, *Workers, Managers, and Welfare Capitalism*, 106.

8. Williams, *What's on the Worker's Mind*, 281.

9. Montgomery, *The Fall of the House of Labor*; Baron, *Work Engendered*; Williams, *What's on the Worker's Mind*, 47–48.

10. William, *What's on the Worker's Mind*, 13–21, 62.

11. Mary Blewett, "Manhood and the Market: The Politics of Gender and Class among the Textile Workers of Fall River, Massachusetts, 1870–1880," in Baron, *Work Engendered*, 92–113.

12. Quoted in Brandes, *American Welfare Capitalism*, 138.

13. "Wage Bonus Plan, Merit Pay . . . 1910–1923," Box 4, Accession 1615, Series II, Part 2, DPC.

14. "Employee Relations Department: Management Deliberations—Bonus Plan 1902–1923," and "Wage Bonus Plan, Merit Pay . . . 1910–1923," Box 4, Accession 1615, Series II, Part 2, DPC.

15. "Wage Bonus Plan, Merit Pay . . . 1910–1923," Box 4, Accession 1615, Series II, Part 2, DPC.

16. Ozanne, *A Century of Labor-Management Relations at McCormick and International Harvester*, 36–39, 86–92. Much of the problem at International Harvester, as at other firms, stemmed from the fact that management continued repressive labor practices alongside the more gentle methods of the welfare system. Under these circumstances, workers were not inclined to believe that reciprocity could be mutually beneficial.

17. "Stenographer's Notes of Lectures by Miss Elizabeth Briscoe . . . April 21, 1913," 12, Subject Files: Lecture, Box 84, NCF; Brandes, *American Welfare Capitalism*, 138–9.

18. Peiss, *Cheap Amusements*, 164.

19. Meyerowitz, *Women Adrift*.

20. Beeks, "Report of 1901 Factory Tour," 18, Box 27, Subject File 3B, NFM; *National Civic Federation Review* (March–April 1906): 9.

21. National Civic Federation, *Conference on Welfare Work*, 107, 161–63; *National Civic Federation Review* (December 1, 1913): 18; Elizabeth Briscoe to

Gertrude Beeks April 12, 1907, and Elizabeth Briscoe to J. H. Bragdon & Co., November 26, 1907, Bancroft and Sons Collection, Hagley Museum and Library; "Report of W. E. C. Nazro, August 1, 1912–August 1, 1913," Case 48, and "Summary of History and Present Status of Welfare Work," Folder: Welfare—Mr. Marshall's Reports early 1920s, Case 47, PCC; "The Welfare Work of the Metropolitan Life Insurance Company: Reports for 1914," 24, Folder: V.F. Welfare Division General, 1909–1949, MLICA.

22. Beeks, "Report of 1901 Factory Tour," Subject File 3B, Box 27, NFM.

23. Ibid.

24. *National Civic Federation Review* (December 1, 1913): 18.

25. Gertrude Beeks to F. A. Flather, December 2, 1902, File: F. A. Flather, 1902, File 3B, Box 30, NFM.

26. "Stenographer's Notes of Lectures by Miss Elizabeth F. Briscoe . . . April 21, 1913," 4, Subject Files: Lectures, Box 84, NCF.

27. Beeks, "Report of 1901 Factory Tour," 12, Subject File 3B, Box 27, NFM.

28. National Civic Federation, *Conference on Welfare Work*, 185–97.

29. "Summary: History and Present Status of Welfare Work," Folder: Welfare—Mr. Marshall's Reports, early 1920s, Case 47, PCC.

30. Quoted in Shuey, *Factory People and Their Employers*, 197.

31. "Report by Miss Van deCarr," ca. 1905, Box 78, NCF; "Summary: History and Present Status of Welfare Work," Folder: Welfare—Mr. Marshall's Reports, early 1920s, Case 47, PCC.

32. Williams, *What's on the Worker's Mind*, 66.

33. Ibid., 68–69, 117.

34. Ibid., 145.

35. Cleveland Hardware Company to Ralph Easley, April 17, 1901, Box 72, NCF. See Brandes, *American Welfare Capitalism*, 138, for a list of other welfare companies that experienced strikes.

36. "Welfare Work May Conquer Great Labor Problems," *New York Times*, November 17, 1912. Emphasis added.

37. Nelson, *Managers and Workers*, ch. 2. Nelson notes that building technology allowed for improvements such as better ventilation and more window space long before they became a standard part of new building design in the 1910s. Although he attributes these developments to both technological capabilities and managerial initiative, he does so without giving credit to the welfare ideal that lay behind those managerial initiatives.

CHAPTER SEVEN

1. Gertrude Beeks to Edward A. Filene, March 23, 1904, Folder: Filene Store, Box 78, NCF.

2. "Stenographic Report of Proceedings of Conference of Welfare Workers . . . Jan., 11, 1911," Box 83, NCF; "Remarks of William R. Willcox . . . at Formal Opening . . . New York University . . . February 10, 1913," Box 85, NCF; *National Civic Federation Review* (March 1914 and May 1914); Green, *The National Civic Federation and the American Labor Movement*, 270.

3. Gilson, *What's Past is Prologue*, 122, 290.

4. American firms continued to use the language of "family" to describe relations with both their employees and their customers. However, in the 1920s and beyond, the public relations functions of this language, which had co-existed with its labor relations functions, came to be the sole reason for its use.

5. Since the effort here is to explore employer initiatives, I will use the employers' preferred term of "employee representation" rather than "company unionism."

6. Mintz, *Domestic Revolutions*; Sheila Rothman, *Woman's Proper Place*.

7. Meyerowitz, *Women Adrift*. Meyerowitz carefully distinguishes between the real lives of workingwomen and the ways in which popular imagery and reformers' perceptions of those women changed over time.

8. U.S. Bureau of the Census, *Women in Gainful Occupations, 1870–1920*, 19.

9. For discussions of the adjustments made in offices as a result of the increased employment of women, see Aron, *Ladies and Gentlemen of the Civil Service*; Fine, *The Souls of the Skyscraper*; Kwolek-Folland, *Engendering Business*.

10. "The Use of Research in Employment Stabilization" (New York: Metropolitan Life Insurance Co., 1927), 13, MLICA. Hundreds of firms established or enhanced their Americanization programs during the World War I.

11. Chandler, *Strategy and Structure*, 286–87. Chandler refers specifically to the difficulty of assigning personnel responsibilities (which integrated general planning with on-site activities) within the line and staff structure (which required a clear separation of general planning and plant-level activity).

12. Gerard Swope had also been a settlement worker at Hull House in the 1890s. While that experience shaped his long-term commitment to employee welfare, it is highly unlikely that it exposed him to any examples of employer-employee intimacy.

13. Chandler, *The Visible Hand*, 438–39.

14. The ties to corporate welfare work were sometimes quite explicit. C. W. Price, who headed the first government-employer safety council in Wisconsin, gained his expertise in factory safety as director of welfare work at International Harvester.

15. Among the attributes of a profession are the autonomy of the professional, and his or her claim to possess expertise not possessed by nonprofessionals. Recent scholarship reveals that those in feminized professions had much less autonomy than those in male professions, and that they shared their specialized knowledge with their clients much more than those in male professions.

16. Kohn, "The Significance of the Professional Ideal," 3.

17. *National Civic Federation Review* (July 15, 1913); Gertrude Beeks to Ralph Easley, December 27, 1906, Box 72; H. D. W. English to Beeks, June 5, 1914, Box 75, NCF; Benson, *Counter Cultures*, 135–36. The distance between these two groups of reformers widened further after 1910 as social work moved in the direction of individual case work.

18. Gertrude Beeks to Matae B. Cleveland, n.d., Box 72, NCF. Although Jane Addams supported the McCormick's decision to hire Beeks as a welfare worker, Beeks considered Addams and the Hull House residents as too radical, and thus the wrong kind of settlement workers.

19. For examples of the ways in which the network among public sector re-

formers sustained reform initiatives in the face of opposition by business, government, and others, see Muncy, *Creating a Female Dominion in American Reform*, and Ware, *Beyond Suffrage*.

20. Gertrude Beeks to Dexter Kimball, March 29, 1904, Box 73, NCF.

21. National Civic Federation, *Conference on Welfare Work*, 53–54, 87ff.

22. Gertrude Beeks to Miss Demarest, September 14, 1904, Box 72, NCF.

23. Gertrude Beeks to Dexter Kimball, March 29, 1904, Box 73, NCF.

24. *Social Service* (July 1904), Folder: American Institute of Social Service, Box 76, NCF.

25. After 1904, the AISS limited its efforts in this area to safety work. Kryder, "Humanizing the Industrial Workplace," 42.

26. See, for example, Gertrude Beeks to Charles H. Hubbard, May 14, 1906, Subject Files, Box 86; L. H. Brittin to Beeks, February 10, 1911, Folder: Clothescraft Shops, Box 77; Mrs. Edward S. Ogden to Beeks, October 3, 1913, Folder: DuPont, Box 78. The Welfare Department's correspondence fills twenty boxes in the NCF Collection.

27. Comstock, "A Woman of Achievement," 448.

28. Ibid. The previous year, Beeks wrote Metropolitan Life president Haley Fiske to *thank him* for the "beautiful lunch rooms you have installed." After expressing her approval of the furnishings and service, Beeks concluded by chastising Fiske for providing free meals in these model lunchrooms. Gertrude Beeks to Fiske, August 3, 1912, Box 80, NCF.

29. N. V. Moore to Gertrude Beeks, April 29, 1904, Folder: National Cash Register, Box 80, NCF.

30. S. M. Darling to Graham Taylor, March 16, 1905, Box 72, NCF.

31. S. M. Darling to Professor Graham Taylor, March 16, 1905, Box 72; Gertrude Beeks to Charles Hubbard, June 23, 1906, Box 72; Winifred Lyford to Secretary, Welfare Dept., August 26, 1909, Box 88, NCF.

32. Robert C. Auld to Gertrude Beeks, June 17 and July 7, 1913, and Secretary to Gertrude Beeks to Robert C. Auld, July 9, 1913, Box 72, NCF.

33. Beeks's efforts to establish a formal training course for welfare workers began as early as 1904 when she attempted to interest Harvard University in including welfare theory in their curriculum. By 1907, she had written her own course on welfare work and begun searching for a university to sponsor the class. Although she lectured sporadically to students of social work at schools of philanthropy around the East and Midwest, Beeks wanted a course and students devoted specifically to her understanding of corporate welfare work. Negotiations with Columbia University in 1909 probably broke down because of Beeks's insistence on controlling the content of the course. The 1913 and 1914 courses at New York University were the fruition of this decade-long effort.

34. M. W. Alexander to Gertrude Beeks, January 9, 1911, Box 72, NCF.

35. John Soby to Gertrude Beeks, May 19, 1914; Gertrude Beeks to John Soby, May 1914, Box 72, NCF. Beeks agreed to provide a list of the graduates of the recent New York University welfare class when she found the time to copy it. Although she lived in New York City, she made no offers to assist Soby's efforts. They apparently never got off the ground.

36. Anna Sears to Gertrude Beeks, July 29, 1909, and Beeks to Anna Sears, July 30, 1909, Box 85, NCF.

37. Gertrude Beeks to Lucia B. Chapman, April 15, 1909, Box 72, NCF.

38. The following discussion draws heavily from Zerzan, "Understanding the Anti-Radicalism of the National Civic Federation," as well as from my own reading of the *National Civic Federation Review*.

39. *National Civic Federation Review* (April 10, 1919): 4–5, 16–18.

40. Lemons, *The Woman Citizen*, 214–15; Cott, *The Grounding of Modern Feminism*, 242, 249–50. The Spider Web Chart, circulated first by the Chemical Warfare Division of the War Department and later by an array of conservative groups, purported to show that prominent female reformers and their organizations were part of a vast socialist network working toward the overthrow of capitalism and democracy. Although the War Department later disassociated itself from the Chart, it had a chilling effect on public support for progressive reform.

41. Lemons, *The Woman Citizen*, 97–98; Ralph Easley to Helen Harmon-Brown, January 31, 1912, Box 73; Helen Varick Boswell to Gertrude Beeks, May 31, 1906, Box 83, NCF. This latter citation documents Beeks's strategy to combat those within the General Federation of Women's Club who had submitted a resolution calling for women's suffrage.

42. Gertrude Beeks married Ralph Easley, director of the NCF, in 1917, which quite likely accounts for some of the decline in her public role. Other prominent welfare managers also faded from the scene by 1920: W. C. Nazro left the Plymouth Cordage Company around 1919, Elizabeth Briscoe of Bancroft and Sons died the same year, and Diana Hirschler left Filene's in 1912 to join the vocational education movement.

43. Jacoby, *Employing Bureaucracy*, ch. 4.

44. Similar to welfare work, these new methods were known by a variety of terms: personnel management, employment management, and, later, industrial relations.

45. Benge, *Standard Practice in Personnel Work*, 8.

46. Ching, *Review and Reflection*, 153–54.

47. Rachel Lewis, "Personnel Work in a Factory." Turnover, which had been a motivating concern of welfare advocates since the late nineteenth century, became an overriding concern of the personnel management movement.

48. Benge, *Standard Practice in Personnel Work*, 98.

49. As with their adoption of the welfare system, employers did not abandon all other labor relations strategies when they adopted the new system of personnel management. They continued to rely on the speed-up, spying, blacklisting, and a variety of other methods to spur productivity and ensure labor peace.

50. U.S. Bureau of Labor Statistics, *Proceedings of the Employment Managers' Conference*, 22.

51. Robert C. Clothier, "The Function of the Employment Department," reprinted in Bloomfield, *Employment Management: Selected Articles*, 158–65; Benge, *Standard Practice in Personnel Work*, chs. 10–11.

52. In fact, they began promoting welfare work through a new vehicle—the employee manual. The employee manual presented welfare work as the em-

ployer's payment in exchange for the employee's loyal and efficient labor (Employee Pamphlets Collection, Baker Library).

53. U.S. Bureau of Labor Statistics, *Health and Recreation Activities in Industrial Establishments.* The scope of this study was more limited than the earlier 1916 report. Thus, it is not possible to make comparisons in certain areas, such as factory safety, locker rooms, or restrooms. The bureau did not survey the same firms for the two reports, although there was some overlap. Researchers, however, felt that the firms that responded were similar enough to make comparisons between the two periods.

54. Jacoby, *Employing Bureaucracy*, 199.

55. Benson, *Counter Cultures*, 52, 146.

56. Personnel management and employee representation were not mutually exclusive. Both the National Industrial Conference Board and the secretive Special Conference Committee recommended that their members institute both these strategies.

57. Dozens of trade associations held membership in the NICB; thousands of industrial firms participated in the NICB through their membership in these trade associations. National Industrial Conference Board, *A Works Council Manual*, 3.

58. Typical of the sham nature of these industrial democracies, Filene's new welfare secretary and other management personnel dominated the Filene's Cooperative Association. The welfare secretary, Diana Hirschler, actually managed these programs.

59. "Sage Foundation Report Calls Rockefeller Employes' Representation Plan Only Partial Success," January 26, 1925, Folder 134A, Box 16, Business Interests Series-CFI, Record Group OMR, Rockefeller Family Collection, Rockefeller Archive Center.

60. Gilson, *What's Past is Prologue*, 107; "Summary of Accomplishments of Works Committee," Case 1, Henry S. Dennison Papers, Baker Library; A. H. Lichty to Harold McCormick, March 23, 1920, Folder 126, Box 15, Industrial Questions Series, Record Group OMR, Rockefeller Family Collection, Rockefeller Archive Center.

61. The foregoing discussion draws a sharp dividing line between the welfare system and personnel management in an effort to explicate the significant differences between them. In real practice, firms rarely moved from one system to the other in a clear, well-defined transition. Rather, the continuation of welfare activities often masked a gradual and uneven transition.

62. Jacoby, *Employing Bureaucracy*, 137, 189; Berkowitz and McQuaid, *Creating the Welfare State*, 55.

63. Firms with large female workforces generally did not adopt employee representation plans. Employers assumed that these plans demanded a type of maturity and qualities of citizenship that women did not possess. At the same time, women's lower rates of trade union membership meant that employers of women felt less need to turn to this anti-union strategy. Slichter, "The Current Labor Policies of American Industries," 397; Nelson, *Workers and Managers*, 161–2; Derber, *The American Idea of Industrial Democracy*, 211, 214, 260.

64. This was part of the larger decline in Progressive Era maternalist movements. Ladd-Taylor, *Mother-Work.*

65. Taylor Society members Morris Cooke and Mary Van Kleeck wrote the Ordnance Department directive that established the right of employees to some form of collective bargaining, as well as requiring employers to provide fair wages and decent working conditions. Greenwald, *Women, War and Work.*

66. Fisher's interest in personnel management grew out of his involvement in the vocational guidance movement. He was particularly interested in developing systems of internal promotion for employees, which he believed would reduce labor turnover. Jacoby, *Employing Bureaucracy*, ch. 4.

67. Twenty-four men completed this first course. Enrollment was strictly limited to pupils sent by firms engaged in war production—thirteen representing shipyards, arsenals, and other government departments, and eleven from private companies. Quote is from Jacoby, *Employing Bureaucracy*, 145; Nelson, *Managers and Workers*, 154; U.S. Bureau of Labor Statistics *Proceedings of the Employment Managers' Conference*, 19–27.

68. Jacoby, *Employing Bureaucracy*, 141–44; Nelson, *Managers and Workers*, 154.

69. U.S. Bureau of Labor Statistics, *Proceedings of the Employment Managers' Conference*, 8. The success of the movement that was organized at the Rochester convention is attested by the dramatic growth of the National Association of Employment Managers' membership in the next few years. The 600 delegates at the 1918 convention grew to 2,000 in 1919 and rose to 5,000 in 1920. By that time, the organization had established a journal, *Personnel*, and employment management associations were meeting in over fifty cities.

70. Jacoby, *Employing Bureaucracy*, 146.

71. U.S. Bureau of Labor Statistics, *Proceedings of the Employment Managers' Conference*, 71–72.

72. Ibid., 21.

73. Gilson, *What's Past is Prologue*, 168; Miller and Coghill, "Sex and the Personnel Manager."

74. The wartime draft of young men may have accentuated the maturity and experience of the men who enrolled in these courses.

75. U.S. Bureau of Labor Statistics, *Proceedings of the Employment Managers' Conference*, 228–49. The fact that a number of welfare workers attended the conference may be a sign that they were interested in adapting their own work to this emerging field and that their own efforts to systematize welfare work was fully compatible with the kind of systematization promoted by the advocates of personnel management.

76. Gilson, *What's Past is Prologue*, ch. 15.

77. Bloomfield, *Employment Management*, 137–47.

78. Miller and Coghill, *The Historical Sources of Personnel Work.*

79. Benge, *Standard Practice in Personnel Work*, 87.

80. Ibid.; Meyer Bloomfield, "Aims of the New Science: The New Profession of Handling Men," in Bloomfield, *Employment Management*, 35–36.

81. Marshall, "Incentives and Output," 734.

82. Mark Jones to Mary Gilson, April 12, 1920; Gilson to Jones, April 19, 1920; Jones to Gilson, April 27, 1920, Folder: General Letters 1920–1929, Box 4, Mary Barnett Gilson Papers, Wellesley College Archives.

83. It was at this convention that L. C. Marshall claimed that the duties of the personnel manager called for a "full-grown man."

84. See Jacoby, *Employing Bureaucracy*, 180–86, for an account of employer strategies to control the liberal wing of this movement, which was most committed to professionalizing personnel management.

85. The concurrent masculinization of salesmanship certainly added legitimacy to claims that personnel management was a manly endeavor. Salesmen were engaged in a parallel gendering process, asserting that certain characteristics, previously considered feminine but now associated with sales, were in fact, characteristics of virile and manly men.

86. Charles Carpenter, director of the nation's first labor department at the National Cash Register Company, had previously been a plant superintendent at NCR. Cyrus Ching moved into labor relations from a supervisorial position with the Boston Elevated. When the DuPont Company decided to include labor relations as a formal position within its managerial hierarchy, it chose a former plant engineer and production superintendent, William Foster, as director of the new Service Department.

87. Fine, *Souls of the Skyscraper*; DeVault, *Sons and Daughters of Labor*; Kwolek-Folland, *Engendering Business*, 4, 30.

88. Adams, *Women Professional Workers*, 18–19.

89. Hatcher, *Occupations for Women*.

90. Armstrong, "A Woman in Wall Street"; Armstrong, "Uneasy Business"; Armstrong, "Fear in Business Life"; Armstrong to George Eastman, August 4, 1919, and Manager Industrial Relations to George Eastman, December 13, 1919, Box 32, George Eastman Papers; Lemons, *The Woman Citizen*, 232.

91. Adams, *Women Professional Workers*, 196–97, 243; *Independent Woman*, a publication of the National Federation of Professional and Business Women, July 1920, January 1921, February 1921.

CONCLUSION

1. Melosh, *"The Physician's Hand"*; Muncy, *Creating a Female Dominion in American Reform*; Lubove, *The Professional Altruist*; Glazer and Slater, *Unequal Colleagues*; Trolander, *Professionalism and Social Change*; Garrison, "The Tender Technicians."

2. When universities began offering courses in social work, for example, male academics gravitated to the more theoretical side of this field, which they split off as sociology. Women found their opportunities limited to the practical side of case work. Muncy, *Creating a Female Dominion in American Reform*; Lubove, *The Professional Altruist*.

3. Jacoby, *Employing Bureaucracy*. Jacoby documents the struggles between liberals within the personnel management movement who sought to establish them-

selves as independent professionals and conservatives who represented employer interests in limiting personnel managers to dependent staff positions.

4. Jacoby, *Employing Bureaucracy*, ch. 4.

5. Gilson, *What's Past is Prologue*, 177ff.

6. Gilson, *What's Past is Prologue*, 215–16. Harvard also informed Gilson that women were not permitted in the library after 6:00 P.M.; the library closed at 10:00 P.M. Gilson lost her job at Joseph Feiss and Company following a conflict within the family that resulted in Richard Feiss's ouster from the firm. Apparently, other family members were not willing to support the elaborate labor relations program that Richard Feiss and Mary Gilson had created.

7. Gilson, *What's Past is Prologue*, 283.

8. Gilson's personal achievements owed much to the strong network of reformers who supported her throughout her varied career. Unlike other women in welfare work, Gilson maintained close associations with leading reformers, many of them women.

9. Fones-Wolf, "Industrial Recreation, the Second World War, and the Revival of Welfare Capitalism."

BIBLIOGRAPHY

MANUSCRIPT COLLECTIONS

Baker Library, Harvard University, Cambridge, Mass.
  Henry S. Dennison Papers
  Employee Pamphlets Collection
  Employer Pamphlets Collection
  A. Lincoln Filene Papers
  Plymouth Cordage Company Papers
Hagley Museum and Library, Wilmington, Del.
  Joseph Bancroft and Sons Company Collection
  E. I. duPont de Nemours and Company Papers
  Pierre S. DuPont Papers
  Special Conference Committee Papers
  Frank Tallman Papers
Metropolitan Life Insurance Company Archives, New York, N.Y.
  Metropolitan Life Insurance Company Papers
New York Public Library, New York, N.Y.
  National Civic Federation Collection
Rockefeller Archive Center, Sleepy Hollow, N.Y.
  Rockefeller Family Papers
  Russell Sage Foundation Papers
State Historical Society of Wisconsin, Madison
  Nettie Fowler McCormick Papers
Wellesley College Archives, Wellesley, Mass.
  Mary Barnett Gilson Papers

BOOKS

Adams, Elizabeth Kemper. *Women Professional Workers: A Study Made for the Women's Educational and Industrial Union.* New York: The Chautauqua Press, 1921.

Alberts, Robert C. *The Good Provider: H. J. Heinz and His 57 Varieties.* Boston: Houghton Mifflin Company, 1973.

Aron, Cindy Sondik. *Ladies and Gentlemen of the Civil Service: Middle-Class Workers in Victorian America.* New York: Oxford University Press, 1987.

Baron, Ava, ed. *Work Engendered: Toward a New History of American Labor.* Ithaca: Cornell University Press, 1991.

Bender, Thomas. *Community and Social Change in America.* New Brunswick: Rutgers University Press, 1978.

Bendix, Reinhard. *Work and Authority in Industry.* Berkeley: University of California Press, 1956, 1974.

Benge, Eugene J. *Standard Practice in Personnel Work.* New York: The H. W. Wilson Company, 1920.

Benson, Susan Porter. *Counter Cultures: Saleswomen, Managers, and Customers in American Department Stores, 1890–1940.* Urbana: University of Illinois Press, 1986.

Berkowitz, Edward, and Kim McQuaid. *Creating the Welfare State.* New York: Praeger Publishers, 1980.

Bernstein, Irving. *The Lean Years: A History of the American Worker, 1920–1933.* Baltimore: Penguin Books, 1960.

Bloomfield, Daniel, ed. *Employment Management: Selected Articles.* New York: H. W. Wilson Company, 1919.

Boettiger, Louis A. *Employee Welfare Work.* New York: The Ronald Press Company, 1923.

Bonnett, Clarence E. *History of Employers' Associations in the United States.* New York: Vantage Press, 1956.

Brandes, Stuart D. *American Welfare Capitalism, 1880–1940.* Chicago: University of Chicago Press, 1970.

Braverman, Harry. *Labor and Monopoly Capital.* New York: Monthly Review Press, 1974.

Brecher, Jeremy. *Strike!.* San Francisco: Straight Arrow Books: 1972.

Breckinridge, Sophonisba. *Women in the Twentieth Century.* New York: Arno Pres, 1933.

Brody, David. *Steelworkers in America: The Nonunion Era.* New York: Harper & Row Publishers, 1960.

———. *Workers in Industrial America.* New York: Oxford University Press, 1980.

Carnes, Mark C. *Secret Ritual and Manhood in Victorian America.* New Haven: Yale University Press, 1989.

Carnes, Mark C., and Clyde Griffen, eds. *Meanings for Manhood.* Chicago: University of Chicago Press, 1990.

Carson, Mina. *Settlement Folk: Social Thought and the American Settlement Movement, 1885–1930.* Chicago: University of Chicago Press, 1990.

Chandler, Alfred D. *Strategy and Structure: Chapters in the History of the American Industrial Enterprise.* Cambridge: The M.I.T. Press, 1962.

———. *The Visible Hand: The Managerial Revolution in American Business.* Cambridge: Harvard University Press, 1977.

Ching, Cyrus S. *Review and Reflection: A Half-Century of Labor Relations.* New York: B. C. Forbes and Sons Publishing Company, 1953.

Clark, Neil M. *Common Sense in Labor Management.* New York: Harper & Brothers Publishers, 1919.

Cohen, Lizabeth. *Making a New Deal: Industrial Workers in Chicago, 1919–1939.* Cambridge: Cambridge University Press, 1990.

Common, John R. *Industrial Goodwill.* London: McGraw-Hill Book Co., 1919.

Cott, Nancy. *The Grounding of Modern Feminism.* New Haven: Yale University Press, 1987.

Crowther, Samuel. *John H. Patterson: Pioneer in Industrial Welfare.* New York: Doubleday, Page & Company, 1923.

Curtis, Susan. *A Consuming Faith: The Social Gospel and Modern American Culture.* Baltimore: Johns Hopkins University Press, 1991.

Davies, Margery. *Woman's Place is at the Typewriter: Office Work and Office Workers, 1870–1930.* Philadelphia: Temple University Press, 1982.

Derber, Milton. *The American Idea of Industrial Democracy, 1865–1965.* Urbana: University of Illinois Press, 1970.

DeVault, Ileen A. *Sons and Daughters of Labor: Class and Clerical Work in Turn-of-the-Century Pittsburgh.* Ithaca: Cornell University Press, 1990.

Dienstag, Eleanor Foa. *In Good Company: 125 Years at the Heinz Table.* New York: Warner Books, 1994.

Dubbert, Joe L. *A Man's Place: Masculinity in Transition.* Englewood Cliffs, New Jersey: Prentice-Hall, 1979.

Dublin, Thomas. *Women at Work: The Transformation of Work and Community in Lowell, Massachusetts, 1826–1860.* New York: Columbia University Press, 1979.

Edsforth, Ronald. *Class Conflict and Cultural Consensus: The Making of a Mass Consumer Society in Flint, Michigan.* New Brunswick: Rutgers University Press, 1987.

An Epoch in Insurance: A Third of a Century of Achievement. New York: Metropolitan Life Insurance Company, 1924.

Fass, Paula S. *The Damned and the Beautiful.* New York: Oxford University Press, 1977.

Filene, Edward A. *The Way Out: A Forecast of Coming Changes in American Business and Industry.* New York: Doubleday, Page & Company, 1925.

Filene, Peter G. *Him/Her/Self: Sex Roles in Modern America.* New York: Harcourt, Brace, Jovanovich, 1974.

Filing as a Profession for Women. New York: Library Bureau, 1919.

Fine, Lisa M. *The Souls of the Skyscraper: Female Clerical Workers in Chicago, 1870–1930.* Philadelphia: Temple University Press, 1990.

Foerster, Robert F., and Else H. Dietel. *Employee Stock Ownership in the United States.* Princeton: Princeton University Press, 1927.

Folsom, Marion B. *Executive Decision Making: Observations and Experience in Business and Government.* New York: McGraw-Hill Book Co., 1962.

Fox, Richard Wightman, and T. J. Jackson Lears. *The Culture of Consumption.* New York: Pantheon Books, 1983.

Frankel, Lee K., and Alexander Fleisher. *The Human Factor in Industry.* New York: The Macmillan Company, 1920.

Gilson, Mary Barnett. *What's Past is Prologue.* New York: Harper & Brothers, 1940.

Gitelman, H. M. *Legacy of the Ludlow Massacre: A Chapter in American Industrial Relations.*

Gladden, Washington. *Working People and Their Employers.* Boston: Lockwood, Brooks, and Company, 1876. Reprint. New York: Arno and the New York Times, 1969.

Glazer, Penina Migdal, and Miriam Slater. *Unequal Colleagues: The Entrance of Women into the Professions, 1890–1940.* New Brunswick: Rutgers University Press, 1987.

Glenn, John M. Brandt, Andrew Lillian, and F. Emerson. *Russell Sage Foundation, 1907–1946.* New York: Russell Sage Foundation, 1947.

Gordon, David M., Richard Edwards, and Michael Reich. *Segmented Work, Divided Workers: The Historical Transformation of Labor in the United States* Cambridge: Cambridge University Press, 1982.

Gordon, Linda. *Pitied But Not Entitled: Single Mothers and the History of Welfare.* New York: The Free Press, 1994.

Gordon, Michael, ed. *The American Family in Social-Historical Perspective.* New York: St. Martin's Press, 1973.

Green, Marguerite. *The National Civic Federation and the American Labor Movement, 1900–1925.* Westport, Conn.: Greenwood Press, 1956.

Greenwald, Maurine Weiner. *Women, War, and Work: The Impact of World War I on Women Workers in the United States.* Westport, Conn.: Greenwood Press, 1980.

Grossman, James R. *Land of Hope: Chicago, Black Southerners, and the Great Migration.* Chicago: University of Chicago Press, 1989.

Haber, Samuel. *Efficiency and Uplift: Scientific Management in the Progressive Era, 1890–1920.* Chicago: University of Chicago Press, 1964.

Hartness, James. *The Human Factor in Works Management.* New York: McGraw-Hill, 1913. Reprint. Easton: Hive Publishing Company, 1974.

Hatcher, O. Latham. *Occupations for Women.* Atlanta: Southern Woman's Educational Alliance, 1927.

Hawley, Ellis W. *The Great War and the Search for a Modern Order.* New York: St. Martin's Press, 1979.

Hayes, E. P., and Charlotte Heath. *History of the Dennison Manufacturing Company.* Cambridge: Harvard University Press, 1929.

Heermance, Edgar L. *The Ethics of Business: A Study of Current Standards.* New York: Harper & Brothers Publishers, 1926.

Henderschott, R. C., and F. E. Weakly. *The Employment Department and Employee Relations.* Chicago: LaSalle Extension University, 1918.

Henderson, Charles Richmond. *Citizens in Industry.* New York: D. Appleton and Co., 1915.

Hicks, Clarence. *My Life in Industrial Relations: Fifty Years in the Growth of a Profession.* New York: Harper & Brothers Publishers, 1941.

Higham, John. *Strangers in the Land: Patterns of American Nativism, 1860–1925.* New Brunswick: Rutgers University Press, 1988.

Hounshell, David A. *From the American System to Mass Production, 1800–1932.* Baltimore: The Johns Hopkins University Press, 1984.

Houser, J. David. *What the Employer Thinks: Executives' Attitudes Toward Employees*. Cambridge: Harvard University Press, 1927.

Jacoby, Sanford. *Employing Bureaucracy: Managers, Unions, and the Transformation of Work in American Industry, 1900–1945*. New York: Columbia University Press, 1985.

―――. *Modern Manors: Welfare Capitalism Since the New Deal*. Princeton: Princeton University Press, 1997.

―――, ed. *Masters to Managers: Historical and Comparative Perspectives on American Employers*. New York: Columbia University Press, 1991.

James, Marquis. *The Metropolitan Life: A Study in Business Growth*. New York: The Viking Press, 1947.

Johnson, Edith. *To Women of the Business World*. Philadelphia: J. B. Lippincott Company, 1923.

Kessler-Harris, Alice. *Out To Work: A History of Wage-Earning Women in the United States*. New York: Oxford University Press, 1982.

―――. *A Woman's Wage*. Lexington: University Press of Kentucky, 1990.

Kessner, Thomas. *The Golden Door: Italian and Jewish Immigrant Mobility in New York City, 1880–1915*. New York: Oxford University Press, 1977.

Korman, Gerd. *Industrialization, Immigrants and Americanizers: The View From Milwaukee, 1866–1921*. Madison: State Historical Society of Wisconsin, 1967.

Krooss, Herman. *Executive Opinion: What Business Leaders Said and Thought on Economic Issues, 1920–1960*. New York: Doubleday, 1970.

Kwolek-Folland, Angel. *Engendering Business: Men and Women in the Corporate Office, 1870–1930*. Baltimore: Johns Hopkins University Press, 1994.

LaDame, Mary. *The Filene Store: A Study of Employes' Relation to Management in a Retail Store*. New York: Russell Sage Foundation, 1930.

Ladd-Taylor, Molly. *Mother-Work: Women, Child Welfare and the State, 1890–1930*. Urbana: University of Illinois Press, 1994.

Lamoreaux, Naomi R. *The Great Merger Movement in American Business, 1895–1904*. Cambridge: Cambridge University Press, 1985.

Lasch, Christopher. *Haven in a Heartless World: The Family Besieged*. New York: Basic Books, 1977.

Layton, Edwin T., Jr. *The Revolt of the Engineers: Social Responsibility and the American Engineering Profession*. 1971.

Lee, James Melvin. *Business Ethics: A Manual of Morals*. New York: Ronald Press Company, 1926.

Lemons, J. Stanley. *The Woman Citizen: Social Feminism in the 1920s*. Urbana: University of Illinois Press, 1973.

Litchfield, P. W. *The Industrial Republic: Reflections of an Industrial Lieutenant*. Cleveland: The Corday & Gross Co., 1946.

Lubove, Roy. *The Professional Altruist: The Emergence of Social Work as a Career, 1880–1930*. Cambridge: Harvard University Press, 1965.

McCarthy, Kathleen D. *Noblesse Oblige: Charity and Cultural Philanthropy in Chicago, 1849–1929*. Chicago: University of Chicago Press, 1982.

May, Elaine Tyler. *Great Expectations: Marriage and Divorce in Post-Victorian America*. Chicago: University of Chicago Press, 1980.

Melosh, Barbara. *"The Physician's Hand": Work Culture and Conflict in American Nursing*. Philadelphia: Temple University Press, 1982.

Meyer, Stephen. *The Five Dollar Day: Labor Management and Social Control in the Ford Motor Company, 1908–1921*. Albany: State University of New York Press, 1981.

Meyerowitz, Joanne J. *Women Adrift: Independent Wage Earners in Chicago, 1880–1930*. Chicago: University of Chicago Press, 1988.

Milkman, Ruth. *Gender at Work: The Dynamics of Job Segregation by Sex During World War II*. Urbana: University of Illinois Press, 1987.

Miller, Frank, and Mary Ann Coghill. *The Historical Sources of Personnel Work: An Annotated Bibliography of Developments to 1923*. New York: Cornell University Press, 1961.

Mintz, Steven. *Domestic Revolutions: A Social History of the American Family*. New York: Free Press, 1988.

Mitchell, Neil J. *The Generous Corporation: A Political Analysis of Economic Power*. New Haven: Yale University Press, 1989.

Montgomery, David. *Beyond Equality: Labor and the Radical Republicans, 1862–1872*. Urbana: University of Illinois Press, 1967.

———. *The Fall of the House of Labor: The Workplace, the State, and American Labor Activism, 1865–1925*. Cambridge: Cambridge University Press, 1987.

Moody, J. Carroll, and Alice Kessler-Harris, eds. *Perspectives on American Labor History: The Problems of Synthesis*. DeKalb: Northern Illinois University Press, 1989.

Muncy, Robyn. *Creating a Female Dominion in American Reform, 1890–1935*. New York: Oxford University Press, 1991.

National Civic Federation, Welfare Department. *Conference on Welfare Work*. New York: Press of Andrew D. Kellogg Co., 1904.

National Convention of Employers and Employes. *Employers and Employes*. Full text of the addresses before the National Convention of Employers and Employes, held at Minneapolis, Minnesota, September 22–25, 1902. Chicago: Public Policy, 1903.

National Industrial Conference Board. *Employee Magazines in the United States*. New York: National Industrial Conference Board, 1925.

———. *Employee Stock Purchase Plans in the United States*. New York: National Industrial Conference Board, 1928.

———. *Industrial Relations: Administration of Policies and Programs*. New York: National Industrial Conference Board, 1931.

———. *Industrial Relations Programs in Small Plants*. New York: National Industrial Conference Board, 1929.

———. *A Works Council Manual: Research Report Number 26*. Boston: National Industrial Conference Board, 1920.

Nelson, Daniel. *Managers and Workers: Origins of the New Factory System in the United States, 1880–1920*. Madison: University of Wisconsin Press, 1975.

Noble, David F. *America by Design: Science, Technology, and the Rise of Corporate Capitalism*. New York: Alfred A. Knopf, 1977.

Norwood, Stephen H. *Labor's Flaming Youth: Telephone Operators and Worker*

Militancy, *1878–1923*. Urbana: University of Illinois Press, 1990.

Ozanne, Robert. *A Century of Labor-Management Relations at McCormick and International Harvester.* Madison: University of Wisconsin Press, 1967.

Pascoe, Peggy. *Relations of Rescue: The Search for Female Moral Authority in the American West, 1874–1939.* New York: Oxford University Press, 1990.

Peiss, Kathy. *Cheap Amusements: Working Women and Leisure in Turn-of-the-Century New York.* Philadelphia: Temple University Press, 1986.

Perkins, Agnes F. *Vocations for the Trained Woman: Opportunities Other Than Teaching.* New York: Longman's, Green, and Company, 1910.

Pleck, Elizabeth, and Joseph Pleck, eds. *The American Man.* Englewood Cliffs, New Jersey: Prentice-Hall, 1980.

Ramirez, Bruno. *When Workers Fight: The Politics of Industrial Relations in the Progressive Era, 1898–1916.* Westport, Conn.: Greenwood Press, 1978.

Reyburn, Samuel W., et al. *For Top-Executives Only.* New York: The Business Bourse, 1936.

Ripley, Charles M. *Life in a Large Manufacturing Plant.* Schenectady: General Electric Company Publications Bureau, 1919.

Rockefeller, John D., Jr. *The Personal Relation in Industry.* New York: Albert and Charles Boni, 1930.

Rodgers, Daniel T. *The Work Ethic in Industrial America, 1850–1920.* Chicago: University of Chicago Press, 1974, 1978.

Rosen, Ruth. *The Lost Sisterhood: Prostitution in America, 1900–1918.* Baltimore: Johns Hopkins University Press, 1982.

Rosenberg, Rosalind. *Beyond Separate Spheres.* New Haven: Yale University Press, 1982.

Rosenzweig, Roy. *Eight Hours for What We Will: Workers and Leisure in an Industrial City, 1870–1920.* Cambridge: Cambridge University Press, 1983.

Rotella, Elyce J. *From Home to Office: U.S. Women at Work, 1870–1930.* Ann Arbor: UMI Research Press, 1981.

Rothman, David. *The Discovery of the Asylum.* Boston: Little, Brown and Company, 1971.

Rothman, Ellen K. *Hands and Hearts: A History of Courtship in America.* New York: Basic Books, 1984.

Rothman, Sheila. *Woman's Proper Place: A History of Changing Ideals and Practices, 1870 to the Present.* New York: Basic Books, 1978.

Rotundo, E. Anthony. *American Manhood: Transformations in Masculinity from the Revolution to the Modern Era.* New York: Basic Books, 1993.

The Russell Sage Foundation: Social Research and Social Action in America, 1907–1947. Guide to the Microfiche Collection. David Hammack, Editorial Advisor. Frederick, Md.: UPA Academic Editions.

Ryan, Mary P. *Cradle of the Middle Class: The Family in Oneida County, New York, 1790–1865.* Cambridge: Cambridge University Press, 1981.

Schacht, John N. *The Making of Telephone Unionism, 1920–1947.* New Brunswick: Rutgers University Press, 1985.

Scott, Joan Wallach. *Gender and the Politics of History.* New York: Columbia University Press, 1988.

Shuey, Edwin. *Factory People and Their Employers*. New York: Lentilhon & Col, 1900.

Sklar, Kathryn Kish. *Catharine Beecher: A Study in American Domesticity*. New York: Norton & Co., 1973.

Smith-Rosenberg, Carroll. *Disorderly Conduct: Visions of Gender in Victorian America*. New York: Oxford University Press, 1985.

Strom, Sharon. *Beyond the Typewriter: Gender, Class, and the Origins of Modern American Office Work, 1900–1930*. Urbana: University of Illinois Press, 1992.

Taussig, F. W., and C. S. Joslyn. *American Business Leaders: A Study in Social Origins and Social Stratification*. New York: The MacMillan Company, 1932.

Tedlow, Richard S. *Keeping the Corporate Image: Public Relations and Business 1900–1950*. Greenwich, Conn.: J.A.I. Press, 1979.

Tentler, Leslie. *Wage-Earning Women*. New York: Oxford University Press, 1979.

Tomlins, Christopher L. *The State and the Unions: Labor Relations, Law, and the Organized Labor Movement in America, 1880–1960*. Cambridge: Cambridge University Press, 1985.

Tone, Andrea. *The Business of Benevolence: Industrial Paternalism in Progressive America*. Ithaca: Cornell University Press, 1997.

Trolander, Judith. *Professionalism and Social Change: From the Settlement House Movement to Neighborhood Centers, 1886 to the Present*. New Brunswick: Rutgers University Press, 1987.

Walker, Pat, ed. *Between Labor and Capital*. Boston: South End Press, 1979.

Ware, Susan. *Beyond Suffrage: Women in the New Deal*. Cambridge: Harvard University Press, 1981.

Weinstein, James. *The Corporate Ideal in the Liberal State*. Boston: Beacon Press, 1968.

Wiebe, Robert H. *The Search for Order, 1877–1920*. New York: Hill and Wang, 1967.

Wilensky, Harold L., and Charles N. Lebeaux. *Industrial Society and Social Welfare*. New York: Russell Sage Foundation, 1958.

Williams, Whiting. *Mainsprings of Men*. New York: Charles Scribner's Sons, 1925.

———. *What's on the Worker's Mind: By One Who Put on Overalls to Find Out*. New York: Charles Scribner's Sons, 1920.

Williamson, Joel. *The Crucible of Race: Black-White Relations in the American South Since Emancipation*. New York: Oxford University Press, 1984.

Wilson, Elizabeth. *Women and the Welfare State*. London: Tavistock Publications, 1977, 1982.

Winslow, Mary N. *Women at Work: The Autobiography of Mary Anderson as Told to Mary N. Winslow*. Minneapolis: University of Minnesota Press, 1951.

Woloch, Nancy. *Women and the American Experience*. 2nd ed. New York: McGraw-Hill, 1994.

Wren, Daniel A. *The Evolution of Management Thought*. 2nd ed. New York: John Wiley & Sons, 1979.

Wyllie, Irvin G. *The Self-Made Man in America: The Myth of Rags to Riches.*
New York: The Free Press, 1954.

Yates, JoAnne. *Control Through Communication: The Rise of System in American Management.* Baltimore: Johns Hopkins University Press, 1989.

Young Men's Christian Association. *Summary of the Industrial Conference on 'Human Relations in Industry': Silver Bay, New York, August 27–29, 1920.*
New York: YMCA, 1920.

Zahavi, Gerald. *Workers, Managers, and Welfare Capitalism: The Shoeworkers and Tanners of Endicott Johnson, 1890–1950.* Urbana: University of Illinois Press, 1988.

Zunz, Olivier. *The Changing Face of Inequality: Urbanization, Industrial Development, and Immigrants in Detroit, 1880–1920.* Chicago: University of Chicago Press, 1982.

———. *Making America Corporate, 1870–1920.* Chicago: University of Chicago Press, 1990.

ARTICLES, ESSAYS, AND OTHER SOURCES

Armstrong, Anne. "A Woman in Wall Street." *The Atlantic Monthly* (August 1925): 145–58.

———. "Fear in Business Life." *Harper's Monthly Magazine* (April 1927): 607–14.

———. "Have Women Changed Business?" *Harper's Monthly Magazine* (December 1928): 10–16.

———. "Uneasy Business." *The Atlantic Monthly* (January 1927): 101–14.

Baker, Paula. "The Domestication of Politics: Women and the American Political Society, 1780–1920." *American Historical Review* 89 (June 1984): 620–47.

Barker, G. A. "Nothing Slow About These New Englanders." *Light* (September 1926): 12.

Berkowitz, Edward, and Kim McQuaid. "Businessman and Bureaucrat: The Evolution of the American Social Welfare System, 1900–1940." *Journal of Economic History* 38 (March 1978): 120–42.

Brittin, Emma. "Two Years of Successful Welfare Work in a Factory Employing One Thousand People." *Human Engineering* 1 (April 1911): 86.

Carpenter, Charles. "The Working of a Labor Department in an Industrial Establishment." *Engineering Magazine* 25 (April 1903).

"The Changing Character of Big Business." *The World's Work* (June 1926): 168.

Cohen, Miriam, and Michael Hanagan. "The Politics of Gender and the Making of the Welfare State, 1900–1940: A Comparative Perspective." *Journal of Social History* 24 (Spring 1991): 469–84.

Comstock, Sarah. "A Woman of Achievement: Miss Gertrude Beeks." *The World's Work* (August 1913): 444–48.

Conway, Jill. "Women Reformers and American Culture, 1879–1930." *Journal of Social History* 5 (Winter 1971–72): 164–77.

Cookingham, Mary E. "Combining Marriage, Motherhood, and Jobs Before

World War II: Women College Graduates, Classes of 1905–1935." *Journal of Family History* 9 (Summer 1984): 178–95.

Cranston, Mary Rankin. "The Social Secretary—An Opportunity for Employer and Employee to Understand Each Other." *The Craftsman* (July 1906): 489.

Crowther, Samuel. "The Fetish of Industrial Democracy." *World's Work* (December 1919): 23.

Davies, Margery. "Woman's Place is at the Typewriter: The Feminization of the Clerical Labor Force." *Radical America* 8 (July–August 1974): 1–28.

Deutsch, Sara. "Learning to Talk More Like a Man: Boston Women's Class-Bridging Organizations, 1870–1940." *American Historical Review* 97 (April 1992): 379–404.

Dye, Nancy Schrom. "Creating a Feminist Alliance: Sisterhood and Class Conflict in the New York Women's Trade Union League, 1902–1914." In *Class, Sex and the Woman Worker*, edited by Milton Cantor and Bruce Laurie. Westport, Conn.: Greenwood Press, 1977.

Eilbirt, Henry. "The Development of Personnel Management in the United States." *Business History Review* 33 (Autumn 1959): 345–64.

Elliott, Margaret, and Grace Manson. "Some Factors Affecting Earnings of Business and Professional Women." *Annals of the American Academy of Political and Social Science* 43 (May 1929): 137–45.

Filene, Edward A. "A Simple Code of Business Ethics." *The American Academy of Political and Social Science* 101 (May 1922): 223–28.

Folsom, Marion B. Interview by Peter Corning, June 1965. Oral History Collection, Part III. Butler Library, Columbia University, New York.

Fones-Wolf, Elizabeth. "Industrial Recreation, the Second World War, and the Revival of Welfare Capitalism." *Business History Review* 60 (Summer 1986).

Frazer, Elizabeth. "Miss Graduate Hunts a Job." *The Saturday Evening Post* (October 19, 1929): 14.

Freeman, Estelle B. "The New Woman: Changing Views of Women in the 1920s." *Journal of American History* 61 (September 1974): 372–93.

French, Lillie Hamilton. "A New Occupation: The Welfare Manager." *The Century* (November 1904): 61–71.

Garrison, Dee. "The Tender Technicians: The Feminization of Public Librarianship, 1876–1905." In *Clio's' Consciousness Raised*, edited by Mary Hartman and Lois Banner, 158–78. New York: Harper and Row, 1974.

Gilson, Mary Barnett. "Management's Responsibility in Industrial Relations." *Wellesley Alumnae Quarterly* 6 (May 1922).

———. "Recreation of the Working Force." *Industrial Management* (October 1917).

———. "The Relation of the Home Conditions to Industrial Efficiency." *Annals of the American Academy of Political and Social Science* (May 1916).

———. "Scientific Management and Personnel Work." *Bulletin of the Taylor Society* 9 (February 1924).

———. "Wages of Women in Industry." *Industrial Management* (June–July 1921).

Gitelman, H. M. "Being of Two Minds: American Employers Confront the Labor Problem, 1915–1919." *Labor History* 25 (1984): 189–216.

Gordon, Lynn D. "The Gibson Girl Goes to College: Popular Culture and Women's Higher Education in the Progressive Era, 1890–1920." *American Quarterly* 39 (Summer 1987): 211–30.

Gwinn, Sherman. "Her Soul Goes Marching On." *American Magazine* (March 1925): 52–53, 76–86.

——. "What Business Men Ought to Know About Women." *American Magazine* (November 1929): 62–63, 180–84.

Hamilton, Diane. "The Cost of Caring: The Metropolitan Life Insurance Company's Visiting Nurse Service, 1909–1953." *Bulletin of the History of Medicine* 63 (Fall 1989): 392–413.

Hurvitz, Haggai. "Ideology and Industrial Conflict: President Wilson's First Industrial Conference of October 1919." *Labor History* 18 (Fall 1977): 509–24.

The Independent Woman. Publication of the National Federation of Business and Professional Women. 1920–29.

Jacoby, Sanford M. "Employers and the Welfare State: The Role of Marion B. Folsom." *Journal of American History* 80 (September 1993): 525–56.

Kelly, Roy. "Hiring the Worker." *Engineering Magazine* 52 (March 1917).

Kerber, Linda. "Separate Spheres, Female Worlds, Woman's Place: The Rhetoric of Women's History." *Journal of American History* 75 (June 1988): 9–39.

Kessler-Harris, Alice. "A New Agenda for American Labor History: A Gendered Analysis and the Question of Class." In *Perspectives on American Labor History: The Problems of Synthesis*, edited by J. Carroll Moody and Alice Kessler-Harris. DeKalb: Northern Illinois University Press, 1989.

Kohn, Robert D. "The Significance of the Professional Ideal: Professional Ethics and the Public Interest." *The Annals of the American Academy of Political and Social Science* 101 (May 1922): 1–5.

Kryder, Elizabeth A. G. "Humanizing the Industrial Workplace: The Role of the Early Personnel Manager: 1897–1920." Ph.D. diss., Bowling Green State University, 1982.

Kwolek-Folland, Angel. "The Business of Gender: The Redefinition of Male and Female and the Modern Business Office in the United States, 1880–1930." Ph.D. diss., University of Minnesota, 1987.

Lewis, Lawrence. "Uplifting 17,000 Employees." *The World's Work* (March 1905): 5939–50.

Lewis, Rachel. "Personnel Work in a Factory." *Prince Alumnae News* (October 1920).

McClymer, John F. "Gender and the 'American Way of Life': Women in the Americanization Movement." *Journal of American Ethnic History* 10 (Spring 1991): 3–20.

MacIver, R. M. "The Social Significance of Professional Ethics." *The Annals of the American Academy of Political and Social Science* 101 (May 1922): 5–7.

McQuaid, Kim. "Henry S. Dennison and the 'Science' of Industrial Reform,

1900–1950." *American Journal of Economics and Sociology* 36 (January 1977): 79–98.

Mansfield, Justine. "Business Girls as 'Office Housekeepers.'" *The Office Economist* 8 (May 1926): 7–14.

Marshall, L. C. "Incentives and Output: A Statement of the Place of the Personnel Manager in Modern Industry." *The Journal of Political Economy* 28 (November 1920): 713–34.

Meiksins, Peter. "The 'Revolt of the Engineers' Reconsidered." *Technology and Culture* 29 (April 1988): 219–46.

Miller, Frank B., and Mary Ann Coghill. "Sex and the Personnel Manager." *Industrial and Labor Relations Review* 18 (October 1964): 21–44.

National Civic Federation Review. 1905–20.

Nelson, Daniel. "The New Factory System and the Unions: The National Cash Register Company Dispute of 1901." *Labor History* 15 (Spring 1974): 163–78.

———. "'A Newly Appreciated Art': The Development of Personnel Work at Leeds & Northrup, 1915–1923." *Business History Review* 44 (Winter 1970): 520–35.

Nelson, Daniel, and Stuart Campbell. "Taylorism Versus Welfare Work in American Industry: H. L. Gantt and the Bancrofts." *Business History Review* 46 (1972).

Opportunity. Journal of the National Urban League. 1923–24.

Petersen, Peter B. "Elizabeth F. Briscoe: Pioneer in Personnel Management." *Southern Management Association 1986 Annual Meeting Proceedings.* Atlanta, Georgia. (November 1986).

Philbrick, Inez C. "Women, Let us be Loyal to Women!" *The Medical Woman's Journal* 36 (February 1929): 39–42.

Porter, H. F. J. "The Higher Law in the Industrial World." *Engineering Magazine* 29 (August 1905).

Rikard, Marlene Hunt. "An Experiment in Welfare Capitalism: The Health Care Services of Tennessee Coal, Iron and Railroad Company." Ph.D. diss., University of Alabama, 1983.

Rindge, Fred, Jr. "Can the Human Side of Engineering be Taught?" *Industrial Management* 52 (November 1916).

Robinson, Grace. "The Office Wife." *Liberty Magazine* (June 2, 1928): 43.

Roe, Joseph W. "How the College Can Train Managers." *Engineering Magazine* 51 (July 1916).

Scheinberg, Stephen J. "The Development of Corporation Labor Policy, 1900–1940." Ph.D. diss., University of Wisconsin, 1966.

Slichter, Sumner, "The Current Labor Policies of American Industries." *The Quarterly Journal of Economics* 43 (May 1929): 393–435.

Swope, Gerard. "Management Cooperation with Workers for Economic Welfare." *The Annals of the American Academy of Political and Social Science* 154 (March 1931): 131–42.

Sumner, Graham. "Do We Want Industrial Peace?" *The Forum* 8 (1889): 406–16.

System Magazine. 1913–20.

Tead, Ordway. "The Problem of Graduate Training in Personnel Administration." *The Journal of Political Economy* 29 (May 1921): 353–67.

Van Kleeck, Mary, and Graham Taylor. "The Professional Organization of Social Work." *The Annals of the American Academy of Political and Social Science* 101 (May 1922): 158–68.

Walkowitz, Daniel J. "The Making of a Feminine Professional Identity: Social Workers in the 1920s." *American Historical Review* 95 (October 1990): 1051–75.

"Welfare Work May Conquer Great Labor Problems." *New York Times* (November 17, 1912).

Wolfe, Allis Rosenberg. "Women, Consumerism, and the National Consumers' League in the Progressive Era, 1900–1923." *Labor History* 16 (Summer 1975): 378–92.

Zerzan, John. "Understanding the Anti-Radicalism of the National Civic Federation." *International Review of Social History* 19 (1974): 194–201.

GOVERNMENT PUBLICATIONS

U.S. Department of Commerce. Bureau of the Census. *The Integration of Industrial Operation.* Census Monographs III. 1924.

———. *Statistics of Women at Work.* 1907.

———. *Women in Gainful Occupations, 1870–1920.* Census Monographs IX.

U.S. Department of Labor. Bureau of Labor Statistics. *Health and Recreation Activities in Industrial Establishments, 1926.* Bulletin No. 458. February 1928.

———. *Personnel Research Agencies.* Bulletin No. 299. November 1921.

———. *Proceedings of the Employment Managers' Conference, Rochester, N.Y., May 9, 10, 11, 1918.* Bulletin No. 247. 1918.

———. *Welfare Work for Employees in Industrial Establishments in the United States.* Bulletin No. 250. February 1919.

U.S. Department of Labor. Women's Bureau. *Women's Occupations Through Seven Decades.* Women's Bureau Bulletin No. 218. 1947.

INDEX

fare Department, 90; and professionalization 92–94, 111, 116, 131

National Industrial Conference Board, 144, 145

Natural Foods Co., 55, 56, 123

Nazro, W. E. C., 60, 87–88, 94, 96, 99, 108, 111

Nelson, Daniel, 5

Nye, Isabelle, 22, 85, 86, 111, 113

Paternalism, 6, 13, 16, 21–22, 69

Patterson, John, 1–3, 15, 19, 23, 24–25, 35, 54–55, 98

Pension plans. *See* Welfare work: and financial benefit plans

Personnel management, 6, 7; and consumer model, 10, 142–43; and welfare work, 136, 143–44; functions of, 142–43; and number of departments, 146; and World War I, 146–48; and gender and professionalization, 148–52, 156; employer control of, 157

Plymouth Cordage Co.: and welfare work, 20, 44, 60, 87, 94, 96, 99, 108, 111; employer attitudes in, 104; employee attitudes and actions in, 119, 125, 126, 128

Profit sharing. *See* Welfare work: and financial benefit plans

Ray, Laura, 42, 67, 93–94, 109, 111

Reading rooms. *See* Welfare work: educational, recreational, and social

Repression: and labor practices, 11, 13, 21

Restrooms. *See* Welfare work: educational, recreational, and social

Rochester School for Employment Managers, 147–50

Rockefeller, John D., Jr., 35, 105, 145

Savings plans. *See* Welfare work: and financial benefit plans

Scientific management, 142

Sears, Roebuck and Co., 41, 45, 73, 80–81

Self-made man, 31–32, 105–6, 117

Settlements, 36, 84, 137, 156–57

Social Darwinism, 105

Social Gospel, 18–19, 35, 86–87, 137

Social secretary. *See* Welfare managers

Solvay Process Co., 94, 125

Strikes, 2, 11, 50, 120, 128

Stock purchase plans. *See* Welfare work: and financial benefit plans

Suggestion systems. *See* Welfare work: systematization of

Systematic management, 142

Taylor, Graham, 140

Taylor Society, 142, 147

Tennessee Coal and Iron Co., 45

Tone, Andrea, 5–6

Unions, 2, 4, 18, 118, 128

Urban League, 45

Vacations. *See* Welfare work: and financial benefit plans

Van Kleeck, Mary, 137, 149, 151

Victorian family: as model for welfare work, 6, 8–9, 26–32, 42, 51–68 passim, 89, 101, 130, 133–36, 158; applied to welfare workers, 6–7, 36–39, 53, 55; masculinity and femininity within, 27–28, 86, 105–6, 117; crisis of, 29–31; compared to workingwomen and immigrants, 42–44

Visiting nurses. *See* Welfare work: and health and safety

Wanamaker, John, 58, 66, 109

War Industries Board, 147

Welfare managers: duties and skills of, 8, 33–34, 37–39, 85; and professionalization, 9, 92–94, 99–100, 131, 136–37, 155–56; and corporate motherhood, 33, 36–39, 68, 84, 133–34; salaries of, 34; prior experi-